THE GOLDEN PARTNERSHIP

Robin Holleyhead

with a foreword by Mark Johnston

Robin Holleyhead.

Cover Picture: Silvestre de Sousa on Dark Vision. From an oil on canvas by Stuart Herod

Published by Robin Holleyhead and
printed by G H Smith & Son of Easingwold

First published in 2021
by Robin Holleyhead

E-mail: robinholleyhead@icloud.com

First Edition 2021

ISBN 978-1-5272-9333-5

Printed and Bound by

DESIGN PRINTING PUBLISHING

Market Place, Easingwold, York YO61 3AB
Tel: 01347 821 329
E-mail: info@ghsmith.com

" O for a horse with wings"

William Shakespeare

"Cymbeline"

"There have been as many plagues

as wars in history: yet always plagues

and wars take people equally by surprise"

Albert Camus

"The Plague"

ACKNOWLEDGEMENTS

"Publish or Perish" was the mantra of my first mentor, Stuart Stanley Kind one of the founders of the Forensic Science Society, and it is quite remarkable that I should pick up my pen again with a nudge from a pandemic, which had its origins in late 2019 in the Far East, only to spread like a forest fire to Europe and beyond by the spring of 2020. As I was writing this book two groups of people stood out for special mention. The professional medical personnel who have valiantly fought against it and saved lives sometimes at the cost of their own and scientists from all over the world who have worked tirelessly to develop vaccines. At least the troubled times forced me to get my head down and write.

Many people have contributed to this book. Some before it was even thought of and also those who have been generous with their time in its preparation and publication. First and foremost it would not have been possible without Mark and Deirdre Johnston who set up their first training yard some 34 years ago. To the present day, firstly under the Mark Johnston Racing banner and latterly as Johnston Racing they have pursued a relentless search for excellence in their operations. They and their expert team, now at Kingsley Park, are thanked for making the telling of my tale possible. Mark's many articles, his expertise and our numerous conversations over the years have contributed greatly to the book and he is thanked for allowing me to include them. He has kindly written the "*Foreword*".

Three others deserve special mention for the supply of ideas and copy in the book's preparation. Mikaelle Lebreton for her many photographs taken on the gallops, at the race tracks and in one instance from Mark's plane. John Scanlon for his guidance in the early stages of the thought processes of writing this book and who has documented most of the Johnston's operation since 2000 in the Kingsley Klarion. He has kindly written the "*Epilogue*". Also Paul Walker, whom I had not met before the formation of Kingsley Park 10, for his constant supply of the analysis of horses and races, and throughout the Golden Partnership's years a daily supply of interesting e-mail messages.

I have quoted James Willoughby and Simon Rowlands both of whom have written widely about rating horses and sectional timing. They are thanked for their erudition.

Many fellow travellers through some 50 years of an interest in racing are thanked for their company and many good times at the track and sometimes afterwards. Especially those regular attendees at York who have shared "our spot" on the Members' lawn between the rails bookmakers and the finish line, and those who are no longer with us to be able do so deserve special thanks. Some for making it necessary for me to extend my years of employment as a result of following their tips. Those days are amongst the most happy events in my memories of horse racing.

Several of the Dramatis Personae have allowed me to reproduce their stories of how they became interested in racing and how they were fortunate enough to join Johnston Racing. Adele Brown, Ruth Carty and Catherine Ross, were on hand to take a plentiful supply of photographs when they attended the tracks and have submitted them for publication. Many have sent their observations of particular events. These submissions have been used liberally in the text. They are all thanked for these and their companionship. Ruth Carty coined the title "The Golden Partnership."

Racecourse Photographers have been very helpful and co-operative with the supply of their high resolution files. Many have found their way into the chapters. The Racehorse Owners Association publishes a list of photographers and the following are thanked for allowing me to use the results of their fine work: Hannah Ali; Francesca Altoft; Steven Cargill; Steve Davies; John Grossick; John Hoy; Jonathan Hipkiss; Tony Knapton; Bernard Parkin; Jeremy Phillips; Megan Ridgewell and Matthew Webb. It is a pleasure to single out two of these for special mention: Jeremy Phillips (York) who has also allowed me to use his work on the covers of the book and Bernard Parkin who took his first photograph of a horse race in 1946 and at the age of 90 years was also writing a book. Stuart Herod has allowed me to use his oil painting of Dark Vision and Silvestre de Sousa, on the front cover inspired by a photograph taken by Steve Davies.

The Racing Post, The Racehorse Owners Association, Weatherbys and the British Horse Racing Authority have kindly allowed me to use some of their copy. The Racing Post's database accessible to Premium Members has been indispensable for the research of events and its membership is enthusiastically recommended. Their race analysts saw most events with a discerning eye, many of which have been adapted with their kind permission.

Having edited The Forensic Science Society's journal for a short spell in the 1970's I am aware of the task Graham Charlton, who is this book's editor, has had. We were colleagues in the now disbanded Home Office Forensic Science Service and also for a large part of our careers in Dr J H Burgoyne and Partners. Over those 45 years Graham has helped with the preparation of many of my publications. He has waded through page after page of this text with unrelenting enthusiasm and corrected my grammatical misdemeanours, loose expression and repetition. Thank you. I claim full responsibility for any errors that have survived to the finished article. A second ex-colleague, Janine McAndrew has remembered how to interpret my fountain pen and ink handwriting scrawl and has typed up most of the chapters. Having had a go at typing some myself I have very much appreciated her professional contributions. Further expert preparation has been carried out by Alexander Roberts, at the printers G H Smith and Son Ltd, and has put his first class honours degree in graphic design (from the York St John University) into practice.

THE GOLDEN PARTNERSHIP

CONTENTS

FOREWORD

When Robin first told me of his intention to write this book I did my best to dissuade him as I had some idea of the amount of work that would be involved and indeed there may be a limited market for it. Well having now read the book I can see that even I underestimated the task. Robin's enthusiasm for horse racing in general and the exploits of the Kingsley Park 10 partnership in particular are clear to see.

Horse racing is an extremely expensive sport for owners. I make no apology for that as it is, and always will be, very labour intensive. In my stable we employ one member of staff, from grooms and skilled riders to tractor drivers and veterinary surgeons, for every two horses. It goes without saying, therefore, that, with half a wage to pay before you consider all the other expenses, to own and race one of these animals is beyond the means of most people. Furthermore, fierce competition for the best stock, in a sport famous for its association with kings and sheikhs, has brought us to a situation where the most valuable substance on the planet is Galileo's semen and yearlings commonly change hands for seven figure sums before there is any indication, apart from that suggested by their parentage, of their ability to run.

The British Horseracing Authority and much of the racing media seem to think that syndicate ownership is the future for British racing but, to me, this demonstrates a naivety and lack of understanding of the costs involved in ownership. The high costs will probably remain but the outgoings can be in some instances mitigated against by an increase in income. Compared with our neighbours near and far the prize money in British racing (apart from a few high profile events) is derisory and owners' support relies on those who perhaps don't need the money or are just involved through their love of the sport.

While money is no guarantee of success in racing, and that is a large part of the allure for many, the odds against achieving success with a modest outlay should never be underestimated. It is quite remarkable, therefore, that 'The Golden Partnership' should enjoy such success with not just one or two but all three of its horses. Robin has been in racing for a long time and fully appreciates what an extraordinary achievement this was.

On reflection, I am pleased I did not put him off putting his pen to paper as this book is very good, I was impressed with the detail and I enjoyed reading it. He has been inspired by the success of the three horses to write it and, in doing so, he has rekindled many wonderful memories for those of us who were lucky enough to be involved along the way and, hopefully, he has provided some valuable insight and information for those who dream of dabbling in the Sport of Kings.

Mark Johnston
April 2021

PREQUEL

Glorious Goodwood

Up until 1801 a group of army officers, titled the Sussex Militia, and the Goodwood Hunt had held their annual races in Letchworth Park on land owned by the Earl of Egremont. This agreement was withdrawn in 1801 and the Duke of Richmond stepped in to allow the races to continue on "The Harroway", a ridge at the top of the escarpment on the South Downs. Such was the success of the new venue that a decision was made to hold a three day public race meeting in 1802.

The meeting grew in popularity, partly because of the beautiful setting, and it was soon referred to as "Glorious Goodwood". It is regarded by many as the most beautiful place in racing. The north western slopes which overlook the final straight and finish line, known as "the Trundle" became famous not only for the view it afforded, but it was an area where it was free to have a picnic and watch the action. In 1953 the first day of racing attracted 55,000 spectators. I know it is people that matter rather than places, but Goodwood racecourse on a warm summer's day is the place to be.

Now there are several meetings throughout the year and the Glorious Goodwood Festival held at the end of July and the beginning of August, can attract 100,000 racegoers over its 5 days. It is now sponsored by Qatar and many of the races are a firm fixture on the card and are the aim of the racing world to win. The prize money matches the quality of the racing.

It is no secret that Mark Johnston looks forward to Glorious Goodwood. Claire Balding once interviewed Mark and Deirdre on a boat just to the south of the track with their two young sons (Charlie and Angus) in attendance. They looked so relaxed they appeared to be on holiday. They were not. The stable targets the 5 days and he has been top trainer 13 times at the festival including 5 out of the last 7 years. He saddled his first winner there in 1991 and now has 88 winners, which is more than any other trainer.

The Vintage Stakes

This was first run at Goodwood in 1975, when it was a Listed race. Riboboy trained by Dick Hern and ridden by Joe Mercer won it and did so again the following year with Sky Ship. In fact Dick Hern trained the winner of four of the first five runnings. It was elevated to a Group 3 race in 1986 and to its present status of Group 2 in 2003. As one of the premier races for 2-year-olds of the season, it is run over a distance of 7 furlongs and in 2018 the total prize money was £200,000. Horses that have won the Vintage have gone on to win Classics. Troy, for example, won the Derby in June 1979 after he had been successful in the Vintage the previous year, as did Dr Devious in 1991/92.

Mark Johnston had success in the race with Mister Baileys in 1992 and he followed up the following year with the 2000 Guineas. He trained Shamardal to win it in 2004 and Lucky Story in 2005. The former went on to be champion 2-year-old. The most recent winner to achieve Classics glory was Galileo Gold in 2015, trained by Hugo Palmer and ridden by Frankie Dettori. He also won the 2000 Guineas and the St James's Place Stakes at Royal Ascot in 2016 with the same combination of trainer and jockey.

Willie Carson is the leading Jockey (to date) with 6 wins and the leading trainers with 6 wins each are the late Sir Henry Cecil and the late Dick Hern. Richard Hannon Snr had a remarkable run from 2010 to 2013 with 4 consecutive wins with Richard Hughes in the saddle for all four of them.

The scene is set for one of the important races of the Glorious Goodwood Festival. Nine of the last 12 runs have been won by the favourites and all twelve have been won by a horse in the first three of the betting.

INTRODUCTION

"Here now comes Dark Vision down the centre, Silvestre has got this one out of trouble and is storming down the centre. He has come from last and has won."

This is how Ian Bartlett, the course commentator described the finish of the most thrilling 2018 Qatar Vintage Stakes. The race is often won by one of the best 2-year-old horses of a particular year. The win came only a few days after one of the other horses in the Kingsley Park 10 (KP 10) partnership, Victory Command, had won a Listed race at Ascot. This is the story of not only those wins, but also of a tremendous two years of racing experienced by the partners and their friends in Johnston Racing's KP 10 partnership: **The Golden Partnership.**

It is a success story beyond an owner's wildest dreams, a rags to riches story, akin to a "Black Beauty" tale. It describes how many of those involved in this happy enterprise were brought together to become friends as they embarked on the journey of a racing lifetime. Perhaps a one in a million occurrence. They joined for many different reasons, were from a variety of racing backgrounds, but all experienced and achieved their dream.

It started with 19 people joining one of the famous Johnston Racing partnerships. They are all now broadly of the same structure with mainly 3 horses in each one (see Appendix). Each partner paid a one off sum of £7000 for one year's racing. The option of further payments of £1500 per horse for a second year was available at the end of the first year should Mark Johnston consider a horse worth keeping. At the end of the second year, ie the horses' 3-year-old careers, they are sold at public auction.

Johnston Racing (Mark and his son Charlie Johnston) originally bought the horses at public auction and in the first chapter their approach and methodology prior to and at the sales is explained. They are trained at their Kingsley Park stables in Middleham, North Yorkshire. The three horses in Kingsley Park 10 were bought at the Tattersalls October Yearling Sales at Newmarket; two at Book 2, purchased in October 2017 and the third in the December Sale of the same year.

In Chapter 2 "Dramatis Personae" the reasons why the partners bought into the partnership, and the origins of their interest in racing to become fans is disclosed. The viewing of the horses once they had settled in at the stables is illustrated in Chapter 5, as are the early days of their development leading to their first steps on to the racetrack. Chapter 6 follows on with a description of the detailed and skilful application of the stable's wide knowledge of a racehorse's ability used every day to plan and to choose in which races to enter horses, and ultimately where to declare them to run. Their illustrious careers as 2-year-old and 3-year-old racehorses are described. The story will take the reader to all of the Grade 1 tracks namely the best racecourses in Great Britain and Ireland and includes a brief spell at Meydan in the United Arab Emirates.

The present Kingsley Park partnerships have developed over a period of more than 20 years. Inaugurated in 2000 they went under the name of the stable's motto "Always Trying". A history of these and some of their variations is included in Chapter 4. Not only in these partnerships are the stories of the horses told, but some of the partners are identified, who survived to join KP 10. There is a longevity of interest by owners (and indeed staff) at Johnston Racing.

There is a description (Chapter 3) of the many types of races and how horses qualify for them. For the majority of races this is via a handicap system and how a horse is allotted a handicap mark or rating is explained.

The joys and disappointments of the experience of being an owner, which is not always plain sailing will be described. Such was the success of the horses that inevitably offers were received to buy them. Although there was a clear pathway of how to deal with any offers made the associated emotions of whether to sell or to keep the horses were not so uniform.

It is also emphasised how being involved with one of the most successful stables in the country is a great help in the pursuit of winners. In fact during the course of KP 10's existence Mark Johnston became the trainer who had won the most races in the history of Flat racing in Britain by breaking the previous record held by Richard Hannon Snr. On 23rd August 2018 Poet's Society won the one mile Clipper Logistics Handicap at York ridden by Frankie Dettori to record Mark's 4,194[th] winner. The owners of the horse, a Ready to Run partnership (Kingsley Park 9) were delighted along with Mark, Frankie and everybody else connected with Johnston Racing, see Chapter 8. There was splendid coverage of the achievement by the very professional ITV Racing.

Never a stable to stop there a year later another record fell. This time the number of wins in a calendar year was broken when yet another Kingsley Park partnership recruit Bavardages (KP 11) ridden by Joe Fanning won at Kempton Park to pass the old record of 235 wins held jointly by Richard Hannon Snr. and Richard Fahey.

Every month the "Kingsley Klarion" magazine is published by Johnston Racing with articles which cover a wide range of topics on racing. It has been a rich source of information for this book, and has been quoted widely, as has Mark's "Straight Talking" column which appears in every publication.

CHAPTER 1

THE HORSES

1.1 The Sales Strategy: Yearlings

From the start of summer to the end of the year trainers, owners or their representatives and bloodstock agents descend on the sales. In Europe these take place in England, France, Germany and Ireland. There are such events in the USA and other parts of the world but Johnston Racing in the form of Mark and his son Charlie now attend only those in Europe. The 2018 schedule is set out in the Table.

Table: Sales Attendance 2018

Arqana August Deauville
Goffs UK (Doncaster) Premier
BBAG Baden-Baden
La Teste – New
Ascot Yearlings – New
Tattersalls Fairyhouse
Goffs Orby
Goffs Sportsman
Tattersalls Book 1 – Newmarket
Tattersalls Book 2 – Newmarket
Tattersalls Book 3 – Newmarket
Arqana October – Deauville
Tattersalls December - Newmarket

Before they arrive at the venues, where hundreds of yearlings are available for inspection a detailed study of the sales catalogue is undertaken. The breeding (pedigree) of each horse is set out on a single page of the catalogue. A particular stallion may be responsible for several of the lots to be auctioned but obviously there will be only one offspring for a broodmare or dam. She will in most cases have raced and a record of her performance and handicap ratings will be recorded. If these races include Class 1 events then the information is included in bold type – hence the term "Black Type." There is an apt saying about breeding prevalent in horse racing circles.

You put the best with the best and then you hope for the best. Thus the progeny of a Group 1 winning stallion and Group 1 winning mare is definitely not guaranteed to be a fabulous racehorse.

Snaafi Dancer, a colt foaled in February 1982 sired by the great "Northern Dancer" out of "My Bupers" sold for US$10 million (the current payment would have been perhaps nearer twice that sum in today's money). The colt never raced and it was reported that he was so slow in training that it would have been embarrassing to have run him in public.

This is a salutary reminder of the potential pitfalls of buying horses. It also gives people whose pockets are not bottomless some hope of buying a potential winner, with a much more modest sum compared with US$10 million. This story is about such an occurrence and for it to happen, with all three of the Kingsley Park 10 horses is quite remarkable.

Mark Johnston buys horses "on spec" with the hope and expectation his loyal band of owners will buy them. He also has commissions where a potential owner will ask him to buy a horse perhaps within a certain price range. He has explained his thoughts and details on this particular part of the buying process in his "Straight Talking" article in August 2018's Kinglsey Klarion:

"I started buying horses on 'spec' and, in the early days, sent a list out, of horses available for resale, by fax. The system remains to this day but now all but one owner receive the list by email. It works well and I have no doubt that it stimulates business and encourages owners to buy horses, especially when there is movement in the list and owners feel that they have to get in quick to secure a particular animal that has caught their eye.

On the other hand, the fact that I make the initial purchase and take the risk has a very significant effect on the average price of the horses I buy and, in particular, on the maximum amount I can risk on any one animal. That average and limit has come a long way from the time when I had to keep all speculative purchases under £10,000 but it still means that I cannot compete at anything near the highest level. I think long and hard before venturing into six figures and I try never to have more than one purchase at that level left on the 'shelf'.

It can be said, to some extent, with horses as with most other products, that you get what you pay for and we all envy the owners and trainers who have large strings of extremely well-bred youngsters. But the fact that there are no guarantees of ability when buying untried horses, and that paying a lot extra can only give you a relatively small advantage, makes horse racing what it is and allows us all to dream.

James Willoughby conducted one study into the relationship between yearling price and Timeform rating and concluded that an average yearling price of around £50,000 offered the best value for money. This was not to say that there wasn't a correlation between purchase price and racing ability but rather that if, for example, you bought two horses for £50,000 each and trained them for two years, your total outgoing would be around £220,000 and this would give a greater chance of success than buying one horse for £160,000. However, if you bought three horses for £13,333 and trained them for two years, your outgoings would be the same but your chance of a return would be less.

It is a principle that I recognised right from the beginning of my career and, when Brian Palmer gave me my first opportunity to buy a horse and train it, he told me that he had £20,000 to spend and asked for my advice. I told him to buy two horses and he jokes to this day that it never occurred to him that I simply needed the training fees. But it was sound advice and it got us both our first winner.

This, of course, is not to say that those who can afford to have several horses, all at an average price well into six figures, should not do so and that their chance of success would not be greater than mere mortals who do not have such deep pockets. But James Willoughby's study, as with all his studies, was based on facts and the laws of probability.

However, one of the other great attractions of horse racing for most of us, whether we be owners, trainers, or punters, is the opportunity to beat the odds through skill. And this, for me, is what makes the sales season the most exciting time of the year.

There are bargains at all levels in the sale ring and I am often frustrated by my inability to speculate large sums on those 'superstar' lots which I still perceive as great value for money but, on the other hand, I still love scraping around in the 'bric-a-brac' of horse sales looking for gems.

Our Kingsley Park partnerships fall into that bargain-basement level where James's study concluded that you would be better to buy two horses for more money than three at under £15,000. But for those owners taking a small share in a partnership and still putting out a significant amount of money, the biggest disaster is if they don't have runners, let alone winners. I, therefore, concluded that I must spread the available money over as many horses as possible and the policy is providing heaps of fun for the participants."

Mark enjoys the period of the sales. It is hard work and I have been with him both in Ireland and the UK where he has systematically gone through his assessment routine over and over again, looking at 60 to 70 horses per day sometimes more. One day at Newmarket we were drenched and frozen to the bone at the December Sale. Bear in mind he will have trained thousands of thoroughbreds over the years and watched them run in tens of thousands of races. He is well on the way to training 5,000 winners. He is also a lover of animals and a vet. He knows what he is doing and has an eye for a good horse.

James Willoughby also has accompanied Mark to the sales and commented in July 2015's Kingsley Klarion on his experiences. *"After just a few weeks of working with Mark at sales, the strength of his approach is not difficult to discern. He has the same structured dynamic to vetting horses, analysing catalogue information and bidding; nothing is haphazard; there is a clearly understood reason for everything. I think we can take "Always Trying" for granted now after 3,500 winners. Another motto which could be applied just as much to Mark Johnston racing is "Trust the Process."*

On arrival at the sales venues he and Charlie are armed with the notes of their studies of the sales catalogues. He looks for racing ability, which is the be-all and end-all as far as he is concerned. The first dam must have, as an absolute minimum, a rating of 90, and or have produced stock rated over 90. If a horse has not been selected prior to the sales in the "basic" criteria he will not look at it when he is there.

He explained to James Thomas of the Racing Post that :

"very, very few from the shortlist would be completely rejected once they have been selected on paper … Pedigree decides whether we're interested in the horse, and then the physical decides how much we'll be willing to pay for it."

"I love it, but it's very hard on the people at home", he said without a moment's hesitation when asked how he feels about facing another demanding round of yearling sales. "Some people may feel that their time is better used elsewhere, but I like to see the horses myself."

The "physical" is an inspection of each horse on the interested list. The yearlings have grooms in attendance and they are asked to remove the horse from its box for inspection. As soon as they emerge into the yard they are scrutinised. Some horses are excited and sometimes difficult to hold still. Bending down to touch a fetlock joint needs some willingness on the part of the horse to stand nice and calm. Such things are noted. Charlie Johnston has set out in the Klarion (August 2018) his vet school's (Glasgow University) five stage, pre-purchase examination and points out:

"most veterinary inspections of horses for sale are based around this model. It involves exercising the horse", but he points out that *"vettings at the yearling sales take a very different make up, largely because the horses are not exercised prior to the sale.*

As a result, the main part of a yearling vetting is the physical evaluation of the horse along with assessment of its conformation and gait at walk in hand.

There are many conformational 'faults' that cause people to remove horses from their list of potential purchases, even though there is no evidence that these faults have a limiting effect on performance. At most of the yearling sales this autumn, every yearling on our shortlist will be viewed by Dad and me.

At this point we take detailed notes on all the conformational imperfections a horse may have but, using experience and veterinary knowledge, differentiate between those that we feel are manageable and trainable and those that we consider will be of concern going forward.

Those conformational faults that we feel are trainable are factored into our valuation of the horse when it comes to purchasing in the sales ring, but it remains a possible purchase.

If, when performing our physical examination, there are any clinical signs of injury or physical abnormalities that we believe may have an effect on future athletic ability, we will request radiographs of the yearling and examine these to determine whether our suspicions are correct.

We will be seen at the sales palpating the front limbs of every horse, paying particular attention to the fetlock joints as we try to identify any possible sesamoid fractures, an injury that we have found has a very poor prognosis.

The only other people frequently seen palpating a horse's legs when viewing them at the yearling sales are James Tate and Andy Oliver, both previous vets at Kingsley Park!

After a yearling has been sold it is then subject to a 'Wind Test' where it is cantered on the lunge in both directions and listened to by a vet. A horse may be deemed returnable if it is heard to make a characteristic abnormal inspiratory noise when actively exercised as well as showing evidence of laryngeal hemiplegia when examined with the endoscope.

The majority of vettings at the sales are looking for reasons not to purchase an individual. Our methodology is to try to identify those with major issues we must avoid, but for the majority, to note their faults and factor them into our valuation, but not remove them from consideration. That method means we do not prevent ourselves from purchasing competitive racehorses, something that has been reinforced on countless occasions this summer with the success of horses we have purchased.

All the pedigree analysis, physical examinations and veterinary inspections we perform at all the yearling sales over Europe this autumn are done with no cost or commissions passed on to our owners."

1.2 The Kingsley Park 10 Horses

Until they are sold and named, foals and yearlings are known by their sire's and dam's name. In fact in a stable where there maybe several horses by the same sire they are known by their dam's name. The first to be foaled (on 16th February 2016) of the KP 10 trio was a Dream Ahead colt out of Black Dahlia.

Dream Ahead ex Black Dahlia

Shamardal ex Sexy Lady

He was bred by Ballylinch Stud, owned by an American John Malone, situated in County Kilkenny in Ireland. He is thanked for sending the photograph and indeed for breeding the horse.

The second to be born (10th April 2016) was a Shamardal colt out of Sexy Lady. He was bred in Germany in Westfalia at Stud Hof Ittlingen. Lisette de Jong is thanked for the photograph.

The star of the stud photographs was without doubt Platinum Bloodstock's War Command colt out of Aquinaga. He was a late foal (25th May 2016) and the last of their season. The young lad is Robert Byrne's son, Hogan, who was five years old at the time. The horse was only a few minutes in this world. Robert Byrne is a well known figure in the Irish bloodstock industry. Having formed Platinum Bloodstock in 2013 Robert has enjoyed success both in the sales ring and on the track.

War Command ex Aquinaga

Mill House 1961 being long reined.

A Curragh native, Robert's family has always been involved in horses and breeding. His great grandmother, Bridgit Lawlor bred Mill House from her Punchestown farm. His father John Byrne is a vet and partner in Sycamore Lodge Veterinary Practice on the Curragh. Many thanks Robert.

The black and white photograph shows Mill House being lunged (on a long rein) during the breaking process, probably circa 1961. The gentleman on the left was Old Tom Taaffe with dog Hardy. The man with the long rein was Paddy (Blob) Hannon, the father of my great friend Pat Hannon.

Shamardal ex Sexy Lady November 2017. *Mikaelle Lebreton*

Dream Ahead ex Black Dahlia November 2017. *Mikaelle Lebreton*

The three colts were lined up and advertised in the Klarion (December 2017) to race for the partnership and their "pages" are included as an Appendix.

The first was a chestnut colt, by the former MJR Group 1 winner **Shamardal** out of the Danehill Dancer mare, **Sexy Lady**, bought by Mark as part of Book 2 of the Tattersalls October Yearling Sale for 12000 guineas. Shamardal is, of course, one of the leading sires in Europe, with 18 individual Group 1 winners to his name and several of his sons standing as sires in their own right.

War Command ex Aguinaga December 2017. *Mikaelle Lebreton*

Sexy Lady won four races in France and Germany, including the Group 3 Prix Chloe at Maisons-Laffitte and the Listed Festa-Rennen at Baden-Baden, both over nine furlongs as a three-year-old. In the paddocks, she has produced three winners from three runners, out of five foals of racing age. Sexy Girl, Salamati and Showtime are all multiple winners in Germany.

Also purchased for Kingsley Park 10 was a bay colt, by **Dream Ahead** out of the Dansili mare, **Black Dahlia** at Tattersalls Book 2 for 15000 guineas.

The Diktat stallion Dream Ahead was joint champion two-year-old in Europe in 2010 (with Frankel), having won the Prix Morny and the Middle Park Stakes, and Champion Sprinter in Europe in 2011, after July Cup and Betfred Spring Cup successes. Retired in 2012, he has proved popular at stud having produced the likes of Al Wukair, Donjuan Triumphant and Raucous. At Kingsley Park, Dream Today, Love Dreams, Peach Melba and Haley Bop have kept his flag flying.

At ages three and four, Black Dahlia won five races between seven furlongs and a mile and a quarter. She was placed no fewer than 18 times, and finished second in Kempton's Listed Ladybird Stakes over a mile. She also produced two winners from her two previous foals. Al Hayyah, by Lope de Vega, won a race in France and was three times Listed placed in 2016; Another Eclipse, also by Lope de Vega, won a three-year-old maiden over 10 furlongs at Brighton in July 2017.

Completing the trio of colts was a bay colt, by first-season sire **War Command** out of the Machiavellian mare, **Aguinaga.**

This fellow was picked up by Mark at Tattersalls December Yearling Sale for 6000 guineas. War Command, a son of War Front, was an exciting juvenile, winning the Group 2 Coventry Stakes by six lengths before going on to land the Group 1 Dewhurst, in the process becoming only the second colt to land the Coventry/Dewhurst double since Mill Reef in 1970.

Aguinga won once, at three, when she won a Thurles maiden over an extended mile and a half. She ran just once as a juvenile, finishing third in a mile maiden at Navan behind subsequent Group 3 winner, Chiang Mai.

Her four winners in the paddocks include Second Serve, a winner for Johnston Racing at three, and Conquest, by Invincible Spirit, who won the Gimcrack Stakes (Group 2) at York and an Ascot Group 3 as a four-year-old.

Purchased yearlings travel to Middleham rather than return to their stud farms and undergo familiarisation training with the tack they are to wear and to get used to being in close proximity to handlers. They start work the day after they arrive at Middleham. High quality feed is provided to build up muscle, put on condition and help them grow. They are exercised in the lunge ring on a long rein. They are taught how to steer and broken in to accept being ridden away. Hours are spent in the trotting ring going round in both directions. Eventually they will be put on a daily exercise routine of walking, trotting, and cantering. Assuming everything goes to plan, namely they suffer no injuries or soreness they will canter and gradually build up distance travelled and pace. Going up the gallops upsides with another horse follows and eventually they will gallop. They start to run fast but not as fast as they would in a race itself. Starting stalls training is also fitted into the schedule.

Needless to say they are at this very young age prone to injuries and the riders/grooms and yard managers call in the vets to inspect any signs of soreness, lameness and unusual lack of interest in their food. A spell of swimming can be used to warm up a horse before cantering and or to exercise a horse without the impact of the gallops.

They grow very quickly and most people are surprised to see the big difference in their physique between the time they arrive at Middleham or the first viewing at the partners' day in December and the next partners' day visit in April of the following year when, of course, the horses will be two-year-olds. All horses have their "birthday" on January 1st. However on this date some "two-year-olds" may only be 18 months old.

CHAPTER 2
DRAMATIS PERSONAE

2.1 Mark Johnston : Trainer and Managing Director Johnston Racing

In August 2018 Mark became the trainer with the most wins in British racing history. A special edition of the Kingsley Klarion was issued and the following is an adapted description of his career based on an article written by John Scanlon, which appeared in the special edition.

Since setting up his first training yard in 1986 at North Sumercotes, Lincolnshire, a place which Mark recalls as being *"the coldest place on earth"* and where the gallops had to be used only when the RAF weren't undertaking bombing practice on the adjacent range, Mark Johnston has been on a journey - a journey in the pursuit of excellence in training the thoroughbred horse. From those humble beginnings, where he and his wife Deirdre virtually rebuilt the dilapidated Bank End Stables themselves and sent out in the summer of 1987 their first winner Hinari Video, ridden by Bobby Elliot at Carlisle, Mark has built a tremendous and unparalleled record of success in British horse racing.

With the help of owners Brian and Val Palmer, the Johnstons in 1988 acquired the historic Kingsley House stables in Middleham in North Yorkshire. Straightaway, Mark set about revolutionising the way his horses were fed, prepared and raced. Using the traditional Low Moor and High Moor gallops high above Middleham, Mark patiently added to his empire. When in 1994 he trained Mister Baileys, ridden by Jason Weaver to win the first British Classic of the season, the 2000 Guineas at Newmarket, it allowed him to acquire and refurbish another yard, Warwick House opposite to and across the road from Kingsley House.

Having transformed Kingsley House into a modern racing yard with equine pool and all mod cons, and having added Warwick House to the estate, further substantial expansion took place when in 2003 Mark purchased the 270-acre Park Farm, this has now become the centre of operations for the business. Mark set about installing his own Tapeta gallops, lunging rings, an all-weather arena and, of course, a landing strip for his plane. In 2016, facilities at Kingsley Park were significantly upgraded by the construction of an aqua complex, housing a second equine swimming pool, a water walker and a treadmill. The investment had been significant, and results on the track have matched his ambitions.

Mark differs from many of his peers in the training profession in that he buys many of the horses in his string himself at the annual round of yearling sales. He has proved time and time again, as witnessed in this book, that he is a fantastic judge of a horse; he has a record of buying them cheaply and many have turned out to be more than useful.

Mark has always held strong views about racing and has always been willing to state them. Over the years he has contributed columns to The Sporting Life, The Racing Post, The Times and Horse and Hound, and of course his "Straight Talking" columns in the Klarion are required reading for anyone who follows the sport.

Every aspect of horse husbandry is noted in meticulous detail. The facilities he has put in place to ensure the yard's horses are given every chance to succeed are second to none, and the systems he has employed in managing staff and horses in separate yards, each with a yard manager, together with his ongoing investment at the highest level of staff training, ensure that there is a constant focus on each horse and its performance. This thoroughness is encapsulated in the Johnston Racing motto "Always Trying", effectively a guarantee to his customers that no stone will be left unturned in the quest for success.

In 1994, the year of Mister Baileys' breakthrough success, Mark trained 100 British Flat race winners for the first time, reaching a total of 117 for the year. Since then, his stable has sent out at least 100 winners in Britain every year. This represents an unprecedented and unbroken chain of success which stretches over 25 years. It is also one with which no other training establishment can compete. In 2009, Mark became the first flat race trainer to score 200 wins in a calendar year and, having broken remarkable new ground in doing so, he has gone on to consolidate the achievement by repeating the feat seven times. It is hardly surprising that Kingsley Park is acclaimed as the most consistent winner-finding stable in British horse racing history.

2.2 Some of the Cast at Kingsley Park

Deirdre Johnston: Director/Assistant Trainer

Jock Bennett, Hayley Kelly, Andrew Bottomley and Charlie Johnston: Assistant Trainers

John Martin Senior Vet

John is from the town of Stradbally in County Laois in Ireland's Midlands. He was raised on a farm and from a young age had ambitions to become a vet. He trained at University College in Dublin and it was there that he first took an interest in horse racing, which nurtured an ambition to eventually specialise in working with horses as a vet. After graduating he took up a post at a veterinary hospital in Navan in County Meath, before moving to England to join a practice in Louth, Lincolnshire. Interestingly, Louth is the nearest town to North Somercotes where Mark had his first stable. He joined Johnston Racing at the start of 2010, staying for more than two years before returning to Ireland for a brief spell and then resuming his position at the yard in April 2013.

Becky Dinsdale : Vet

Erin Allinson, Dora Leng: Vet Assistants

Rachel Fox Barnett, Mairhead Heap, Liam Conway, Kim McGiven, Andrew Larnach, Luke Evans and Louis Blanchet: Yard Managers.

Michael Flory: HR and Transport Manager.

Kieran Bray: Racing Secretary.

Coral Eastment: Racing Secretary.

Cathy Pettigrew: Secretary

Alex Stearn: Racing Secretary

Robynne Watton: Senior Travelling Manager.

Tristan Burton-pye, Tim Jarvis, Rhona Bagnall, Mark Billingham, Calvin McCormack: Travelling Managers.

Needless to say the above is a description of just a few of the many members of staff. There are Farriers, Box Drivers, Assistant Yard Managers, Grooms-Riders, Riding Coach, Part-time Riders, Maintenance staff, Chefs/Cooks, a Housekeeper, and last but not least Alexandra Adams is the Embroiderer. Each member of the KP 10 partnership has a Johnston Racing Musto jacket with the wearer's name embroidered on it.

2. 3 Jockeys

A large number of Jockeys rode the Kingsley Park 10 horses with the most prominent of them being Joe Fanning, Franny Norton, Silvestre de Sousa and P J McDonald.

Dream Ahead ex Black Dahlia (Dark Vision): F Norton, D Probert, S de Sousa.

Shamardal ex Sexy Lady (Seductive Moment): W Buick, F Norton, J Fanning, R Kingscote, S de Sousa.

War Command ex Aguinaga (Victory Command): P J McDonald, J Mitchell, J Fanning, S de Sousa, R Ffrench,

R L Moore, C Beasley, C Y Ho, J Hart.

Joe Fanning

Joe Kevin Fanning was born on 24th September 1970 in Dublin, but spent his early years in Roundwood County Wicklow. At the age of 16 years he graduated from the Irish Racing Academy and had his first rides for Kevin Connolly. In 1988 he came to England at the age of 18 years to work in Middleham for Tommy Fairhurst. His first winner was for Mr Fairhurst in a four-runner hurdle race at Sedgfield. He suffered a bad fall afterwards and broke two neck vertebrae. This not surprisingly made his mind up to switch to the Flat.

He has in fact always thought that he was too light to be a jumps jockey. In 1993 he rode Highflying, trained by George Moore to win the Northumberland Plate. Soon after, he took up with another Middleham training establishment: Mark Johnston Racing. His association has lasted to this day. Joe's first big winner was Three Green Leaves in 1998 for Mark in a Listed race, the "Silver Tankard " at Pontefract. The following year he won the Group 3 September Stakes on Yavana's Pace at Kempton Park. The horse was a stalwart for the stable in the late 1990's and Joe came second on him twice in the Irish St Leger.

Group 2 success came in 2003 on board Darasim, trained by Mark when he won the Prix Kergorlay. He went on to win, on Darasim, the Prix Gladiateur, Barclay Rennen, and the Goodwood Cup. That year (2004) he won more than £1 million in prize money. Since 2009 he has won more than 100 races in Britain every year. He has been champion All-Weather jockey twice in 2009/10 and 2011/12.

In September 2016, on his 46th birthday he secured his first Group 1 winner on The Last Lion in the Middle Park at Newmarket. *It was a feeling of relief* he said after the win as he did not want to retire without a Group 1 success. After The Last Lion's victory Mark said:

"He's ridden a huge number of winners for us over the years. He usually doesn't get the opportunities to ride in Group Ones. Hopefully he will get a few more before he retires. He gives us loyalty. He came to us when he was just out of his apprenticeship. Many times he has been jocked off over the years and had to play second fiddle to a chain of jockeys. He turns up every day and never lets us down. He's always been there for us when we need a jockey."

Joe did not like being "jocked off" a decent horse although he agreed that he didn't complain. In 2019 he won his 2500th race and was one of only two active jockeys to have reached that total. He has ridden a winner on every track in Britain and regards Kieren Fallon as the toughest opponent he has ridden against. On Monday 7th September 2020 at Leicester racecourse Eton College, trained by Mark provided Joe with his 2,594th winner, which took him to ninth place in the all-time list of most successful Flat jockeys in Britain. Joe had further success at Group 1 level with Subjectivist trained by Mark in the 2020 running of the Prix Royal-Oak at Longchamp and the 2021 Royal Ascot Gold Cup.

I have known Joe for over 20 years and he won at Southwell on Cheeney Basin, my first horse with Mark Johnston Racing. When we meet we often compare what cars we are driving and I am always amazed how many miles he does in a year. He drives himself to the races and must know every take-away coffee shop/ machine on Britain's motorways.

Joe with yours truly at Ayr about to get the leg up on my Byres Road

Franny Norton

Franny was born in 1970 in Belle Vale in Liverpool. He lives in Liverpool with his wife Rachel. He is well known and respected in the area, especially at Haydock and Chester (his local tracks) and in May 2019 he rode Making Miracles, trained by Mark Johnston to win the Chester Cup. This success followed his best ever year in 2018 when he rode 112 winners.

He was one of four brothers and his father and family had no background or previous experience of horse racing. However because of his stature he decided to give riding horses a go and was given an opportunity at Peter Arthur's stable in Didcot. He was 16 years old when he moved south but was confident he would be able to look after himself away from Liverpool as he had a black belt in Judo and was an accomplished amateur boxer. In fact at one stage he considered taking up boxing as a career rather than racing.

Thankfully he chose to be a jockey and had his first ride in 1989. He was almost immediately successful and on 13th July 1991 he won the John Smith's Cup on Halkopous, trained by Mark H. Tomkins. Later that same year on 21st August he won the Ebor Handicap at York on Depose, trained by Sir Michael Stoute. He weighed in at 7st 3 lbs for both rides.

Franny on Victory Command at Royal Ascot 2019. *Mikaelle Lebreton*

He admits on reflection that he *"had too much too soon"* and began to struggle when he lost his claiming allowance. He was back boxing and was picked to go to the England boxing camp to train for the 1994 Commonwealth Games, but a chance to ride at Sandown offered by Mick Channon steered him back figuratively and literally to the track. Soon after he joined Dandy Nicholls near Thirsk.

He is not entirely sure when Mark Johnston came knocking but it was while Folkestone was still in business as a race course- it closed in 2012. *"He reinvented me.. and I'm a better rider and a better person since I started riding for him. It's all because of him. The first thing a jockey must accept is that we don't have a God-given right to ride any horse. As soon as you can get your head round that you can crack on. Mark has so many runners I might win on one and Joe would ride it next time or vice versa."*

"Franny is in a better place now [in 2018] than he has ever been ," Mark told the Klarion. *"I'm absolutely delighted for him that he's reached his first century and it's an achievement he has thoroughly deserved. I often think it's a shame we didn't discover the value of putting Franny up on our horses 10 years ago. He's a clever quick-witted jockey who looks after himself and works hard at his craft."*

He won on Dark Vision, first time out at Yarmouth and in 2014 enthused about the staying power of Maid in Rio (of the New Fairyhouse Partnership) after winning at Haydock. Franny rode her several times. Like me, as he is also a Liverpool Football Club supporter, he would have been equally pleased when the famous Liverpool and England footballer, Roger Hunt MBE presented the prizes at Haydock.

At the 2020 Dante meeting at York (delayed until 9th June 2020 due to the Covid-19 pandemic) Franny rode the Dante/ Musidora double for Mark. The Al Basti Equiworld Dubai Dante Stakes (Group 2), under normal circumstances is regarded as a Derby trial and the Tattersalls Musidora Stakes (Group 3) an Oaks trial. Rose of Kildare, owned by Kingsley Park 14 (bought by Charlie for 3000 euros) was an impressive winner of the latter race, seemingly beaten over 2 furlongs out she rallied in great style to win by 2½ lengths going away. Thunderous, owned by "Highclere Thoroughbred Racing- George Stubbs " artistically wore down the favourite to stay well and win by a neck in the Dante.

Charlie Johnston at York said: *"It's fantastic for Franny. Every year that goes by people try to write off our stalwart jockeys and we get the odd troll or others sending e-mails and messages saying they're past it and to get some new blood in, but they've proven it year on year that they're still riding at the top of their game. The two most important factors for a jockey are experience and confidence and Franny has them in spades."*

Franny's Group race successes in 2020 continued when on 11th September Dark Vision won at Baden-Baden in the Group 2 Kronimus Oettingen Rennen 1 mile event. A great driving finish by horse and jockey.

Silvestre de Sousa

Silvestre was born on New Year's Eve 1980 in Sao Francisco do Maranhão, Brazil. He is the youngest of 10 siblings and moved to Sao Paulo at the age of 17. One year later he sat on a horse for the first time. He was introduced to Fausto Durso, a leading jockey at that time, and he suggested Silvestre had the build of a jockey. Silvestre recalled in an interview he gave to the Thoroughbred Owner and Breeder magazine that: *"I started very badly…. it took me six months to get my first ride, but 16 months later I was champion apprentice and had lost my claim."*

In 2006 he joined David Nicholls, like Franny Norton before him, at his stables near Thirsk in North Yorkshire. By the end of his first season he had ridden 27 winners from 195 runners. The following year he decided to offer his services as a freelance jockey. In 2010 he achieved his maiden century of winners. In a BBC interview Mark Johnston said: *"I noticed him last season [2010] when he rode 100 winners for mainly small trainers, often on horses at long odds."*

Silvestre flanked by Sue Russell and Catherine Ross

His career at Kingsley Park flourished and after lots of winners in the late spring and early summer of 2011 he was leading in the jockeys' title race. He won two races at Royal Ascot on Fox Hunt and Namibian. Paul Hanagan retained his title and Silvestre was only four wins short of his tally. The following year he was again runner up, this time to Richard Hughes and in 2013 he was third to Richard Hughes. However in 2015 he won the title. The Klarion reported that : *"Mark is very clear about the qualities Silvestre brings to the saddle. His combination of physical strength and utter determination to win have seen him win countless races in recent seasons for the yard which might have been beyond many perfectly competent jockeys."*

The jockey's title trophy was presented by Richard Hughes and Lester Piggott. Richard Hughes explained: *"he's the same Silvestre every day, a real Mr Reliable and he doesn't make many mistakes."* Lester Piggott added: *"He's one of the few who rides every day. He's looking to ride all the time and he'll ride anything, anywhere, and that's a big thing."* He also won the title in 2017 and 2018 and is currently retained by King Power Racing.

He rode all three of the Golden Partnership horses with memorable wins on Victory Command at Ascot and Dark Vision at Glorious Goodwood.

Patrick Joseph "PJ" McDonald

PJ was born in 1982 in County Wexford, Ireland. His grandmother had ponies at her cottage and he rode them as a child. He started off as a point-to-point rider mentored by Padge Berry, having been taught to ride by Dusty Sheehy. He rode for Charles O'Brien but was not very successful and on the point of giving up when in 2005 he was persuaded to move to Leyburn in North Yorkshire to join Ferdy Murphy's yard at West Witton. He won on Hot Weld for Murphy in the 2007 Scottish Grand National. It was Murphy who persuaded "PJ" to continue to ride through the summer months on the Flat to keep fit. He liked it, was good at it and his Flat career blossomed from there.

His first major success came in 2016, when deputising for Danny Tudhope, he rode Clever Cookie to win the Yorkshire Cup at York. The following year, also at York he won the Lonsdale Cup on Montally, trained by Andrew Balding. Later in 2017 he won two Group 2 races on Havana Grey; the National Stakes at Sandown and the Holcombe Stakes at Glorious Goodwood.

However, his most famous connection, to date is with the Karl Burke trained Laurens, who was runner up in the 1000 Guineas in 2018 before winning two French Group 1 races; The Prix Saint-Alary and Prix de Diane. Unfortunately, he was thrown from his horse in the parade ring at Newcastle and fractured his heel and ankle. Consequently he missed several weeks of the season during which Laurens won two late season Group 1 races under Danny Tudhope. "PJ" returned to to ride her in the Queen Elizabeth II Stakes on Champions Day at Ascot and finished eighth behind Roaring Lion, but would win another Group 1, the following year, the Prix Rothschild.

He rides regularly for Karl Burke. He also rides for Mark Johnston and often rides Kingsley Park partnership horses. For KP 10 he won the Almada Cup at Hamilton, and a Class 3 handicap at Chelmsford. He was the Professional Jockeys' Association safety officer in the North from 2010 and in July 2018 was appointed Flat President of the PJA. In his last 3 seasons he has broken a century of winners: (2017:128), (2018:120) and (2019:110). He is shown below on Laurens's before her last race at Newmarket in 2019.

On 10th July 2020 at Newmarket he achieved the 1000 winner mark when he rode Zabeel Champion for Mark Johnston to win the bet 365 Class 2 Handicap. Thirty seven of those winners were over the jumps. He said: *"My career probably took off in the last 4/5 years. Before that hard graft on small tracks helped me to keep my feet on the ground and helped me to appreciate the last 4/5 years."*

P J on Laurens at Newmarket Rowley 2019

2. 4 Partners and Friends

One of the advantages of owning a racehorse in a partnership such as those offered by Johnston Racing is the friendships that develop through a common interest. This was one of the highlights of Kingsley Park 10 and, of course, the number of runs and winners facilitated this. I canvassed the partners of KP 10 to provide some insights into their history and racing experiences generally. Several have generously given their time to provide recollections and have also given their permission to adapt pen pictures, which have been published in the Kingsley Klarion.

Lionel and Lorna Beecroft

"In the summer of 2017 a friend sent us a copy of the "Kingsley Klarion", and that was the first time my wife and I became aware of the Kingsley Park partnerships. After a few phone calls with Mark and his team in the autumn, we became owners in KP 8,9 and 10. We joined Johnston Racing hoping to go racing frequently and have lots of fun following the horses- and we have to say it has certainly delivered, exceeding all our expectations. KP 9, the very aptly named "Ready to Run" partnership, gave us racing from January onwards, along with everything we had hoped for and, as an added bonus, more than our fair share of success with Poet's Society and Mambo Dancer winning regularly.

Throughout the year it was interesting to watch the horses in KP 8 and KP 10 grow up and develop from awkward yearlings to stunning two-year-olds, via the frequent e-mail updates, video clips and visits to the yard. What a stunning bunch they have turned out to be. Without exception, we have found everyone at Kingsley Park to be more than helpful and friendly. Mark, Deirdre and Charlie do have an excellent team."

Lionel says *"I have been mad about racing since I was kid. It's a passion I picked up from my father and my uncles, and which Lorna has subsequently picked up from me. We have enjoyed racing throughout the UK and overseas particularly in the USA and France. There are many folk who have contributed to British racing to make it what it is today. From King Charles II, our own Merry Monarch, who had the first common book of rules for racing drawn up circa 1666, thereby making racing the first ever regulated sport in the world, to Admiral Rous, who devised the handicapping system in the mid- 19th Century, which remains largely unchanged today. There is also of course Phil Bull the founder of Timeform, who helped the Jockey Club sort out some of their barmier rules, and also helped the punter to better understand the merit of a horse with his excellent form ratings and speed figures. Even today I look in disbelief as I see some folk at the races grasping the sports pages of some of the daily newspapers (which are devoid of any performance data) vainly pitting hope against experience, trying to make a winning selection.* (Lionel's first book "Unravelling Racing", published in 2008 by Lambee Publications, amongst other things explains how to utilise such data in the attempt to pick a winner).

"You can take your pick, but I think I would plump for Phil Bull as my racing hero, because of his indispensable services to the poor, hapless punter, who needs all the help he or she can get. An equine hero is also difficult to decide upon as there are so many: Frankel, Secretariat, Dancing Brave, Shergar, Nijinsky etc.. All fabulous horses, but we just can't leave out our own Poet's Society, Dark Vision, and Victory Command along with Astrac. The last mentioned in 1998 won the Wokingham Stakes at Royal Ascot, a horse I owned with a good friend, Clive Titcomb. That was another day to really savour."

Adele Brown

"I am from a horsey background and have ridden ponies and then horses in the various disciplines, mainly show jumping. I also had some rides in point to points, which started my interest in jump racing. I gave up with show jumping and horses when money became tight and I was suffering from painful back problems. More recently I started to follow racing more and more. I joined a couple of racing clubs mainly for the stable/ stud visits and other events that they organised. In 2014 I joined my first syndicate with the Racegoers Club, a two-year-old filly trained by Richard Fahey called Clouds Rest, which won 3 races that year and ran in the Queen Mary at Royal Ascot. It was really good fun and I met a lot of friendly like-minded people including Paul Walker of KP 10. I then joined another Racegoers Club syndicate that had many of the same people in it, and a mare trained by Malcolm Jefferson. She won and was placed in both Bumpers and hurdle races. The

rest as they say is history."

Peter Neumark and his Granddaughter Isadora Prytherch.

"We had no idea when we bought Lot Number 8 at a charity auction for a "Day at the Johnston Racing Stables In Middleham", just how lucky it would turn out to be.

We bid for the charity lot in order to take our horse-mad granddaughter, to the yard for a tour of the facilities and a look at the horses. My wife, Maria was especially keen as her family came from North Yorkshire just down the road from the stable near Masham, and she loves that part of the world. In true Johnston style, as we now know, Mark and Deirdre insisted on extending the proposed visit into an overnight stay, dinner and a tour of Kingsley Park, given that we had paid quite a lot of money for the prize. We could not have been treated more kindly.

Isadora, then 13 years old, was mesmerised by the horses and facilities at Kingsley Park, as indeed were we with the sheer quality of the Johnston operation. We were treated to dinner that evening at the excellent Wensleydale Heifer by Mark and Charlie in nearby West Witton. After breakfast the following morning, we ventured out on to the gallops. Despite the atrocious weather, we had a tremendous time there as Mark shared his time with us and gave us a running commentary on the horses we saw working. I was so impressed with the whole operation and the wonderful way in which we had been treated that I decided to buy two shares in one of Mark's partnerships, one for Isadora and the other for my wife and myself. Fortunately for us, those shares just happened to be in the Kingsley Park 10 partnership. The rest, in a sense, is history."

Ruth Carty's Cottage (In Middleham)

"My backstory with racing is quite simple. I bought my cottage in 1996 in the centre of Middleham and from the start, my friend Liz Pescops and I both loved watching the horses pass by on the way to and from the gallops on the moor. We were particularly impressed by the strings from Mark Johnston Racing, in their uniforms for both horses and riders. We also attended the Middleham open days and went round the stables. Mark's operation stood out to both of us.

When in 2000 Liz's 60th birthday came round, I wrote and asked whether there were any partnership shares available at MJR. Not Mark's favourite thing at the time, but as it happened the Shaws (Ian and Fred) had space in a partnership with Danton, which included Lady Bolton, and for that one I was able to tailor a share to whatever I could afford. It was one of my better ideas and we enjoyed Danton so much that we both went into successive partnerships, including the Always Trying ones, which were just at the time starting up. I reluctantly gave up being a partner when I temporarily went part-time at work and things got a bit tight financially. I haven't quite made it back, as I put money into property instead. My mistake. I didn't join KP 10 but fortunately Liz did."

Liz Pescops: " A gift that changed a Life".

A few years ago Liz Pescops, who later became a member of The Kingsley Park 10 partnership, received a surprise present which changed her life. *"On my 60th birthday, I received one of my best presents ever- a 60th share in a racehorse,"* Liz told the Klarion. The horse was Danton, trained by Mark Johnston. It was a dream come true and it led Liz in 2001 to join the first Always Trying partnership, with Ashkalani Star and Thundering Falls. *"I knew little about racing and I am still learning. Currently I'm trying to understand the handicapping and race classification rules. Watching Victory Command win in a Listed race at Ascot was truly amazing"*, but that was not the first time, as she will explain, she had won there with a Johnston Racing partnership.

Over the past 18 years she has been involved in seven partnerships with Mark: five Always Trying partnerships, the Bute Hall lease and then KP 10. *"The horses have turned out to be incredibly successful, but also my fellow partners are a great group of people and we have a core of regular attendees when our horses run, all of whom get so excited about the horses and really care about their welfare. I have tried trainers nearer to home on the South Coast but none of them came near to Johnston Racing's standards. It never ceases to amaze me how Mark, Deirdre and Charlie always manage to make time when I visit. Although I am not an owner outright, I am always made to feel as if I own the top horse in the stables. Nothing seems to be too much trouble, despite having so many pressures on their time.*

I also love the way the team find bargain horses which are then brought on and develop so well. Being part of Johnston Racing has broadened and enriched my life and I will always be grateful for that. One of my best-ever racing days was in 2004 at Ascot when Always Waining won the South Africa Diamond Rated Stakes. It was a thrilling race and we were cheering him all the way. I was standing next to my dear friend the late Phil Marrison and, as Always Waining crossed the finishing line, Phil turned and gave me a huge bear hug, lifting me off the ground. He never knew, but he left me with two cracked ribs that day! It was certainly a day to remember. Always Waining was a character - we used to call him Gnasher and he would stand in his stall with his tongue hanging out, waiting for you to give it a wiggle. Of course he went on in later life to win the Topham at Aintree three times. We would have never have guessed that he'd go on to do that when, as a two-year-old he used to come back regularly from exercise with sore pasterns."

Other than horses with whom she has been involved, Liz has always had a soft spot for the sprinter, Gaelic Storm, who was trained by Mark for six years from 1996, winning 16 times. *"He was one of Mark's high-profile horses when I was in my first [Danton] partnership and he just appealed to me. We used to visit him on stable tours and follow his races."*

"Travelling to most racecourses involves a bit of a trek. However there are compensations like Ascot and Goodwood, so I can't complain! Fortunately I have a friend with a cottage in Middleham, so that it makes it easier to visit the stables. I'm happy to travel many miles to see our partnership horses race. Beverley and back is 532 miles, but I've done that in a day. It's worth it for the anticipation, excitement, fellowship and atmosphere."

Catherine and Billy Ross

Catherine explained that although Billy was not a regular racegoer his father took him a few times to Bogside Racecourse in Irvine, Ayrshire, which was his nearest local track and only about 7 miles from home. At that time Bogside hosted the Scottish Grand National but closed down in the mid 1970's. Until they moved to Chester in 2009 Billy played golf at Ravenspark Golf Club in Irvine, which overlooked the old Bogside course and some of the chase fences were still visible. An annual Marymass Festival is still held on the Bogside site and horse racing is still part of the event.

It was in 1963/64, on a family visit to Hamilton Racecourse when Billy had his first bet on a winner trained by Pat Rohan and ridden by Johnny Seagrave. He recalls the horse's name Christina Rossetta. That day she carried Billy's first ever bet- a *"tanner"* (six old pence, 6d). In the mid to late 1960's, on unauthorised days off from school, a bus trip to Lanark (which closed in the mid 1970's) or Ayr were regular courses of local interest. Billy's first Grand National recollection was Merryman II, trained at Warwick House in Middleham by Neville Crump and ridden by Gerry Scott, winning in 1960 and likewise the Derby, in the same year won by St Paddy. Although Arkle was Billy's favourite horse of those early years the 1968 and 1970 Derby wins by Sir Ivor and Nijinsky respectively are well remembered and really kindled his interest in horse racing.

Catherine, on the other hand, had no interest or knowledge of horse racing and in 1972 when Billy took her to the Ayr Gold Cup and a horse was put down in front of the stands, it did nothing to encourage her to go racing. In fact she would go with Billy racing, but sit in the Paddock with a magazine or a book. They still do not watch the race from the same position or viewpoint. However, when in 2008 they both retired it was a different story and now she goes racing on a regular basis.

They have had a variety of interests in racehorses over the years. Originally associated with Mark through the Always Trying VII partnership (Always Dazzling and Bute Hall) and the New Fairyhouse Partnership (Maid in Rio), Billy and Catherine joined KP 10, like other members of the partnership attracted by the breeding of the three colts. They have also been involved in syndicates with Middleham Park Racing and had an interest in Axel Jacklin, trained by Mark, and in smaller partnerships - Juste Pour Nous gave them a memorable win at Hamilton Park.

Having experienced several syndicates/partnerships they thought that the one-off payment was a benefit of the Johnston Racing partnerships. You know where you stand. Billy pointed out that the partnerships give you the opportunity to go racing regularly and to visit racecourses throughout the length and breadth of Britain throughout the season. Billy and Catherine have had some fantastic days in racing. *"Wearing our Middleham Park Racing hats, we had a share in Captain Dunne who won the Epsom Dash in 2011, which has to be one of our best experiences in racing. Penitent was second in a Group 1 at Longchamp too. He also took us to Dubai and Sha Tin, Hong Kong. Maid in Rio winning the Brown Jack Stakes at Royal Ascot, ridden by Silvestre de Sousa (and six other races too) for the New Fairyhouse partnership was a special moment as well. Flying in Mark's plane to see Maid in Rio run at Deauville has to be right up there as a day to remember."*

The experience of stable visits also appeals to Billy and Catherine. *"There is something special about watching and listening to the horses as they make their way up the gallops towards you. The facilities and outstanding scenery, of course, at Kingsley Park are tremendous and always worth seeing. The staff always go out of their way to make you feel welcome."*

Catherine's equine hero is Frankel, and she considers herself privileged to have seen him win the Guineas at Newmarket as well as races at Ascot, York, Goodwood and Newbury. Although divided as to their equine hero they are as one as to their choice of Sir Anthony McCoy as their racing hero, citing his dedication, work ethic and professionalism.

Bryan and Sue Russell

Bryan and Sue Russell first met Mark and Deirdre Johnston when the Johnstons moved in late 1998 to Middleham from Bank End Stables in Lincolnshire. At that time the Russells had a fuel and lubricant business and they supplied fuel to MJR from Mark's arrival until they sold their business in July 2000 to Total. They became friends with Mark and Deirdre, and in 1994 after what Sue recalls *"was a particularly good party"* they arranged to buy a yearling from Mark. It was a colt by the 1987 2000 Guineas winner Don't Forget Me, whom Bryan and Sue named Needle Knot. *"He wasn't much good"* Sue recalls, *"but we had no regrets about getting involved, he finished third at Thirsk and also ran at Newmarket."*

Once the business was sold in 2000 Bryan and Sue had more time to indulge in their hobbies and jumped at the chance of joining the Kingsley Park partnerships. They joined Kingsley Park 6 and 10. Sue thinks that the Kingsley Park experience is unique. *" What makes these partnerships special for me is the welcome you receive at Kingsley Park. When you visit the stables you are welcomed as if you own the whole horse."*

She was born in Middleham and both her parents were involved in racing. Her father worked for trainers Jack Fawcus and Harry Blackshaw, while her mother worked for Neville Crump at Warwick House, which is of course, now part of the Johnston training estate. *"I left Middleham when I was 10"* Sue said, *"but I have always been involved in show horses and hunting. It was an ambition of mine to come back to Middleham and to have the chance of riding horses on Middelham Moor. After we had sold the business Mark gave me the opportunity of riding some of his horses there. I absolutely loved it."*

Bryan loves his racing and recalls the day at York when Benny the Dip won the Dante. *"I was one leg away from winning the Tote Jackpot that day. It was a marvellous occasion, tremendously exciting and we're still very fond of the track."* Both Bryan and Sue have interests which keep them busy away from racing, and he is also heavily involved in game shooting. He organises goose and pheasant shooting trips for parties from the United States and Canada, who stay in Helmsley and shoot on the local moors and estates.

Some years ago he met his racing hero, Sir Henry Cecil, through shooting; he had the pleasure of spending a couple of days loading for Henry and Jane Cecil on Walden grouse moor. *"Sir Henry always had time for a chat wherever you saw him. He was a top class trainer and a real gentleman to boot."* Her racing hero is Sir Anthony McCoy, for his sheer strength, bravery and determination to win.

Thrilled with the success of KP6 and KP 10 to date, the Russells have one more ambition to fulfil. *"We'd love to have a winner at Thirsk, our local track, as we live in Maunby. Bryan's affinity with Thirsk racecourse started back in the early 1960's when, as a teenager he used to get ten old shillings for picking up a sack full of paper rubbish after race days, usually on a Sunday. On one occasion he found a £5 note and he and his pals lived royally on sweets for the next month! Hence the ambition to have a winner there."*

Bryan and Sue have come close there twice, having had Victory Command, on his first run, placed third adding to Needle Knot's placing all those years ago.

Fred and Muriel Shaw

Fred and Muriel have been associated with the Johnston stable for many years. Their first excursion into joint ownership with the yard was in 2000 when he joined the 4th Middleham Partnership, whose Double Honour gave Mark his 1,000[th] winner.

Fred said: *"I believe my interest in horse racing is inherited. In 1908 my maternal grandfather, Albert, a publican/farmer in Yorkshire, took a group of clients to the old Manchester racecourse to see the November Handicap. As he departed his wife who was heavily pregnant, asked him to call in at the midwife's and request her attendance. On returning that evening, the pub clients suggested that he should go upstairs to see his wife, Ethel. There she presented him with a daughter, my mother. Ethel is reputed to have said " I think we could call her Brenda."*

Grandfather replied: *"I thought we could call her Ruby; I have won this at the races on a horse called Rubio," and held out a fistful of sovereigns. Ethel handed him the child, took the money and said : "for that, you can call her whatever you want." The horse won the day. My mother's interest in racing lasted to the end of her life and she passed on the interest to me. I am told that my first visit to the races was to Wetherby in 1935, in a pram.*

My grandfather became a full-time farmer and I spent a great deal of time with him, both on the farm and delivering milk, all using horses. He gave up farming in the early days of the war due, I understand, to not being able to get labour that could manage the horses. I have to admit that, later in life, I took more interest and involvement in motor racing than in horses, but certainly did not entirely ever lose interest in the turf. Some 20 years ago, when chatting with an old school friend, with whom I share the same surname, we decided that on retirement we should rekindle our interest in horse racing and we took a share in Double Honour, trained by Mark. Since then I, or should I say we, as my wife Muriel has become similarly interested, have maintained our involvement and experienced enjoyment with the Kingsley Park operations.

We have had runners and winners at the big meetings, such as Ascot, Epsom, Newmarket and Doncaster. But for me it is the smaller courses, such as Leicester, Nottingham, Thirsk, Ripon and Bath, where you can get fish and chips and walk about anywhere in the racecourse at leisure, where I am most happy. It is where we can often get to have a good chat about the horse running with a member of staff, and often with Mark, Deirdre or Charlie.

It has been a pleasure to observe, over quite a long period of time, the development of the Johnston operation. The partnership meetings at Park Farm and lunches at Kingsley House were much appreciated, as were the meetings across the road in the old staff canteen, followed by lunch in one of the Middleham pubs. I remember suggested names for new horses being written on a presentation pad and decisions taken by show of hands of those present- only to find later that Weatherby's had rejected the chosen name.

It has been a delight to have been involved in, and be allowed to feel part of, the Johnston operation, with some winners, more losers but, not least, a whole lot of fun.

Paul Walker

"Lying in a hospital bed after my heart attack, on 21st May 2017, I hatched the plan of becoming more involved in flat racing. Since 1983, I have had shares in some winning syndicates run by Racegoers Club, mostly over jumps and a few on the flat. I joined the Harry Fry Racing Club and 40 of us hit the jackpot in 2016 with a hurdler called Unowwhatimeanharry, trained by Harry Fry. He was leased to our group as a

maiden hurdler but he progressed in leaps and bounds and he won a Grade 2 at Cheltenham before winning the Albert Bartlett (Grade 1) at the Cheltenham Festival itself.

I was looking for the best flat trainer who ran syndicates and so Mark Johnston was an obvious choice. I was also looking for colts and was immediately struck by the three in Kingsley Park 10, with strong dam lines- the War Command with Rose Bowl as the 3rd dam stood out for me. I remembered her from the 1970's and I was hooked.

Rose Bowl was bred in the purple by Habitat out of Roseliere who won the French Oaks. Rose Bowl's outstanding performance was to beat Star Appeal and Allez France in the 1975 Champion Stakes. Timeform rated her 133- one of the best ever fillies. In 2018, I went to Blewbury where she had been trained by Fulke Johnson Houghton. His daughter Eve now trains there and she kindly found the lad who had looked after her. He told me that Rose Bowl was tough and so genuine and I left hoping that she had passed that on to the once raced maiden Victory Command."

Reg Witheridge

Reg and Val Witheridge first got involved with Mark Johnston Racing as partners in Favourites Racing. They signed up for some of the early Kingsley Park partnerships and I first met Reg as a fellow member of KP 2 when Star Focus was successful at Beverley. With regard to the Kingsley Park partnerships Reg likes that there is always plenty of activity and that Mark appreciates that horses are for racing, and likes to get the horses out. Reg and Val enjoy travelling, preferably by train. They have had some great days out travelling to some very diverse courses, and in particular when they had a wonderful excursion to Ripon, made all the better when their horse won.

Reg reckons the main selling point of the Kingsley Park partnerships is the value for money and the partnerships do he says *"give really good value for money. It's a real buzz having a day at the races as an owner."* Asked to nominate his racing heroes, Reg recalled his fondness for the great filly Petite Etoile. *"I used to enjoy watching her on television, with Lester Piggott in the saddle. She was a special filly. In terms of betting, I'll always remember having a bet on Urban Sea at 66/1 when she won the Arc in 1993."*

"One specially memorable day was when Poetic Steps won first time out at Hamilton. The filly won in great style, and it was all the more enjoyable as it was unexpected. I enjoy my racing and I like seeing courses such as Nottingham, Carlisle and Beverley." Reg is looking forward to supporting more horses in the Kingsley Park partnerships and who knows where that will take him. Indeed, and as this pen picture was written before the inception of KP 10 he and Val probably could not have imagined the riches that were to come.

2. 5 The Kingsley Klarion

John Scanlon

In March 2000 John Scanlon took over the editorship, from Colin Woods, of the monthly official Mark Johnston Racing Newsletter entitled " Kingsley Klarion." John was born in Hamilton, Scotland within a stone's throw of Hamilton Park Racecourse. His parents' home overlooked the course, and his earliest memories of racing date back to the early sixties when attendances at his local track were considerably higher than they are today. With his parents he used to look from the upstairs window of the family home while pickpockets plied their trade on the unsuspecting racegoers at the bus stop outside the house.

John was bitten by the racing bug early on, attending meetings at Hamilton whenever he could. Embarking upon a course in 1975 in Public International law (Honours) at Glasgow University presented him with an opportunity to step up his interest in the sport while studying only occasionally. Despite an ever-increasing predilection for Timeform rather than the Statutes, he began a career in Law. Over the years his interest in racing has developed into a passion for the turf, and having enjoyed the ups and downs of a small ownership interest in a number of horses, John became the owner, in 1994 of Tam Tain, a two-year-old gelding by Contract Law trained by

Linda Perrat at Cree Lodge, Ayr. John insists to this day that despite having shown no hint of ability in three outings, Tam Tain was destined for stardom had he not sustained a broken leg when being prepared for his seasonal debut in 1996.

Undeterred by this tragic episode and keen to expand his interest further, John in 1997 began writing about racing. In 1999 he was delighted when Mark agreed to co-operate with him in a book project in which he set out the stable's fortunes throughout a calendar year. The resultant book "Always Trying" was published in 2000 by Portway Press Ltd.

2.6 The Good Old Days

It is interesting to read why and how people became involved in horse racing let alone subscribing, with not an insignificant amount of money to join a racehorse partnership. An interest in a sport often stems from what youngsters are good at during their school years. In the good old days boys used to play soccer, rugby and cricket whereas girls played netball, tennis and hockey. It has changed now. Parental background, location and for some sports, availability of equipment would sometimes not allow youngsters to take part.

The interests of parents were sometimes passed on to their children. My father was a cyclist, a supporter of rugby league, a gardener and a musician. I am all of those but only aspire to the last mentioned at which he excelled on the violin. Certainly in my case horses, perhaps apart from the ones that pulled the rag and bone man's cart, were not a common feature of our mining village and definitely not readily available to ride. Perhaps what also deterred me from taking an early interest was the smell of the fresh droppings I was told to rush out and collect (before anyone else did) so the manure could be put around the rose bushes. Thus it is a fair bet that many of the people that are involved in racehorse ownership and the crowds that flock to the tracks to watch, have never sat on a horse. It makes some of the comments about a jockey's ability from punters almost laughable. *That Piggott got the horse in no end of trouble."*

The operative phrase is "a fair bet" and many of us will have taken an interest in racing owing to the thrill of winning a wager. This thrill together with an increasing understanding of the sport through a study of the "form" adds to the pleasure of trying to pick a winner. Not all are covered by the above circumstances and some just love animals and especially horses. Is there any wonder they do when thoroughbreds at the top of their game speed past the observer standing by the rail; such an exhibition of speed, athleticism and beauty. A long tail sailing in the slipstream, a look of determination in their eyes and with ears pricked. The jockeys in harmony with their charges timing the winning surge to perfection. More of that later.

The BBC in the 1950s pioneered the broadcast of racing and I remember watching coverage of the Derby and the Grand National. ITV showed racing from its start up in 1953 until in 1988 coverage was transferred to other commercial channels. There was no gambling in our house and my parents were unaware of how to place a bet. My father had been brought up by his aunt and as a strict Primitive Methodist. He couldn't even play cards.

I added an interest in horse racing to my sports in the late 1960s soon after I was taken on at a local building site by its clerk of works. It was in one of my long summer breaks from university and he set me on to hold the measure while he took levels. Sheds soon arrived to accommodate the site office and most importantly the canteen. I was promoted to tea boy and had to make sure it was ready for breakfast and lunchtimes. A second task was to fetch fish and chips on a Friday for lunch. A small group of pipe layers arrived and once I got used to their Irish twang I could hear them discussing what was going to win at the races in the afternoon. A tall crane was installed and its driver, when the machine was not in operation, could be seen from below to be avidly reading the daily newspaper. They wrote out their selections at lunchtime and I, with their money, walked up to the local bookmakers only 50 yards away to place the bets. My pockets were full of shilling pieces and half crowns. This was in the days prior to decimalisation when there were 12 pennies in a shilling and 20 shillings in a pound. A "guinea" was and still is 21 shillings. The clerk of works sometimes influenced by his workforce risked ten shillings (ten "bob").

Walter Peplow's Turf Accountant shop in Kippax was typical (I learned later) of many that had opened up after betting shops were legalised in 1961 by Rab Butler the then Home Secretary. Perhaps 10,000 opened in the first six months of the new rules. Butler decreed that the activity inside the shops should not be visible from the outside. He noted in his memoirs that *the House of Commons was so intent on making betting shops as sad as possible, in order not to deprave the young, that they ended up more like undertakers premises.* This suited me as the bookies was almost next door to the Primitive Methodist chapel.

The crane driver usually went along with name association for his selections and had a "round robin": or a "yankee". I was impressed that a form of bet was named after me and I had not even started. Walter Peplow's premises had one large room with access from a side door. A front door on "Crosshills" led to a very small space with a front counter, where Mr Peplow's wife (Greta) could be found, and she took bets from people who did not wish to enter the room at the rear. This room which was almost completely devoid of furniture apart from a couple of chairs placed in there (illicitly) by Greta for a couple of regulars who were *"not so good on their pins"* had at one end a counter for the bookmaker. He would invariably be reading the racing pages of the "Sporting Life". He took your money and gave you a receipt, which took the form of a cloakroom ticket; the number on it corresponded to the ledger entry for the bet. Walter kindly used to write out the names of the horse or horses backed on the rear of the tickets. Secured to one corner of the counter by a piece of string was a copy of the Sporting Chronicle (founded by Edward Hulton in 1871 which survived until 1983). The racing pages of the "Mail" and "Express" were pinned to the long wall opposite the side entrance.

The wall opposite the counter had a large blackboard (the "board") on which the runners for each race that day had been added in the morning prior to the start of racing with meticulous skill. Eventually betting shops were supplied with printed sheets for each race which were pinned to *"the board."* The information about non-runners, withdrawals and odds was relayed to the shops by a wire service from "Extel". As the odds changed the man at the board would chalk the new odds against the horse mentioned. Unlike the difficulty sometimes encountered with partners agreeing on the name for a partnership horse he was universally known as the "the Chalkman". He stood on a small stage to elevate himself from the shop floor.

The race commentary was broadcast through the same system ("the blower") via a tannoy speaker. The description of events was often without emotion but that was provided by the punters inside the premises. When people shout at a television screen to tell the jockey or even the horse to hurry up it raises a smile but to shout at a loud speaker takes the biscuit. I remember as well as there being nowhere to sit (to deter lingering), apart from the two reserved, special chairs there were no toilets. There were public toilets just round corner on *"Crosshills"* but invariably there was a steady stream (no pun intended) of punters crossing the road between the shop and the Royal Oak pub opposite. They often would encounter the landlord's wife "Tamar" shuffling across the road in her dressing gown and slippers to place her daily bets.

I can't remember the exact sums of money I took every day to the shop but I knew some of the bets had come up as on some occasions I picked up the winnings. As the work progressed and the number of workmen grew naturally everything increased. More tea, more fish and chips and more bets and winnings. I did not try to work out how successful my work mates were, in other words what were the total returns on the wagers but the sums grew and some days my pockets were full of money which represented much more than my week's wages.

So the almost inevitable happened, I had a go. The first win I can remember was on a horse called "Maddox Court". I won just over a pound (after tax) for a one shilling each way bet. To put this in perspective a portion of fish and chips in those days cost one shilling (12 old pence). Nine pence for the fish and three pence for the chips- scraps, salt and vinegar were free. I don't know how I wangled it but I did sometimes go to listen to the races especially when I had placed a bet. Despite the government plan to evoke *"the atmosphere of a funeral parlour"* I remember the thrill of hearing that my horse was coming to the front and going away at the end to win. That is how I got started in following horse races and as Graham Greene said: *"There is always one moment in childhood when the door opens to let the future in."*

Fortunately because I had used Mr Peplow's to place my bets, I picked up perhaps the most important and certainly my first piece of advice about gambling. Mr Peplow was a friend of my dad's as he and Greta had followed him wherever he played. Walter owned a grey and cream, two-tone Humber Sceptre motor car, with white walled tyres, leather seats, a heater and a radio. My dad had a very basic and very old Jowett (made in Idle, Bradford) with none of the extras of the Humber. *"What car do I drive and what car has your dad got?"* asked Walter. A rather rude question and a somewhat demeaning one too, but I soon saw plainly and understood what Walter meant that the job of a coal miner was not as lucrative as being a "Turf Accountant."

Billy Ross and I have discussed on a few occasions how we both became involved in horse racing and our early memories of it. His interest started in the early 1960's and "Arkle" dominated his "early racing memories". Between the years 1962 to 1966 Arkle won 27 of his 35 races. Timeform consider him to be the greatest steeplechaser of all time. Ironically his early equine idols and mine (Night Nurse and Sea Pigeon trained by Peter Easterby) were National Hunt superstars. I have never owned a horse that ran in that code and the Ross's have not had many either.

In 1983 Bregawn, Captain John, Wayward Lad, Silver Buck and Ashley House were the first five home in the Cheltenham Gold Cup. Michael Dickinson trained the horses at Harewood near to where I live. Several jockeys including Steve Youlden and Graham Bradley used to sweat it out in the sauna at Wetherby swimming pool, where I and a few mates went to prepare ourselves for a gruelling night out in the local pubs. I became friends with Steve (who is now in Dubai) and Graham, friendships which have lasted to this day.

My first trip to a racecourse was almost certainly in the middle of the 1970's to Goodwood. I lived then in Theale near Reading and joined a trip from the local Red Lion pub. Who could have foreseen that some 45 years later what I was to witness on the South Downs? In the late 1970's I moved back north and this annual outing was replaced with a trip to the Ebor meeting at York. Again a pub trip from the Royal Oak opposite where Walter Peplow's bookies had been. My recollection of these trips is a bit blurred which was inevitable when the itinerary involved a few pints before we left for York, a few more in the Cygnet near the track and a session in Copmanthorpe Working Men's Club on the way home to resume drinking in the Royal Oak. Fortunately my parents lived a few hundred yards from the pub.

The racing was not a complete blur and in 1979 I remember being thrilled when Sea Pigeon won the Ebor ridden by Jonjo O'Neil carrying the current record weight of 10 stones. Jonjo appeared to ease off in the last few yards and the result of the subsequent photo finish, in the days before digital images, took an age to be announced. The result brought a cheer from the crowd and was only bettered when Frankel, many years later won the Juddmonte International, trained of course by the late Sir Henry Cecil. Only those who attended saw the Ebor that year as in 1979 there was a long ITV strike.

Jack Cowes, a local builder, was a great friend of my parents and one day he suggested that I should upgrade my Ebor day experience and join him and his son Nick and their racing pals in the County Stand. I learned a lot from them and that there was a much more scientific way of studying form, rather than, for example, name association, but also that picking winners at York was very difficult. Jack introduced me to many of his pals who had been racing at York since just after the

Second World War. He was well liked and connected. I put my name down to become a member. There was a waiting list then of about 10 years. One of his regular gang was Brigadier Ponsonby of West Witton. I mentioned that I fancied a share in a horse and the Brigadier put me on to his son Henry, who was one of the first to set up racing partnerships. He is still going strong and having winners with several trainers.

I signed up to a 10 person syndicate with a horse called "Gracie" trained by Paul Cole to run in the colours of Christopher Wright, one of the members who had his own colours. She was a disaster so the following year (1994) I had another go with a horse, also trained by Paul Cole. Crystal Gift was by Dominion and out of Grain Lady and his first race was at Newmarket. I distinctly remember Henry's chat line on the morning of the race implying that as the horse was having his first run he was there for the experience and that the hope would be that he would come in at a further date. Willie Carson was on board and was beaten by a head at 25/1 by Blue Ocean. Willie had obviously not listened to the chat line.

The Racing Post gave him a RPR rating of 80. Twelve days later at Lingfield, on the All -Weather in a one mile race, he was ridden by T Quinn and went off at odds-on (1/3) favourite. He led until the last furlong and was beaten by ¾ l by Soldiers' Leap. That was another lesson learned on the path of a lifetime in racing about the pitfalls of betting on odds-on favourites.

One more run in December 1994, again as a short priced favourite (6/4) saw him come 7th of 12 to the winner Rome to Nome. Injury struck and after 144 days off the track he returned to have two more runs (Brighton and Southwell) where he was beaten by 9 lengths and 12 lengths respectively.

On 24th June 1995 he ran at Redcar, ridden by Kevin Darley I was the only partner there. Henry had indicated on his tipping line earlier that day that in view of the fact there were only 4 runners and it was a poor race; "This was the one." He came third at 3/1 beaten by 6 lengths. Kevin Darley told me on dismounting something on the lines that if I were to trace the pedigree back far enough I would find this horse was related to a rattlesnake. My face dropped and after lame excuses during the post-race analysis, about the rain (a sea fret) having affected the ground, I submitted my resignation the next day. I am not sure now if I could have done so and I do not remember what the financial arrangement was, or the terms of the partnership were but I did not want to be the owner of a racehorse anymore. So much nervous anticipation, many dashed hopes and very disappointing.

In 1995 I was persuaded, or I seem to remember cajoled in view of my fairly recent experiences with Gracie and Crystal Gift, to join a partnership with my good friend Nick Cowes and Brian and Nigel Plows who he knew. Brian Plows had in turn been persuaded by Dean McKeown to have a horse with Jimmy Leigh who trained at "Mount House " stables in Lincolnshire. In 1990 Dean had ridden On Tiptoes, trained by Jimmy Leigh to victory in the Queen Mary at Royal Ascot and of course had ridden for Mark Johnston Racing.

A horse had been bought in 1994 at the Doncaster Sales and was by Chillibang. We called him 'Chillam'. This was not the first horse I was to help name with a hidden meaning of which I was completely oblivious (eg Golden Fountain in the Kingsley Park 11 Partnership). Chillam ran several times as a 3-year-old, mainly at Southwell and was winning every race at the four furlong marker but never stayed on to win. He just did not stay and it confirmed what I had overheard Peter Easterby telling Jim that the offspring of Chillibang 'Just don't get home'. Not long after my failed, second/ third attempt to become a successful racehorse owner my racing fortunes changed.

On Boxing Day 1998 at Wetherby races Nick Cowes was successful in a charity auction. The prize donated by Mark and Deirdre was a visit to Kingsley House for breakfast, the gallops followed by a trip to the races. Peter Neumark also a KP 10 partner, joined Johnston Racing via a similar charity donation route some 20 years later. Off we went on 21st April 1999 and had breakfast in the old kitchen accompanied by Mark and Deirdre with Darryll Holland in and out of the room.

Mark had runners at Catterick and we went to support Doonaree a three-year-old colt. The owner had recently died. We stepped into his shoes with suitable decorum until the last 100 yards when "Dazzler" Holland with the race seemingly won eased off a bit and only just got up on the line urged on with extremely loud backing vocals from Deirdre, Nick and myself. We were well and truly hooked. Champagne flowed and we asked Mark to buy us a horse. Two days later Debbie Albion wrote to me with terms and conditions; the training fees were 39 pounds per day.

A King's Signet colt ex Gratclo was purchased for 9,500 guineas at the St Leger sales. The following winter and spring he (Cheeney Basin, named after an ancient fort, now a hollow at the highest point of Kippax, our village) showed some promise and was ready to run when he cocked his jaw on the High Moor gallops, got rid of Keith Dalgleish and attempted to jump a stone wall overlooking Park Farm. He failed to do so. He was a mess (Keith broke a finger) but eventually they got them both back together and the following year with some justice Keith rode him to win his maiden at Catterick .

Cheeney Basin and Keith Dalgleish 19th November 2001 at Southwell. *Tony Knapton*

During his short career at Kingsley House he won three times. One of the wins after his maiden success was on 19th November 2001 at Southwell. It was in the Robert Louis Stevenson Handicap over 6 furlongs, again ridden by Keith Dalgleish. It was a Class 4 race and his first race on sand with £4, 065.75 to the winner. He led more or less from the off and the Racing Post's analyst described it as *"an emphatic victory"*. Horse and jockey are shown below flying home.

 Bobby Elliott, who was representing the stable said:

"You can never be sure how they'll go on the sand, but this one obviously loved it. He had the worst of the draw so I told Keith Dalgleish to make plenty of use of him early on, otherwise he would have to race 10 wide on the bend. Keith thought it wouldn't be a problem bringing the horse back to five furlongs, so we have got that option for him as well."

Cheeney Basin with Keith Dalgleish at Southwell November 2001. *Tony Knapton*

He went up seven pounds to an Official Rating (OR) of 69. His next four races all at Southwell were tougher but he ran well so did not drop much lower in the handicap. Joe Fanning on 29th January 2002 rode him to success in the betdirect.co.uk Claiming Stakes, and we were mystified that he wasn't snapped up.

Joe Fanning and Cheeney Basin 29th January 2002 at Southwell. *Tony Knapton*

A few days later, again ridden by Joe in a Claimer, at Wolverhampton he was claimed by John Akehurst for 8,000 guineas. He didn't win, but came a short head second to Branston Pickle. Both Nick and I were sure that was the best outcome for us, but I remember feeling a little empty and sad on the long, quiet drive home.

Joe Fanning and Cheeney Basin 29th January 2002 at Southwell. *Tony Knapton*

However, these events at the turn of the century had restored my faith in racehorse ownership. Winning was such a great feeling. Celebrating in our local pub afterwards, the Chequers at Ledsham, drinking champagne out of Southwell's cut glass bowl and telling all and sundry, over and over again how Keith and Joe had sped away and left the fields for dead. What a feeling.

Of course the trick is to pick the right trainer, who in turn can pick the right horse and who employs experts in every field to look after them. This increases your chance of owning winners and is probably the best advice to give someone who is thinking of taking the plunge into racehorse ownership.

Nick and Sue's family increased in size soon after this period and Paul Proud, the third member of the partnership, decided that although he had thoroughly enjoyed his racing, this was the end of his short career. I was not going to give up on my winning streak, after so many earlier false starts and looked around for an alternative route to horse ownership.

CHAPTER 3
FLAT RACING: BHA HANDICAPPING & RATING SYSTEMS

3.1 Types of Races

The fixtures for all races are published in the summer of one year, by the British Horse Racing Association (BHA), for the following season. For example 1,481 fixtures were *"initially"* programmed in August 2019 for the 2020 season. They pointed out that the *"Fixture List balances well being of the sport's participants and the delivery of more competitive racing with commercial consideration."* Little did they know that the 2020 season of fixtures would be changed so much because of the Covid-19 pandemic. Throughout a normal year there is racing on most days initially, for the Flat, in the winter on all- weather (AW) tracks and in spring, horses race on turf, from the end of March at Doncaster's *"Lincoln"* meeting until autumn in early November, also at Doncaster, for the *"November Handicap."* The racing calendar is more-or-less set in stone with the Classics and Festivals taking place at the same part of the spring/summer and autumn every year. Within these events the famous races take place and also include preludes or trials for the Classics. For example the *"Dante Meeting"* in May at York includes trials for the Oaks and the Derby. Such was the disruption in 2020 the "trials' for these races took place after their eponymous races.

In any event only a few races are designated Class 1 and the vast majority of them are at a much lower level or standard. There is a large number of different types of race to accommodate these *"would be superstars"* but unfortunately many are destined not to make it. Nevertheless they provide enjoyment and frustration, sometimes in equal measure for the majority of people who are fortunate enough to own a racehorse.

The following Glossary of race types is based on and adapted from the BHA's publication of that name and their continued co-operation and agreement to allow publication here is much appreciated. They are correct to point out that each category of race has its own variations. The first group are races for horses which are starting their careers, in other words having their first runs. These, will be not necessarily be 2-year-olds but mainly are.

A **"Maiden"** is restricted to horses that have never won a race. They might run in several such races before they lose the *"maiden"* tag but on the other hand they might never win at all. A **"Novice"** is open to *"maidens"* but also a winner of either one or two races. The winners of a previous race usually have to carry extra weight (a penalty of perhaps 5lbs to 7lbs) according to the race conditions. Horses are no longer eligible for some novice events once they have raced more than a specified number of times set out in the race conditions.

Sometimes the conditions of a novice event are combined with an **"Auction"** race or **"Median Auction"** race. The former is confined to horses from the less expensive end of the market where horses have been bought cheaply at the Sales. The race conditions dictate that price limit. The weight they carry is based on the Sales price of the individual horse and weight allowances may be granted for horses purchased at various increments below the stated value. Thus the cheapest horses usually carry the lowest weights in the race. The latter **("Median Auction")** is also confined to horses from the less expensive end of the spectrum. In this case, the median price of a sire's offspring at the sales is the value that determines which horses can run. Horses by a sire who generated a median price at the Sales of not more than the value in the race conditions are eligible to run, with the exception in some cases of individuals bought for more than twice the amount stated in the race conditions.

From the beginning of the 2021 Flat season, changes have been made to the two-year-old novice and maiden programme, which will see restricted races merge into one race type. Horses can qualify for these races through their auction value, or, if they have no auction value their median auction value. This means that there will no longer be two-year-old auction or median auction races, but instead, five classes of novice or median races. The value thresholds for the restricted race bands will be published at the end of 2020 once the autumn sales are over.

One can see immediately that the conditions of these races will allow cheaply bought horses from sires who tend not to produce expensive yearlings to be allowed weight concessions and, thereby, a likely advantage. As this story unfolds it will not be a surprise to see that many of the partnership horses compete as 2-year-olds in these types of races.

The majority of races are, however, **"Handicaps"** where horses are allotted weight according to their handicap rating.

The handicap rating or sometimes called the handicap mark has the aim to give each horse in the race an equal chance of winning and thus make the race competitive and, therefore, hopefully more exciting to watch. It is supposed to be *"the great leveller."* Whether or not this stated aim is entirely successful or not is mentioned later in the book together with potential imperfections in the system. How these ratings are determined is explained later in this chapter. There are Maiden and Novice Handicaps, combining the principles of a Handicap within the restrictions of those race types.

The six categories of handicaps are listed below. Classes 2 to 7, based on the ratings of a horse. Letters A, B, C, D etc were once used to describe the levels of handicap.

Class 2 – Handicaps of rating 86-100, 91-105 and 96-110

Class 3 – Handicaps of rating 76-90, and 81-95

Class 4 – Handicaps of rating 66-80, and 71-85

Class 5 – Handicaps of rating 56-70, and 61-75

Class 6 – Handicaps of rating 46-60, and 51-65

Class 7 – Handicaps of rating 46-50

Horses with the lowest handicaps are the slowest ones and the highest class *"Class 2"* includes some of the most prestigious races in a season, such as Heritage Handicaps; the Ebor at York and the Britannia at Royal Ascot just to name two.

There are also:-

"Restricted Handicaps". These are where handicap races can be limited to a particular group of horses based on other criteria and not merely linked with their handicap rating. For example, age restrictions apply in veteran's races and a Nursery is a Handicap on the Flat limited to two-year-olds. Race conditions can also restrict entry in such a Handicap to those that, for example, have not won since a specified date or that have never won a race above a certain value.

"Classified Stakes" Eligibility for these races is determined by a horse's handicap mark but the weight carried is not. For example, the race might be designed for horses rated 0-65 but they all carry the same weight whether their handicap rating is 65 or not. These races provide an opportunity for horses of a similar ability to compete on level terms. *"A level playing field."*

"Conditions Races" (also known as weight-for-age or allowance races) Contests in which the weights carried are dictated not by a horse's handicap mark but according to the race conditions. These allocate weight according to the weight-for-age scale, the gender of the runners and via penalties for those that have won races of a certain value so that they must concede weight to less successful rivals. The weight-for-age allowance is explained later in the chapter.

"Seller" This can be a Handicap or a non-Handicap. The key element is the winner is offered for auction in the winner's enclosure post-race. All beaten horses in a Seller are available to claim via the same methods outlined for claiming races. A selling race can be, but is not necessarily so the lowest class of race.

"Claimer" Every horse in a Claimer can be bought after the race for the price registered at the time of entry. That price is one of the factors which dictates the weight each horse carries; the higher the "claiming price", the higher the weight to be carried. Some of these races can be quite valuable, but often have the same reputation as a "Seller."If more than one person puts in a 'claim' to secure the horse, lots are drawn to decide the winning claim. A 'friendly claim' is one placed by the horse's existing connections.

"Sales Race" These are valuable races largely limited to horses from a particular auction sale, usually as yearlings. The first entry fee is required soon after the horse is purchased and there are several forfeit stages in the year up to the race. The weight carried is usually influenced by the horse's price tag; obviously the lower the price, the lower the weight.

"Pattern Races" Every racing country runs elite races for their very best horses. In the 1970s, the major European racing nations cooperated to produce a template to specify when and where those elite races should take place. The idea was to avoid clashes of similar races in the racing calendar, which would result in a dilution in quality and field size for each. This framework became known as the Pattern and has been copied throughout the world.

The highest level of contest is known as Group 1 or Grade 1; followed by Group 2 and Group 3 races; the next two levels below in this hierarchy.

The continuing status of these races depends on the official handicappers from around the globe agreeing on their yearly performance figures. The average figure for the first four horses in each year's renewal is then in turn averaged with those from the previous two years. That three-year average must fall within certain parameters in order for the race to retain its status. In rare cases, there can be exceptions to this strict process of upgrades and downgrades.

The International Federation of Horseracing Authorities agree on the standing of each race based on those figures and taking into account the history of the race.

British Group 1s include races like the Derby at Epsom, the Gold Cup at Royal Ascot and the Nunthorpe Stakes at York on the Flat.

In 2018 Britain staged 36 Group 1 races on the Flat, 40 Group 2 races and 73 Group 3 races. Group races are more or less level-weights contests to determine which horse is the best, but the conditions always incorporate allowances for fillies/mares competing against colts/geldings and allowances determined by the weight-for-age-scale. Horses that have recently won at that grade or higher are usually also required to carry a penalty.

Listed races are the stepping-stone between handicap races and the Pattern, with the weights carried determined in a similar way to Group races.

3.2 A brief Guide to Handicapping

The British Horse Racing Authority (BHA) has published a detailed and comprehensive *"Guide to Handicapping"* and it is recommended reading. They start with a mission statement:-

Fair: Every horse will be treated fairly and with the highest level of integrity at all times, strictly on the merit of its form and using good handicapping practice.

Transparent: BHA Handicapping will be accessible and understandable for all customers. BHA methodology will be published, demystified and actively communicated.

Accountable: BHA Handicappers will be available to participants to provide logical and reasonable explanations for their decisions via the appropriate channels at the appropriate time.

Consistent: Using robust data analysis, the BHA Handicapping department will monitor and publish its work to ensure a consistent and equitable approach for all customer groups.

Progressive: The BHA Handicapping department will conduct research and analysis to ensure its policies are optimal in achieving a fair outcome for horses racing in British handicaps.

BHA handicappers or assessors watch every race and a horse is given a *"performance figure"* for a particular race. This is the rating which the assessor thinks each horse has achieved in the race and it is expressed on an identical scale to handicap ratings. A race can be watched *"multiple times"*. Most importantly they: take into account everything they know about each of the runners and the specifics of the race (the racecourse, the distance, the ground, the draw, the relative weights carried, the tempo at which it was run, etc) plus more interpretative factors such as whether a horse had started slowly, raced greenly (showing signs of inexperience) or had been hampered/eased. To illuminate this analysis further, a number of handicapping tools are also used. Performance figures for each run of every horse's career are retained. This profiles what they think a horse has been achieving and how they are performing in comparison to their handicap rating. An initial handicap mark will often be the best performance figure that a horse has achieved in (what will usually be) three qualifying runs.

If a horse wins, for example, its first race it may be given a handicap mark. There are *"numerous tools available to us when assessing a race"*. Some of these are outlined below:-

Time analysis

"When we refer to the time of a race, we are describing the official time taken from the start of the race until the winner crosses the finishing line. On the Flat this is usually recorded electronically. We use calculations to compare the times of races over different distances at the same fixture. These are adjusted for the distance of the race, the weight carried by the winning horse, any weight-for-age, any adjustments to the usual course (rail movements), any significant wind and the respective ability of the horses involved. The resultant figure is referred to as a speed figure, or in some instances a time figure."

Speed figures

"A speed figure tells us which races at any particular fixture on a particular day were truly run, meaning we can largely take the result at face value, and those which perhaps provide a less-than-true reflection of the relative merits of the horses involved. A well-run race would return a speed figure very similar to the performance figure we believe the winner to have achieved in that contest. A falsely run race could reflect the fact the pace was on the steady side or conversely overly strong. In both cases, the result is more likely to be an untrue reflection of the relative ability of the horses involved.

*This information is very useful to us. For example a steadily-run race will almost certainly lead to the runners finishing more bunched than might otherwise have been the case because they tend to tire at a later stage of the race than normal and not to the same extent. In this instance we might adjust the poundage used to calculate performance figures, using a higher multiplier to exaggerate the distances between the finishers. In a race run at an overly strong pace, the horses tend to tire at an earlier stage and to a greater extent. This tends to result in them finishing at longer intervals than under normal circumstances. In this scenario, we might adjust our multiplier downwards to close the distances between them and achieve a fairer reflection of their relative abilities. In both cases, a good race analyst will often arrive at the right conclusion with the naked eye, but speed figures not only confirm what has likely been seen but also quantify the extent of the discrepancy. Speed figures can be a very useful tool when rating a race where there is little proven form to go on. However, you have to delve a little deeper than simply drawing a direct comparison with the time of another race. Are you sure you're comparing like with like? That's where **sectional times** come in.*

Sectional timing

"For further depth of time analysis a race can be broken down into sections, often from jump to jump in National Hunt and furlong by furlong on the Flat. Some Flat courses have the infrastructure in place to record 'sectionals' electronically; others are still a work in progress. For those that don't have the technology yet, it's possible to take sectionals with a stopwatch or a dedicated computer programme, depending on the

camera angles that are provided. Sectional times are particularly useful to help understand the pattern of a race. For example, a speed figure compares the time of a race with other races on the same card, but solely using the time of one race as a guide to another (often where there is little previous form to go on) can be misleading. If the races have been run at different patterns it could be like comparing chalk with cheese. If the sectional times tells us the 2 races have been run at a similar pattern, the first race becomes a much better guide to what the form of the other is worth. Sectional times certainly add detail to speed figures and can confirm whether a race that produces a slow time has been run at a steady pace or an overly-strong one. That information can affect the multiplier we use when working out the poundage differences between horses – we may increase it when a steady pace leads to an overly bunched finish and decrease it when a strong pace has strung a field out. Sectionals on individual horses can also confirm which horses may be flattered by their finishing position and which may be better than the result suggests.

Sectionals can also be used to put a time into context. For example when Coventry Stakes winner Calyx won on his debut he recorded a relatively slow time compared to the handicap run over the same distance. When those races were broken down into sectionals it showed that Calyx was significantly behind the handicap on time by halfway. The fact he was able to get as close as he did to the handicap's final time suggested he was well above average. He also happened to draw upwards of 5L clear of a strung-out field as he did. [In other words he ran very quickly during the second half of the race as demonstrated by the sectional times]. Those distances suggested he might be good but that was dependent on the opposition not being substandard. The clock left no margin for doubt."

Historical standards

When handicapping some races – usually Maidens or Novices– the handicapper has little or no previous evidence to use. Newmarket's race the Wood Ditton, staged every April for unraced three-year-olds, when all of the participants are making their racecourse debuts is an extreme example.

In order to rate these races and ascribe performance figures to the horses involved, the handicapper therefore places greater emphasis than normal on the handicapping tool called "Historical Standards." This is based on the BHA's historical record of all races.

Historical information can often provide a ballpark figure to suggest what the latest running of any particular race is worth. Based on the premise that races will attract similar types of horses each year, past performances can be a useful initial guide to the worth of the latest editions. A simple average of past winners/seconds/third/etc of a particular race would give a basic overview of what has happened previously and what has possibly been achieved in the latest edition. But standards differ from a basic average in that they take into account the finishing distances between the principals in that latest edition, thus producing suggested figures based on what has actually happened interwoven with the historical evidence.

The main thing to remember about race standardisation – or indeed any other handicapping tool – is that it is only a starting point. Race standards provide a historical context and a guide as to where initial calculations suggest the latest edition of a race should fit. Alongside this tool others are used, such as **time analysis** to derive our initial figures. As more evidence becomes clear – that is, as more horses from a race like the Wood Ditton run again – the initial figures that rely more on race standards may need to be raised or dropped. This is called **collateral handicapping** (or back handicapping). This process ensures past performances are reviewed as the form-lines develop and also provides a more accurate record of what happened on the day for when those figures are, in turn, utilised for race standards in the future.

3.3: Weight- for- Age [WFA] Allowance.

"The Laws and Practice of Horse Racing", written by Admiral Henry Rous, a British Member of Parliament and Jockey Club official, was published in 1866 by A H Bailey & Co, London. He introduced the principles of handicapping and in his book was included amongst many other deliberations of events of that period a Weight-for-Age Scale. The rationale behind this scale and the bare bones of it are still in use today but is now compiled by the BHA. He realised, as have many others since, that the performance of horses can improve as they grow up. The WFA scale sets out the weight allowances given to younger horses, usually 3-year-olds, to enable them to compete equally with their older counterparts. It is designed to compensate them for their lack of physical maturity. It also attempts to take into account the physical progress, which the *"average"* thoroughbred horse makes as it matures.

Two-year-olds will not have grown sufficiently to be considered mature. They do in fact develop very quickly especially after they have arrived at training establishments. This maturing, which includes such things as growing, putting on muscle, and filling out are physical attributes which continue into and throughout their three-year-old careers. In addition, with experience horses grow in mental strength and usually are easier to handle (not all of them unfortunately) than when they first arrive at a training yard.

The allowances are usually a few pounds and the amount is dependent of the particular race and its distance. A 3-year-old horse in an open age race would be expected to tire more quickly over a longer distance as it is not fully grown than its older opponents. However, as a season progresses the weight allowances are reduced as of course the three-year-old is older by the end of the season. Only months older but it matters.

The reduction in the allowance is linear and it is based on the assumption that *"the average horse develops at the same rate every half month."* The BHA is open in its admission that: *"It is accepted that different animals develop at different rates-some will be ahead of the scale, whilst others are behind it."* during the season.

For the six years 2010 to 2015 the BHA compiled figures for the strike rate (SR) of 3-year-olds in 8000 Handicaps compared with the SR for their older opponents. Strike rate is the number of wins divided by the number of runs. The results were conclusive and showed that the younger horses had a greater SR than the older ones. The inevitable conclusion was that the allowances gave the 3-year-olds an advantage as they had been too generous. In 2016 one lb was deducted from the allowance for a 10 furlong race, 2 lbs for a 13 furlong race and 3lbs for races of 2 miles and over.

3.4: Racing Post, Racing Post Top Speed and Timeform Ratings

In addition to BHA assessors there are other handicapping teams at work on the racecourse. Perhaps the best known of these are the Racing Post's and Timeform's analysts, who watch and report on every race. In the former's case often within the hour after a race has finished. They also provide a performance figure (in pounds) for every horse which is known as the Racing Post Rating or RPR. These ratings are in fact very similar to the BHA ratings. For example the RPR for Godolphin's Ghaiyyath after the 2020 Juddmonte International at York was 131 whereas the BHA rated him at 130.

To arrive at their RPR many of the factors that have already been mentioned in the description of how the BHA go about their job in the provision of performance figures and handicap weights are taken into account. The RPRs are based on a horses's ability at its current handicap weight. So if a horse wins a race carrying 9 stones and the second carried the same weight the winner's rating will be increased (as would the BHA's figure).

The time it takes for a horse to run a race is recorded. These times are taken into account to arrive at the rating. In addition so are sectional times (sometimes referred to as "splits") recorded at some racecourses. Much is made of these times by at least two well known rating methods: the Racing Post's Top Speed ratings (TS) and Timeform.

The former ratings are figures which give insight into the ability, potential and preferred ground conditions of a horse and are measured in pounds. They attempt to make correction for the different tracks encountered, the going and weather conditions. They claim that a mature horse carrying

9 stones with a rating of 100 has the ability to meet the Racing Post's " standard time" in a race which is run truly and on good ground. All distances are proportional back to 5 furlongs and the ratings are calculated on the basis that 1 second at 5 furlongs equals 22 lbs.

The "standard time" is the average of the ten best times for a particular race over the last five seasons for a mature horse with an official BHA rating of 100 carrying 9 stones on Good ground. There are "track records" for every race but these are the fastest a horse has run in a particular race.

Timeform was founded in 1948 in Halifax, West Yorkshire by Phil Bull. He was born in Hemsworth also in West Yorkshire and died in 1989. The company was bought by Betfair in December 2006 and since February 2016 it has been owned by Flutter Entertainment. Phil Bull set out to derive a mathematical link to describe the performance of a horse, based on how fast or slow (the time) it ran in a race. He will always be remembered not only as Timeform's founder but for the shrewd observation that: *"A time will tell you how bad a horse isn't, not necessarily how good it is."*

Jim McGrath "the Sage of Halifax" was associated with Timeform from 1974 until 2019 and is also a well known broadcaster. At the parade ring at York he once showed me how he and his assessors operate. They watch every race and also record what would appear to be the smallest of detail before and during the race. The attention to detail in the parade ring involves not only recording how a horse looks but how it behaves. For example did it appear to be athletic and a good mover? big? small and or backward? was it coltish? did it need two handlers? and so on.

It may seem so obvious that if a horse runs the fastest time in a race it will win it, and this is true but the objective of a horse race (usually one would think) is to run faster than the competition, which may involve tactics and may include not running as fast as possible throughout the race. Timeform quote a figure that only about 40% of flat races over the minimum distance of 5 furlongs are truly run. This can be seen by the naked eye and most course commentators will often describe the start of a race as a slow or a steady pace and as the business end approaches the pace has picked up or increased. However sectional times are invaluable in putting the meat on the bones of these observations. Timeform's experts do this. On rare occasions sectional times confirm what the eye sees but one can hardly believe it is happening, for example Frankel's Guineas in 2011.

James Willoughby writing in the *"Owner Breeder"* soon after the race ("Owner Breeder", 23 May 2011) described how he had measured the sectional times himself by the use of a *"special video which takes some of the guesswork out of estimating the position of the furlong- markers."* In the article he bemoans the lack of official measured sectional times and although they are more available in 2020 than they were in 2011 their measurement is not widespread and they are not universally available, unlike in America and the Middle East. From my point of view the measurement of times and their compilation is important as the data are absolute and not derived from an opinion based on subjective assessments as to how a horse has run. The data lend themselves to mathematical analysis sometimes using computer algorithms and I feel it is a meaningful step forward in the description of a horses's performance and suggests a more scientific approach to the determination of a handicap rating.

For anyone wishing to read more about the use of "times" I would recommend James Willoughby's article in the Racing Post, *" When rating horses, everything is time and time is everything"* Wednesday March 18 2020. Another expert in this field is Simon Rowlands who has spent many years associated with Timeform. He has written widely on the subject of times and handicapping including a series of articles; *"Simon Rowlands Guide to Handicapping"* for *"At The Races"* and monographs for Timeform in their *"Timeform Knowledge"* series. In March 2019 his article; *"Sectional Timing"* was published in the Kingsley Klarion.

CHAPTER 4
HISTORY OF JOHNSTON RACING PARTNERSHIPS

4.1 The Always Trying Partnerships

The first Always Trying partnership was announced in September 2000 in the Kingsley Klarion along with its terms and conditions.

The partnership was to comprise 20 equal shares in two horses, which were to be purchased at the yearling sales with the aim of racing them as two and three-year-olds. Mark would aim to buy them at an average cost of £15000 each. An initial outlay of £1500 and 24 monthly payments of £250 secured a 5% share. Johnston Racing Ltd underwrote the partnership until October 2002 and standard training fees were charged. Partners received a quarterly financial statement and an AGM was to be held in September of each year. The thirteen Always Trying partnerships are shown in the table below.

Askalani Star and Thunderous Falls were the horses in this first partnership and it was already up and running when we parted with Cheeney Basin. I decided to stay with Johnston Racing and in 2003 joined the second Always Trying partnership. The terms and conditions were very similar to the first one. There were three "nominated partners" namely Liz Pescops, Chris Wilson (accountant) and Phil Marrison. The late Phil Marrison was the man to go to in those early days and he acted as a conduit between partners, always making sure they were introduced to each other and kept up to date with any news. Sadly he passed away on 11th March 2015. He was a thoroughly nice man and has been greatly missed.

Table: The 13 Always Trying Partnerships

Year	Horses	Partnership	No of Wins
2001	Askalani Star Thunderous Falls	AT I	1
2003	Always Waining Always Flying	AT II	7
2005	Always Baileys Always Stylish	The Always Trying Partnership	2
2006	Always Best Always Fruitful	AT III	3
2007	Always A Rock Always Attractive	AT IV	3
2007	Always Bold Always Brave	AT V	5
2008	Always Certain Always Cruising	AT VI	1
2009	Always Dixie Always Dazzling Always De One Always De Man	AT VII	3
2011	Always Et Toujours Always Ends Well Always Eager Copperwood	AT VIII E	8
2013	Always Fabulous Scottish Academy	AT IX	
2013	Bute Hall	AT X	2
2014	Maid in Rio	The New Fairyhouse	7
2013	Broxbourne	Ready to Run	8

Joining this partnership turned out to be a stroke of good fortune. Of course I met Liz , Ruth and Phil for the first time, but I am sure Liz and Ruth will understand and I know Phil would not have minded when I report that the best contributor to this good fortune was that Always Waining was one of the horses. He was an Unfuwain colt out of Glenarff, and was purchased by Mark for 9,000 Guineas.

Always Waining's Races 16 May 2004 to 15 October 2004.

His first race was on 16th May 2004, on Good ground, over 1mile 1 furlong (ridden by Joe Fanning) in a Class 4 Maiden where he showed some promise to come 3rd of 12 runners. He improved on his first run, six days later at Chepstow ridden by Keith Dalgleish again in a Class 4 Maiden. It was slightly further, 1mile 2½ furlongs, and he came third again but this time was well clear of the fourth horse Gjovic in the ten runner field. This early promise was confirmed on 31st May again at Chepstow when Keith Dalgleish rode him to his maiden victory. This time it was over 1mile 4 furlongs and the step up in trip and this performance made up for running green on his first two starts. He was rated at (OR 85) and thereby eligible for Handicaps.

His first run in Handicaps did not go smoothly. It was on 2nd July 2004 at Haycock Park, a 1mile 4 furlongs Class 5 event. Mr W Hogg was on board and he did well to stay there as the saddle slipped during the race. The horse looked to be full of running but with the jockey askew on board there was nothing he could do to drive him home. He came 5th of 9 runners. These unfortunate events were witnessed by Mark from above as he was trying to land his plane in the middle of the track. He did manage to arrive at the unsaddling area (on foot) to meet the disappointed partners and a disconsolate Mr Hogg.

Always Waining at Ascot. *Bernard Parkin*

In spite of this mishap the blossoming of the horse continued when six days later, at Newmarket with Joe Fanning on board he came third in a Class 3 Handicap over 1mile 4 furlongs. There were 15 runners and he was only beaten by 2 lengths. Excitement was mounting and he was entered at Ascot on 24th July on the "King George" day. His race was the Class 3 South African Diamond Rated Stakes again over 1mile 4 furlongs and again with Joe Fanning on board. He was with the field for the early part of the race but burst through in the last two furlongs to pull away from the others to win by five lengths from stablemate Fort. Doyen, trained by Saeed bin Suroor and ridden by Frankie Dettori had won the King George and Queen Elizabeth Stakes earlier that afternoon, a race over the same distance in a time one second slower than Always Waining. As Liz Pescops has already described (in Chapter 2) Phil Marrison was so excited that his congratulatory bear hug cracked two of her ribs.

Glorious Goodwood was just around the corner and off he went four days later to carry a 4lb penalty in a Class 2 Handicap over 1mile 4 furlongs, ridden by Joe Fanning. He battled hard and managed to fight for longer than his stable companion Fort but much to the disappointment of his supporters he came 6th of 16 runners. He was put up 3lbs to a rating of (OR 96) and was the second top weight in his next race on 19th August at York and carried 9st 6lbs. He could not live with his 9lbs lighter rivals and came 9th of 13 runners.

Always Waining at Ascot. *Bernard Parkin*

It proved to be good experience on my favourite track as he returned on 1st September to contest the prestigious Elite Homes Garrowby Lane Handicap. He had only been dropped 1lb for his Goodwood run (OR 95) but put up a tremendous show to come fourth and beat stablemate Etman. Supporters lingered in the unsaddling ring under the 4th sign until we had to make room for the the horses, which came into the parade ring for the next race. A photograph of the horse and a youthful looking Paddy Trainor has been on display at home ever since. That was his penultimate run and the last one was on 15th October 2004 in a Claiming race at Newmarket. It was Soft going and lashing it down with rain but he seemed not to mind and romped home, hugging the nearside rail and running as straight as a die to win. Joe Fanning was to ride the first and this last race for us as not surprisingly he was claimed by Mr P Clinton for £30,000.

He changed National Hunt trainers a few times but ended up with Peter Bowen for whom he famously won three "Tophams" at Aintree. Around this time I was often greeted on the golf course with cries of *"How's that Always Waining doing Robin? I see he has just won another Topham."* I pointed out of course that well done to the new owners but we are partnerships that run horses on the Flat and not National Hunt.

Always Waining's total career earnings amounted to £325,703 of which £57,327 represented his contribution when racing on the Flat for MJR and the Always Trying II Partnership.

Always Waining 4th in the Garrowby Lane Handicap,1st September 2004 with Paddy Trainor. *Mikaelle Lebreton*

<u>Always Baileys</u>, a colt bred by MJR by Mister Baileys out of Dubiously and named by yours truly was the most successful in the "Always Trying Partnership". He won at the third time of asking on 21st May 2005 at Carlisle in the New Fixture Maiden Auction Stakes. It was an evening meeting and Nick Cowes and I drove up after work and met Ken Stenger and George Donaldson (early "Always Trying" stalwarts) at the track. Jock Bennett had only recently been promoted to Assistant Trainer and MJR had four runners that evening. Always Baileys ridden by Kevin Darley made all and beat Bryan Smart's Bad Angel Eye and Mick Easterby's The History Man by 1¾ and 2½ lengths respectively. He had the advantage of an inside draw and the Racing Post analyst considered that the "form is nothing special". Notwithstanding this assessment, which was of course not published until the next day we all were thrilled and enjoyed a complimentary glass of champagne in the Winners' Reception room. MJR's other horses won and as some of their owners had not travelled to Carlisle from Dubai I accompanied Jock in drinking some champagne on their behalf.

Nick took possession of my car keys and I am forever grateful for being driven home to West Yorkshire in the early hours of the next day.

He was successful again at Goodwood on 29th July 2005 ridden by John F Egan in the Scottish Equitable Jockeys Association of Great Britain Nursery (Handicap) a Class 3 race for 2-year-olds over 7 furlongs. He won easily. "BJ" in the Racing Post wrote [Always Baileys] *"could do no more than win readily, with something in hand, although he hugged the favoured inside line unlike many of the beaten horses. Connections reported that the softer ground aided his return to form after jockeys reported he had not liked firmer ground on his last two starts. He finished strongly, suggesting even another furlong would be no problem and as such with a middling rating, he could be one to follow this autumn."*

This prophecy nearly came to fruition on 3rd September at Haydock when he was only beaten by a neck by Genari. A rise to a rating to (OR 81) put a stop to his winning although he came close in four subsequent races. He was sold to Trevor Wall at the end of 2006.

Always Baileys, Kevin Darley, Rob Kelly and happy connections at Carlisle. *John Grossick*

Always Fruitful and Kevin Darley with Neil Hodgson

Always Fruitful (Always Trying III) was bred by MJR Ltd and was by Fruits of Love out of Jerre Jo Glanville. Fruits of Love, owned by Mick Doyle, was the winner of some most prestigious races including the Hardwick at Royal Ascot twice, and under a superb ride by Keiren Fallon the £300,000 Dubai Turf Classic at Nad Al Sheba.

Thus hopes were high for Always Fruitful when on 10th May 2006 he went to post for the "Uredale Maiden Stakes" at Ripon, a Class 5 race over 6 furlongs. Drinbola trained by Barry Hills was favourite. He was bumped at the start and was at the rear when Kevin Darley switched him wide. He ran green ("wandered") over 1 furlong out, but when "ridden" he stayed on and led near to the finish to win. The Racing Post analyst said that he deserved credit for overcoming signs of greenness. He made up a fair bit of ground and knuckled down to get up close home. *"A seventh furlong will be a big help."* Nigel Tinkler told me in the bar afterwards that he noticed it took Kevin quite a while to pull him up, which indicated he was doing his best work at the finish line. He certainly was and a delighted set of owners (notice KP 10's Fred and Muriel Shaw to the right of the view) welcomed the horse and Kevin led in by Neil Hodgson.

Happy connections at Ripon with Always Fruitful and Neil Hodgson, 10th May 2006

Sixteen days later he stepped up in class by three grades to run in the " Youngsters Conditions Stakes" at Pontefract, a Class 2, 6 furlongs race for 2-year-olds. It was Soft going and again Kevin Darley was on board. He met a very good horse that day in Hellvelyn, trained by Bryan Smart and ridden by Ted Durcan and was beaten by him into second by four lengths. The third horse home Tombi trained by Howard Johnson and ridden by Darryll Holland had cost 450,000 Euros as a yearling. The winner was touted as being Royal Ascot bound. Indeed he was and he won the Group 2 Coventry Stakes with the same trainer/ jockey combination.

A week later we were at Epsom on Derby Day. The Derby was won by North Light under another inspired ride from Kieren Fallon. Always Fruitful was in the 6 furlong "Vodafone Woodcote Stakes" (Listed Race). Horses were fractious in the stalls and Kevin Darley was shouting at the Starter to wait. He explained, on dismounting, that he hadn't been ready and had shouted to that effect at the Starter just as the stalls opened. He started slowly, as he missed the break, but gained on the leaders finishing like a train to come home in third only 3/4 of a length behind the winner Sadeek, trained by Kevin Ryan and ridden by Neil Callan and a neck behind Going Straight, trained by Ian Wood and ridden by Ryan Moore. He secured **"Black Type"** for third place and eventually was given a rating of (OR 97). I felt the big highs were just around the corner. A runner on Derby Day!

Debbie Albion watching the race in the office at Middleham immediately said *"The Chesham"* after she'd seen him pick up so well. Indeed that is what happened and on 24th June 2006 Always Fruitful ran in the "Chesham Stakes" a 7 furlong race at Royal Ascot. It was good to firm and there were 11 runners. He went off as the favourite as everybody else, of course, had seen how unlucky he had been in the Woodcote. He came 7th and never got into the race. Again disappointing and hopes and dreams dashed but the reality soon sank in. The fact that the horse had run on Derby Day and then at the Royal Meeting, put it all into perspective.

Always Bold and Always Brave

Always Bold and Always Brave were the horses in Always Trying V partnership until they were sold at the Tattersalls Autumn Horses in Training Sale at the end of October 2008. Always Brave by Danehill Dancer ex Digger Park did well winning only once, but finishing second three times and third once. Always Brave earned £7,766.

On the other hand Always Bold, a colt by King's Best out of Tarahkana turned out to be a bit of a star and whenever Mark is asked to recall which horses were amongst the best in the Always Trying partnerships Always Bold always gets a mention. He fetched 65,000 guineas as a foal and in October 2006, at Tattersalls Book 1 Mark paid 14,000 guineas for him. Sue Russell (of KP 10) was riding work at MJR at the time and can be seen on the Middleham Moor gallops on board Always Bold.

Sue Russell on Always Bold on the
Middleham Moor Gallops, 2007

He ran an incredible 79 times in total, mainly in the National Hunt Code and 14 times for MJR until he switched codes. He achieved a maximum rating of (OR 91) on the Flat and won 4 times, came second twice and third 4 times and earned £35,112. He did not run as a two-year-old and started off over middle distances in the winter of 2008 on the All-Weather. After two creditable runs at Lingfield coming 3rd and 2nd on 5th January and 29th February 2008 respectively, he ran in a Maiden Stakes (Class 5) over 1 mile 4 furlongs at Wolverhampton. He won easily and led from start to finish and was eased down by Greg Fairley in the final furlong. His three runs entitled him to a handicap rating of (OR 85). Upped in class for his next two races he struggled but on 18th July at Hamilton down to an official rating of 79, he put the field to the sword at the 3f marker where Joe Fanning moved him to the front and he stayed on strongly to win the John Smith's Stayers Handicap by four lengths from Jim Goldie's Gordonsville. These two had spread-eagled the remaining four runners.

He was put up 4lbs by the handicapper and just over a month later was again at Newmarket in the Ballygallon Stud, Ireland NSPCC Handicap (Class 4) over a longer (1 mile 7 furlongs) trip.

Joe Fanning on Always Bold, Hamilton. *John Grossick*

Joe Fanning on Always Bold 18th July 2008 Hamilton. *John Grossick*

J P Guillambert was on board and again he was sent into the lead 3f out and stayed on well to win. His last two wins demonstrated that he was a stayer with plenty of stamina. A kind handicapper put him up only 3lbs.

The demonstration of his ability to stay was not unnoticed by Mark and the Cesarewitch, at Newmarket a Heritage Handicap for 3-year-olds + with a nominal first prize of £100,000 to the winner was being considered.

Before that race he ran again on 21st September 2008 at Hamilton in the "Tote super 7 Buttonhook Handicap" a Class 3 race with a first prize of £10,592. It was over 1 mile 5 furlongs. It was Soft ground and no doubt a real test of stamina. He won by ½ length from Linda Perratt's Acropolis and the Racing Post's analyst said that he was *"Always in a decent position to attack, once in front he showed all the tenacity you come to expect from a Johnston runner in a driving finish"*. He was now aimed at the Cesarewitch, for which a 4lb rise in the weights would help his chances of getting in the contest.

Ben Curtis at the Curragh 2013. *Pat Hannon*

He did get in and was down towards the bottom of the weights at 8st 1lb. Nicky Henderson's Caracciola carried 9st 6lbs to win and had come second the year before. This race is always targeted by the National Hunt trainers and the first three home were from National Hunt yards. I looked at the race as a "shop window" opportunity rather than a winning one. The jumps code trainers would see how game he was. In the end he did well coming 13th out of a field of 32 runners, 14½ lengths behind the winner. Donald McCain bought him at the Tattersalls Horses in Training sales soon thereafter for 65,000 guineas.

Maid in Rio *"Horses can make fools of us all"* is an adage I have heard often in racing circles. It is sometimes used to express disappointment when a horse that was thought to be a *"certainty"* to win a race (there isn't such a thing) comes last. Or vice versa when a horse is given no chance in a race but wins it. A good name for a horse would be *"Who'd have thought it"*. Perhaps the most annoying example (for the vendor) is when a horse, thought to be of limited ability is sold on for a song and for its new owner becomes a star. Maid in Rio almost fell into that last combination as she was up for sale by auction after winning a Musselburgh Seller. MJR were bidding to buy her back but when they finally bid 8,500 guineas and they were about to pull the plug no higher bids were received so she was transported back home to Middleham.

Maid in Rio at Newmarket (July) with Scott Doherty

Maid in Rio was one of the four horses bought by Mark at the 2012 Fairyhouse Tattersalls Yearling Sales for the New Fairyhouse Partnership formed in November 2012 which was to run until October 2014. The fee per share was £12,000. The colours were the second colours of Ron Huggins who along with Paul Dean, Bob Barbiaux, David White and Richard Huckerby were long standing owners of MJR. Newcomers were Kingsley Park 10 Partnership's Billy and Catherine Ross, and also Carol Woods and Brian Sleight.

She won 7 times, came third once, earned a total prize money of £54,100 and was sold at the Tattersalls December Mares Sales for 52,000 guineas. Needless to say we were pleased she had not been sold earlier. Perhaps for the want of a few hundreds of pounds from another bidder she would have been.

The first 3 runs in 2013 were hardly impressive. She finished 5th out of 6, last and 15th out of 17. The third race was the Tattersalls Ireland Super Auction Sale Stakes at the Curragh where Atlantic Affair, owned by Ron Huggins came second and picked up a prize of 23,750 euros. Princess Tamay one of the Always Trying Partnership horses came eleventh. Maid in Rio came 15th and was ridden by the up and coming jockey Ben Curtis and was, in view of the two partnership runners and Atlantic Affair in the race, sporting my colours (see photograph above). It was around this time that Mark realised a standard set of colours for partnerships was needed to avoid any confusion.

Connections in the winner's enclosure, Newmarket (July). *Nick Cowes*

On 16th September in the aforementioned Musselburgh Seller (7f) : the Drinks Express Selling Stakes she won with Princess Tamay in third. Mark Brown, the Racing Post's analyst pointed out that she had dropped in Class and was *"readily going clear and seeing it out strongly."* The combination of a drop in grade and step up to 7 furlongs worked in her favour and, on this evidence, she should be competitive in Nurseries. We were up and running (we thought) until a month later at Goodwood, admittedly in a higher Class 4 race over 7 furlongs she came last. What made matters worse she was injured soon after this race which was to be her last in 2013.

After 184 days off the track she returned on 17th April 2014 at Ripon in a 1 mile Handicap with a handicap mark of 71. She was last. However she put in a much better performance on 12th May 2014 with an official rating of 67 in her next race at Lingfield over 1 mile finishing 5th of nine runners.

Joe Isherwood of the Racing Post commented on the race at Lingfield that she *"got left behind when the tempo rose and was keeping on at the finish"*. Signs perhaps that she needed further, I thought. Mark will have seen this and he often told me that he always watches and tries to remember what the horse was doing or how it was travelling at the half way stage of a race as well as at the end. On the last day of May at Haydock Park she was asked to race over 3½ furlongs further than she had ever done before in the "Vanessa Rogers Handicap". It was a Class 5 and she carried 9st 4lbs. A furlong or so from the finish she pulled away from the rest of the field to win by 1¾ lengths. A comfortable victory. She had found her forte namely a longer trip.

On 19th June 2014 at Ripon in the Curvy Bridal Boroughbridge Handicap over 1 mile 4 furlongs off an official mark of 72 she came right away from the field and won by 7 lengths. Paul Mulrennan who had ridden her told me that the further she went the better she got. The step up in trip had been the key to her. I was the only partner there and was interviewed by *"At the Races"*. Obviously I was able to agree with Paul's assessment who was interviewed first. They pressed me to tell them what the future plans were and I finessed for a while and waffled on about the Carlisle Bell (first contested in 1599) until I ran out of steam and advised them that my role in the partnership was to make sure nobody bought any cheap champagne and as to where next the horse was to race those were decisions for the team at Kingsley House.

Maid in Rio strides away from the field in the Brown and Shipley Wealth Management Stakes at Haydock with Franny Norton on board. *John Grossick*

Not surprisingly she went up 6lbs for her next race on 27th June 2014 at an evening meeting on the July course at Newmarket. It was the Invesco Perpetual Handicap Class 4 over 1 mile 5 furlongs. She was second favourite at 100/30. She beat a 200,000 guineas Galileo colt (Battersea) trained by Roger Varian by a neck and battled to hold on at the end having made smooth progress to get there. She had completed her hat-trick.

Catherine and Billy Ross, John Dawson, Nick Cowes and I celebrated with Mark who had three winners on the night. I was very quickly putting the role of champagne quality assessor into practice. Nick and I had my golfing pal Barry Ibbetson as a driver, Carol Woods and Brian Sleight left fairly early to travel back to Durham.

Fifteen days later we met Battersea again, at Ascot in the Neptune Investment Management Handicap Class 2 over 1 mile 4 furlongs with Franny Norton on board. She carried one pound more than him. The ground conditions (good to firm) were the same as they had been at Newmarket. He beat us by 2 lengths and we only lost second place beaten by a neck in the last stride.

Maid in Rio and Franny led back by Hari Singh Bhati. *John Grossick*

Six days later she was again at Haydock in the Brown Shipley Wealth Well Managed Handicap (0-85) 1 mile 6 furlongs. She carried top weight and the track was Good to Firm. She went off at 6/4 favourite and Franny Norton was effusive about her winning performance. He said she stays forever and is such a willing horse and *"she'll probably win the Gold Cup"*. The Racing Post's analyst thought a good long distance race was on the cards and the Melrose at York was mentioned.

Connections receiving the prize at Haydock from Roger Hunt MBE. *John Grossick*

I have the trophy of that win and sitting behind the engraved wine decanter is a photograph of the presentation ceremony carried out by Roger Hunt MBE of Liverpool (my team and Franny's) and England. He gave a fantastic insight to the crowd and told them that he couldn't be sure the disputed crucial goal in the 1966 World Cup Final vs West Germany was over the line or not as he was looking away from goal at the time.

Discussions in the parade ring at Deauville

At this point of Maid in Rio's career she had scored plenty of goals and had won 4 times out of her last 5 races. Could she make it 5 out of 6? On 25th July 2014 both a big step up in class and in trip (2 miles), in the famous John Guest Brown Jack Stakes (Handicap) awaited. She annihilated the field with Silvestre de Sousa on board and won by 9 lengths from Hassle. She was 5/2 favourite and the only 3-year-old in the field.

She was entitled to a weight allowance, because of her age. Some of the other connections, although complimentary about her performance did point out this weight difference between their horse and ours.

This race cemented the growing love affair we, Catherine and myself, had with Silvestre de Sousa. Again, we could not have dreamt what this mercurial rider had in store in the future for us. Just short of £20,000 was the prize.

Five days later she ran at Goodwood. It was a big turnout of partners and Mark had to hire a box to accommodate us all with badges. Guest of honour was the terminally ill Phil Marrison, and the photograph of him with Jane Knight and myself belied his condition.

This race, the Goodwood Stakes (Handicap) was over 2 miles 4½ furlongs, a Class 2, 0-95, 3-year-olds + handicap. She led well into the home straight but as the extra distance took its toll she faltered and finished seventh beaten by Teak. Mark said after the race that *"There could be factors like the ground and the race coming quickly but I think it is just she didn't stay. She looked all over the winner 3f out and didn't stay. She was very very tired at the finish."*

Maid in Rio returns to the winners enclosure with a smiling SDS and Hari Singh Bhati. *Steve Cargill*

The presentation of the John Guest Brown Jack Trophy. *Steve Cargill*

Jane Knight flanked by Phil Marrison and the Author at Goodwood

Joe Fanning and the Author at Bagby International Airfield, Thirsk, North Yorkshire setting off to Deauville

On 17th August she travelled to Deauville and so did Billy and Catherine (in Mark's plane). I travelled with Joe Fanning from Bagby airfield near Thirsk.

We stopped off in north London to pick up Ryan Moore who was travelling from America having ridden there the day before. Ryan's trans-atlantic flight home was delayed so our pilot had no alternative but to switch off the engine while we waited for him. This was a mistake as once Ryan had arrived we couldn't start the engine up again. Various items of equipment were brought out to give the engine a "kick start" and the propeller turned. We were over the Channel when the pilot told me that he had been having trouble starting the engine so tended once he got it going, he kept it doing so. I was hoping he was correct and not just optimistic. Joe was fast asleep.

Ryan missed his first ride even though we dashed up to the track in the waiting car. Maid in Rio now encountered soft ground in the Prix Michel Honeyvet (Listed Race) for 3-year-olds. She got a 3lb allowance off the colts. She was never at the races. The pace was very slow until the final bend and she just couldn't go with them when essentially a 3 furlong sprint ensued.

On 4th September she went to Salisbury to contest the CGA "Persian Punch" Conditional Stakes. It was the season for flying and Charlie and I set off this time from Middleham in Mark's plane. She was again well beaten and remained out of form. A tendon injury soon after threatened to end her career with the partnership. There was a suggestion to keep her until the following year as the prognosis was a long spell on the sidelines. Maid in Rio was kept and the patience of the veterinary team got her back on four legs. She ran four more times but never really recovered her three-year-old form although fittingly she did win her last race on 10th June 2015 at Haydock with Franny Norton on board. A great servant she was.

The White Horse on the Hambleton Hills- glad to be back in Yorkshire

Preparing to return from Salisbury with Charlie Johnston

After the wonderful experiences with Maid in Rio some of us, Catherine Ross and I and perhaps Billy were walking on water. We discussed having a continued interest in horses with Mark and perhaps with a smaller number of partners. In the meantime we joined a partnership, Always Trying X which had a horse called Bute Hall on a one year lease, with an all-inclusive fee of £2,500 per share. He ran 17 times, won 3 times and came 3rd 4 times with earnings of £17,778.

Torridon at Wolverhampton and the gallops

I persuaded Mark during a stable visit to view the horses he had "on the shelf" to join me in a two-way partnership with a horse which I called Torridon, in memory of my trips to climb the Munros, especially Liathach in the Northwest Highlands of Scotland. He provided much pleasure without actually winning a race. I was perhaps still, but only just at the stage where the experience of owning a horse and going to the stable and racecourses to see it run was what I thought it was all about. This is only partly true, although both experiences are enjoyable ones, winning races is also a very important element of this sport. Coming away from the racecourse having watched your horse run but not feature in the finish and therefore the prizes takes for me the gloss off the day.

Torridon at Hamilton with Joe Fanning just beaten by Her Red Devil. *John Grossick*

Byres Road on the gallops with Katy Tyler (main) and Rachel Fox- Barnett (bottom right)
and his last race at Ayr. *Mikaelle Lebreton.*

Torridon is shown on the gallops in the montage with Adrian Nicholls on board, who is of course now a trainer. His run at Wolverhampton on 11ᵗʰ August 2014 coincided with the opening of the new Tapeta surface developed by Michael Dickinson who is shown in the background of one of the montage photographs (bottom left).

Torridon, ridden by Franny Norton came third, 4 lengths behind Madame Mirasol, trained by Kevin Ryan.

Byres Road as a yearling at Tattersalls December Sales 2014 Newmarket

He was not very successful although he just got touched off in a thrilling finish on 17ᵗʰ July 2014 at Hamilton (by Her Red Devil) with Joe Fanning on board.

So we tried again with a Pivotal colt out of Croeso Cariad and named him Byres Rood an area of Glasgow where I used to live and not far from where Mark and indeed Charlie, Nicky McGrath and John Scanlon went to University. He was bred at Usk Valley Stud and I was there on 24ᵗʰ November 2014 at the Tattersalls December Sales to "help" with his inspection prior to Mark buying him for 12,000 guineas. I visited the Usk Valley boxes before we and he left Newmarket to find his groom in tears at the thought of losing him. She did manage to tell me that he was a well-mannered horse but we would have to be patient with him. Indeed we were and his first race was 12 months after we had bought him. I took the photograph of Byres Road, at the Sales, and he did appear to have some growing to do. He was a "Rig" (one testicle concealed). However, he was a Pivotal offspring and there had to be a reason he was so cheaply bought.

He ran 19 times with two wins. He won at Lingfield on New Year's Eve 2016 with Jason Hart on board. He came second four times and third once with total earnings of £17,501. He was sold at the horses in training sales at Newmarket for 18,000 guineas making him a break even horse and one that I was able to follow from start to finish.

During the same sales season, I accompanied Mark to Ireland and the Tattersalls Fairyhouse Sales. It was enjoyable to be back in Ireland where I once worked and apart from being for a short while on the same flight path as passenger jets approaching Dublin airport, when we were told to lose height (immediately), we had a good flight and landed safely at Weston airfield. We had a good time at the Sales and Robert Smith and Mick Doyle joined us and together with Andy Oliver, who had been one of Mark's vets, we had a great session of reminiscing. We were in the very canteen where Robert had introduced Mark to Mick Doyle many years earlier.

Byres Road winning the Sunbets.co.uk. Handicap Stakes, 31st December 2016 ridden by Jason Hart. *John Hoy*

Three horses bought there were placed in the Kingsley Park 2 – Fairyhouse Partnership. A Rock of Gibraltar ex Real Cat filly named Fast Cat, an Intense Focus ex Star of Sligo filly named Star Focus and a Vale of York ex Livadiya colt named Triassic. It was probably tempting fate to name a horse "Fast" and indeed she proved not to be. Neither was Triassic. They were moved on and Mark kindly added a horse called Furiant to "KP 2". He proved not to be as successful as he had been with Godolphin.

However, Star Focus won at Beverley and the photograph shows the proud owners. Reginald Witheridge a future KP 10 partner was at the far right of the view. Fred Shaw of KP 10 was also in this partnership as were the Ross's.

I will leave Elaine Thompson to provide a fitting epithet to KP 2 adapted from an email of 16th December 2016. "It is not often a partnership fails to return even a small sum to the partners involved, I cannot recall the last one, but, unfortunately Kingsley Park 2 Fairyhouse is such a partnership. There were not quite sufficient funds to settle the final month's training fees, a shortfall of £4,369.55, but as you are aware Mark always underwrites the partnerships and Mark Johnston Racing Ltd will absorb the outstanding fees."

At the same time as this unhappy ending and somewhat financially poor outcome we embarked on a four-way partnership (Holleyhead, Johnston, Ross and White), which lasted a period of two (to three) years 2015-2017.

Star Focus with Joe Fanning and Scott Doherty and connections, on 23rd June 2016 at Beverley

JUSTE POUR NOUS - THINK SO - 19.05.2016

Kirsty Kettlewell on Juste Pour Nous and Mairead Heap on Think So. *Mikaelle Lebreton*

A colt Juste Pour Nous, by - Pour Moi (a Derby winner) ex Steam Cuisine, a filly Miss Van Winkle, by Rip Van Winkle ex Lasso and a colt Think So, by the Australian sprinter So You Think provided us with more problems.

Juste Pour Nous winning a Seller at Lingfield, 14th December 2016 with Joe Fanning on board

Miss Van Winkle was not successful although she did look rather splendid in July 2017 with Franny in my colours at Pontefract. She came 7th from 11 runners.

This was not a successful exercise with all three horses although Juste Pour Nous did win The Digby Brown Maiden Stakes on 1st September 2015 at Hamilton, and in addition to the prize money we picked up a "plus 10" (£10,000) bonus.

We all hoped that as he was a fine, strong looking horse he would do well as a three-year-old. That was not the case although he did take us to Royal Ascot, where he put up a respectable performance in the King George V Stakes. He went to the Horses in Training sales at Newmarket. Mark attempted to get the bidding started with an opening bid of 5,000 guineas. There were no other bids so "he was bought back in." Mark asked if we wanted to remain in the partnership. True to his generous style Mark transferred ownership into my name and colours, as David White and Billy Ross had opted out. A drop in class saw him on 14th December 2016 win a Seller, the Betway Classified Selling Stakes over 1mile 2 furlongs at Lingfield ridden by Joe Fanning.

He won well and when Joe was asked about the impressive performance he did point out that this was his form, i.e. Selling Class. David Pipe bought him for 7,000 guineas.

The partnership involving Think So, who cost 32,000 guineas as a yearling, was an expensive and chastening experience, which is worth a mention in view of what was to come and also amongst the undoubted, remarkable success story told in this book of what can also happen with racehorses. Unfortunately after some very promising early steps he developed a breathing problem. After one race Charlie Johnston described *"The noise he makes is as dramatic as I have heard and is clearly audible when the horse is being unsaddled never mind when he is galloping."* We were stuck and although wind operations are not always what they are cracked up to be with regards to increasing performance, without one the horse had no prospects. He underwent a "wind operation", which surgically was successful and after a period of recovery raced again. Typically in his races he would run well for most of the race but would falter at the sharp end. He did not make the grade and was sold locally for £500.

Miss Van Winkle in 2017 at Pontefract with Paddy Trainor and Franny Norton. *Brian Lunn*

4.2 The Kingsley Park Partnerships

While this adventure of owning 25% or 50% of horses and paying the same percentages of the training fees was wearing thin and was also draining away my patience and resources, the Kingsley Park partnerships were taking off. These were a very similar idea to the Always Trying partnerships but inevitably the passage of time had meant a slight increase in the fees. These new ventures mainly had three horses in each of them.

Table: A summary of the winning horses in the first 9 Kingsley Park partnerships

Kingsley Park 1 – Ready To Run – 11 wins	
Duke Street	5 wins
Atlantic Affair	2
Sur Empire	2
Cassandane	2
Rennie Mackintosh	0
Kingsley Park 2 – Fairyhouse – 1 win	
Star Focus	1 win
Triassic	0
Fast Cat	0
Furiant	0
Kingsley Park 3 – Originals – 5 wins	
Cape Speed	3 wins
Lido Lady	2
Lord of the Valley	0
Kingsley Park 4 – Ready to Run – 3 wins	
Kelvin Hall	2 wins
Ravenhoe	1
Stetchworth	0

Kingsley Park 5 – 9 wins	
La Casa Tarifa	4 wins
Teofonic	3
Celestation	2
Daleelak	0
Kingsley Park 6 – 5 wins	
Poetic Steps	3 wins
Ravenhoe	1
Villa Tora	1
Galitello	0
Kingsley Park 7 – Ready to Run – 4 wins	
Sennockian Star	3 wins
Gold Merlion	1
Pennington	0
Sennockian Song	0
Kingsley Park 8 - 2 wins	
Diviner	2 wins
Aisling	0
Copper Rose	0
Arms of the Angel	0
Kingsley Park 9 – Ready to Run – 9 wins	
Poet's Society	6 wins
Mambo Dancer	3 wins

I made enquiries (in November 2017) about joining Kingsley Park 8. The prospect of reverting to a 20th share of costs and a relatively lower purchase price had its appeal. However, such was the success of Kingsley Park 5 a large number of its partners simply transferred some of their substantial paid out funds to KP 8. There had been an offer for one of the KP 5's fillies and whether to accept this or not provoked lengthy discussions between partners and apparently resulted without consensus or agreement as to whether the offer should be accepted. This was a watershed moment and convinced Mark that rules with regard to selling horses should be changed. From Kingsley Park 10 onwards he was to make the final decision.

I think Richard Underwood and Fred Shaw also missed out on KP 8 but were to join KP 10. Nicky McGrath wrote to me on 10th November 2017 to answer my enquiry about joining KP 8, to welcome me back, to look forward to seeing me at the forthcoming partnership morning of Saturday 25th November 2017, but to tell me that KP 8 was full. However, owing to extra demand Mark had organised 3 colts to run for Kingsley Park 10. The next step was therefore to go see the horses and decide what to do.

CHAPTER 5
VIEWING: TRAINING TO RUN
5.1 Partnership Day Saturday November 25th 2017

I went along on Saturday November 25th 2017 to the Partnership viewing day at Kingsley Park. Two such events are held every year, at the end of a year, when any new arrivals are on show, and four months later, in the late winter to watch them being put through their early paces. Many are cantering upsides by then. Shamardal ex Sexy Lady and Dream Ahead ex Black Dahlia were viewed being ridden in the trotting ring. The Dream Ahead colt looked big, with a long neck and plenty of·condition. He also held his head slightly down and had a sultry, mean look. The Shamardal colt also looked magnificent with his chestnut coat and white socks. I thought they were going to be big, strong horses. The War Command colt ex Aguinaga had just arrived as he was purchased at the Tattersalls December Sales at Newmarket (which somewhat perversely took place in November).

The horses are shown taking their early steps on the gallops in the sequence of photographs taken by Mikaelle Lebreton.

It could be seen that the two relatively early foaled horses (the Dream Ahead and Shamardal colts) were being ridden away whereas the late (May) foal (War Command colt) was still going through the familiarisation process on a long rein.

Dream Ahead - Black Dahlia 12.12.17

Lauren Hickin up. *Mikaelle Lebreton*

Shamardal - Sexy Lady 30.12.17

Bhanwar Singh. *Mikaelle Lebreton*

After viewing, at a coffee break in the offices, I met Bryan and Sue Russell and we engaged Mark in a conversation about the Shamardal colt. We were aware that Shamardal was rated by Mark very highly and in fact he has said on several occasions that *"he was the best horse I have ever trained."* We were fully aware of Shamardal's reputation as a racehorse and more to the point at that moment his reputation as a sire. I could not understand how Mark had managed to buy the yearling for 12000 guineas as 250,000 guineas would not have been an unrealistic price for a Shamardal offspring.

Bryan Russell suggested that the plan for him would be to run in the Dante at York prior to the Derby. Mark replied that this plan was unlikely as he is likely to be miler, so we'll aim for the 2000 Guineas. I suspect Bryan's tongue was in his cheek, but I'm not sure Mark's was or not.

Apparently there had been a rumour or suggestion that this yearling may have a breathing problem. Mark doubted that the horse had such a condition. I was acutely alert to such information as I had only recently had the experience with "Think So" who undoubtedly had a breathing problem and underwent surgery. Ironically in that month's December edition of the Klarion there was an article written by John Martin discussing *"the topical issue of wind surgery."*

After lunch at Kingsley House Mark gave us all his assessment of the year. He described the three fillies in KP 5 (Teofonic, La Cassa Tarifa and Celestation) as *"arguably the most successful partnership we've ever had."* The KP 5 partners had enjoyed 9 wins. The prize money earned by the horses was £103,000 and the residual sales price £120,000.

Shamardal - Sexy Lady 30.12.17

Bhanwar Singh. *Mikaelle Lebreton*

Dream Ahead – Black Dahlia 12.12.17

Lauren Hickin all smiles. *Mikaelle Lebtreton*

War Command – Aguinaga 30.12.17

War Command ex Aguinaga long reined by Andy Larnach December 30th 2017. *Mikaelle Lebtreton*

Shamardal- Sexy lady with Bela Juszel. *Mikaelle Lebtreton*

John Scanlon wrote that Mark was delighted with the turnout of partners and had told the Klarion that he regarded the success and popularity of the Kingsley Park partnerships as one of the best things about the yard's 2017 campaign.

He repeated what he knew about the Shamardal colt and told us all that it would be a gamble (as buying every horse would be). He as always was at pains to point out at these gatherings that buying a racehorse should not be regarded as what one's bank manager would term *"an investment."*

John Dawson who I knew from the New Fairyhouse Partnership (Maid in Rio) also a vet and an alumnus of Glasgow University was there and I discussed with him my qualms re the Shamardal colt because of the recent experience we had with "Think So". He didn't think the Shamardal colt had a problem and was seriously thinking of joining KP 10. He didn't join. During lunch I met Paul Walker for the first time. He was wearing a Racehorse Owners (ROA) jacket and during our first conversation it was clear he had many bits and pieces of horses in syndicates.

We struck up a lasting friendship fuelled, once racing started, by an almost daily e-mail correspondence about the three horses, their chances, their performance and after a race where they could go next. Many of these conversations have been referred to in this book and at least, hopefully have contributed to the flow of the narrative. On 30th November 2017 the details, photographs and "pages" of all three colts, which were to form KP 10 were distributed. On the same day I wrote to Nick Cowes asking him to do some homework on the new partnership horses. I said *"It would not take much thinking about with a Shamardal colt, one of the three but it was reported at the sales to have a breathing problem – hence Mark got him for £12k instead of £200k."*

Nick liked the look of them and their pedigrees so I joined on 8th December 2017. I was the first of the Holleyhead, Johnston, Ross and White alliance to do so although it could be argued that Mark was the first having bought them. Billy and Catherine Ross had not been able to attend the partners' meeting and after a stable visit in the New Year they joined. David White joined the *"Originals*

Partnership" with *"Summer Moon"* and *"Mister Chiang"* instead. Summer Moon came second in the 2020 Cesarewitch and fetched 100,000 guineas at the Newmarket Horses in Training sale a few weeks later. It is not without some irony that the main reason for me joining and indeed Sue and Bryan Russell's too was the Shamardal colt which, as you will find out, although successful he was the least so of the three horses.

5.2 On the Gallops and Progress Reports

The first report on the horses' progress was issued on 3rd January 2018.*"I am glad to report that your three two-year-olds are fit, healthy and well and are at various stages of the breaking in/ridden process;*

War Command – Ex Aguinaga – *He has been working through and completing the various stages of the breaking in process. This has consisted of him getting lunged, long reined and getting used to commands from someone on the ground which acts as the basis of his educational process. He has since progressed to a rider sitting on him and today was the first day at ridden exercise which he has taken in his stride. From here he will develop his core fitness and will begin his 6 week ridden plan which prepares him for cantering on the All-Weather and full training.*

Dream Ahead – Ex Black Dahlia – *He has progressed well through the breaking in process and is now in the last couple of weeks of the 6 week ridden plan. Since he has been ridden each week his workload has increased and this prepares him for the introduction of cantering on the All-Weather. During this educational process he has also been asked to stop and start as well as turning which continually gets him used to the rider's instructions.*

Dream Ahead-Black Dahlia with Emma Dwyer. *Mikaelle Lebreton*

Shamardal – Ex Sexy Lady – *He is the furthest ahead at this stage of your three two-year-olds and has commenced cantering on the All-Weather completing 2x2 Furlong canters daily. He has taken this in his stride and is completing his work well. In the not so distant future we will be asking you to submit possible name selections for the three 2-year-olds."*

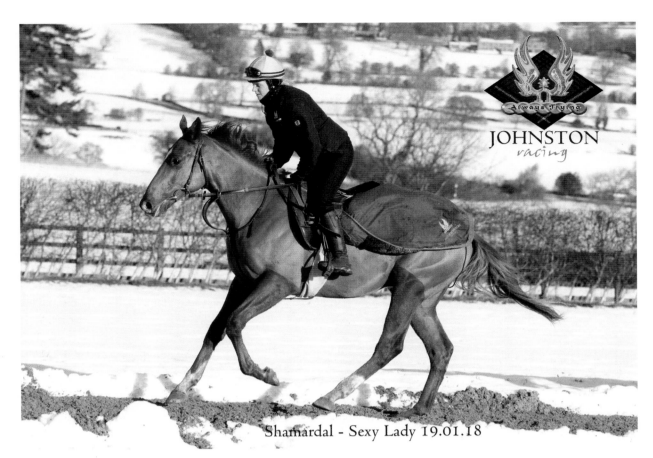

Shamardal - Sexy Lady 19.01.18

Katie Williams. *Mikaelle Lebreton*

This report was followed in January 2018 with photographs (taken on 13th and 19th January) from Mikaelle Lebreton of the Shamardal ex Sexy Lady and The Dream Ahead ex Black Dahlia.

The naming of the horses is undertaken by the partners. Each partner submits a name for each of the three horses. Usually the choice of a name takes into account the names of the dam and sire. Once all the suggestions are in, the office sends the names to the partners who vote with their three choices for each horse. Points are awarded for the choices as follows: 1st (3 points), 2nd (2 points) and 3rd (one point). Obviously the names with the most points are those chosen. On the 1st March the names selected were as follows:-

The Shamardal ex Sexy Lady was called PROVOCATION

The Dream Ahead ex Black Dahlia: DARK VISION

And The War Command ex Aguinaga: VICTORY COMMAND

PROVOCATION was not allowed, as it was discovered, that the first letter of the names of all German bred colts must be the first letter of the sire's name. Thus our horse's name had to start with the letter "S". So *STRICTLY DANCER* (to my dismay) was chosen as a replacement. I was relieved (and of course in the naming of horses or anything for that matter there is no accounting for the different tastes) when Weatherby's deemed the name to be too close to another horse's name for it to be allowed. Eventually and finally my provocative choice of SEDUCTIVE MOMENT (the name associates with the dam Sexy Lady) was chosen.

Prior to the naming process a second progress report was issued:

War Command – Ex Aguinaga. He is on week 5 of a 6 week hacking programme. On completion of his 6 week hacking exercise he will then progress to full cantering, starting initially at 2x2 furlong canters daily and increasing over the coming weeks. He has begun his stalls education by being locked in and walked out. His next step will be to spring out of the stalls.

Seductive Moment with Katie Williams. *Adele Brown*

Victory Command with Harvey Ewart. *Adele Brown*

Dream Ahead – Ex Black Dahlia – This colt is progressing well. He has completed 6 weeks cantering and is going upsides twice a week. He has also been sprung out of the stalls. Shamardal – Ex Sexy Lady – He was found to have some blood from his left nostril earlier in the week. It appears he may have banged his head in his stable overnight. He was given a few easy days of walking and trotting and will resume cantering tomorrow. Prior to this brief stoppage he had been cantering for 6 weeks. He has cantered upsides, jumped from the stalls and will have his first gallop in the upcoming weeks.

On Sunday 4th March 2017 partners and associates were invited to the late winter/spring meeting at Park Farm. The weather was definitely winter; *"The Beast from the East"* and only a few braved the snowy conditions to attend. I got stuck in the snow owing to lack of traction on the driveway up to the offices, which apparently was in full view of the security cameras.

Jock Bennett hurried out to help. The airstrip gallop was used to show the horses doing their stuff. Victory Command came up fluently but looked quite small. Seductive Moment and Victory Command are shown in the snowy conditions.

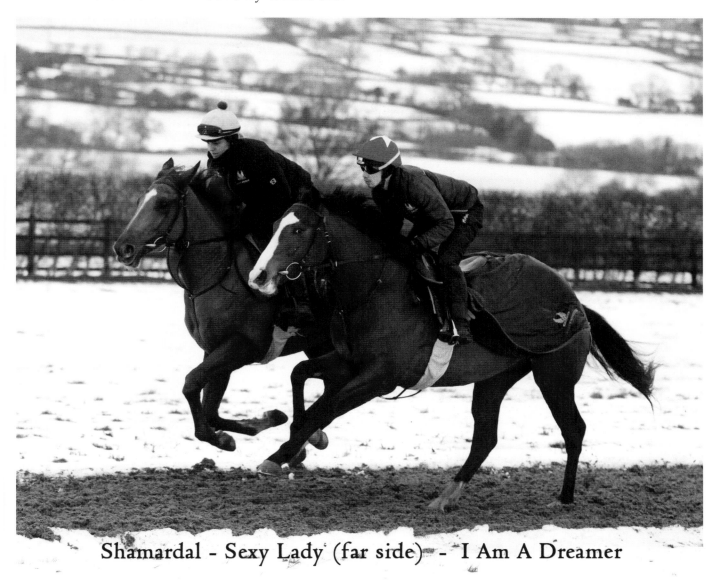

Shamardal - Sexy Lady (far side) - I Am A Dreamer

Katie Williams on Seductive Moment and Michael Tam on I Am A Dreamer. *Mikaelle Lebreton*

Soon afterwards (9th March 2017) Jock Bennett issued a video of Seductive Moment *"having a piece of work with another 2-year-old called I Am A Dreamer"*. Jock noted *"it was a satisfactory gallop and we are pleased with his progress. He also didn't make a noise in the gallop"*. This was good news indeed as a horse with a breathing problem it is most likely to be identified when it is at exercise.

Two of the horses had slight setbacks, whereas the relatively late starter Victory Command was progressing well. The bulletin (from Jock Bennett) on 19th March was as follows:-

Dark Vision – *Has had a bad foot abscess for the last 3 weeks he is now back sound and is currently walking and trotting and will be back cantering in the near future.*

Ex Sexy Lady – *Has unfortunately had a touch of sore shins so his work was reduced to just swimming he is now back walking and trotting and should resume full work shortly.*

Victory Command – *He has now progressed to cantering daily 2x3 furlong canters and is going upsides twice a week.*

Victory Command with Chelsea Butler. *Mikaelle Lebreton*

On 23rd April Mikaelle sent a picture of Victory Command on the gallops looking splendid and Jock Bennett followed up on the same day with enthusiasm for him after he had galloped.

Victory Command – *Had his first gallop out of stalls on Saturday and he galloped very well and continues to please us he is not 2 years old till the 25th May so our normal policy would not be to run until then but Mark may choose to run him sooner.*

Ex Sexy Lady – *Had his first gallop out of stalls on Saturday and we were pleased with the gallop although the other 2 horses in the gallop were a bit sharper he should improve for this and will probably have another gallop out of stalls again in the next few weeks.*

Dark Vision – *He had his first gallop on Saturday just upsides one other horse he was green and needed the experience he will gallop again next week.*

In fact Mark did choose to run Victory Command before his second birthday and he was entered to run on 5th May 2018 at Doncaster in a Novice Stakes. He was also entered at Thirsk in a Novice Auction Stakes on 8th May. Both races were over 5 furlongs.

Dark Vision 06.06.18

Katie Williams. *Mikaelle Lebreton*

CHAPTER 6

MAY/JUNE: FIRST JUVENILE RACES

A very important task for a racing stable, once horses are fit and ready to run, is to place them in races which they can win. The first part of the procedure is to assess the ability of one's own horse. Two-year-olds will have galloped against each other and a pecking order will have emerged and once they start performing in public this order will be either cemented or adjusted in the stable's knowledge of their crop of youngsters. Furthermore an equally important consideration is to assess the standard of the opposition. Again this may become clearer once the horses have run and there is some form on which to base a judgement. Also some horses jump off the page with regard to their pedigree (by Frankel, Kingman etc) but as I have already explained this is not always the best indicator of how good they are, especially if the horses have not run. Over 20 years ago when Cheeney Basin won at Southwell Bobby Elliot, who represented the stable told me that Mark was *"the best placer of horses in Handicaps that he knew"*.

Mark was interviewed on Desert Island Discs in 2020 by the laconic and lovely Lauren Laverne and she asked him about the placing of horses. Mark replied with the adage that the aim *"is to keep yourself in the best of company and put your horses in the worst"*. I had hoped Mark would have then asked Lauren for a sea plane as his luxury item but I suppose his choice of a pair of binoculars was more in keeping with the spirit of the programme.

6.1 Entries and Declarations

Weatherbys look after, amongst other aspects of horse racing, race entries and declarations. They also produce racecards for meetings and they receive and process the race results. Race entries may be made online through the BHA's Racing Administration website. For most races, entries under Rules close five or six days in advance of the race. Entries for major races may close several weeks in advance; in the case of the Derby, on the first Tuesday in December of the horse's yearling year, some 18 months ahead of the race.

There are entry fees for every race, a one off, relatively low sum for minor events, but to pay all the (forfeit) stages to run in the Derby it will cost many thousands of pounds. In prestigious races, where entry fees are substantial, there will always be a risk of not recouping these sums unless the horse wins. At the lower end of the scale even winning a race may leave the owner out of pocket. The funding of prize money is a massive topic and was brought more into focus in 2020 when for the first part of the truncated season the level of prize money was reduced dramatically. It is a really important matter with regard to the future of the sport but a dry, emotive and substantial one. There is insufficient room in this type of book to discuss it other than to say the level is too low.

Once an entry is made and certainly when it results in a declaration this information is often passed on to friends and family. Those who are not familiar with horse racing usually ask at least one of three questions. Is it going to win? How long is a horse's career and what does the jockey get? Obviously "It will be trying" is the answer to the first one; it depends on the horse is the second; and a few percent of the winnings is the third answer. Others receive a percentage of the prize money as outlined in the table below.

Prize Money Breakdown

Participants	% of total Prize Fund
Owners	80
Trainers	7.85
Jockeys	5.77
Stables	4.75
Industry Causes	1.63

Mark described Johnston Racing's entry procedure in an article in his *"Straight Talking" column in* the February 2017 edition of the Kingsley Klarion.

"Once you have trained the horses and got them fit, the next step is to enter them in races and select the race which gives you the best chance of winning. As with everything else, I decided from the outset that we must pay the utmost attention to detail in doing this and so I have employed every aid that I could find to ensure that no stone is left unturned. However, it seems that my openness about the systems we use and the fact that I have always used a computer system to aid in the selection of races has led to many having the ridiculous notion that we just make blanket entries and declarations.

An owner who has been with us for more than 25 years recently referred to my 'automated methods' and then admitted that he 'had a perception of a computer-driven process which forced automated entries for all eligible races'. Nothing could be further from the truth and it made me realise that, at the risk of giving away some of our secrets, I had better tell you all a bit about the process of making entries at Kingsley Park.

I assume that virtually every trainer now makes their entries online so, in that sense, everyone now uses an automated system but I have used a, freely available, software package called Easy Entry for more than 25 years.

It is a tremendously helpful piece of kit but it is, of course, only as good the information you put in and we have to start by entering relevant information such as age, sex, form, handicap ratings, auction price, median auction price, etc and this is now done by our office team. I then, personally, put in my preferred distance range and make selections for certain types of races eg sellers, claimers, Listed races, Group races.

All the details of the weekly Racing Calendar are fed into Easy Entry and then, once a week, I, having had suggestions from every yard manager who, in turn, will have sought suggestions from every member of the team, make the final decision on which horses we will look to make entries for. Then the Easy Entry system sorts those horses, and our 'Entry Diary' is printed in hard copy. It is then taken by one of the racing secretaries and she will manually add to it on a daily basis with up-to-date details on how many current entries the horse holds, whether it has been declared, most recent form, owner preferences, yard manager suggestions, headgear or equipment requirements, and many other details.

I then take this document and mark on my proposed entries, usually at breakfast each morning. It is then passed to Charlie and/or Deirdre for checking and further suggestions and, after that, to the racing secretaries. But they aren't ready to make the entries just yet. First they call all yard managers to tell them of my proposals and our head vet, John Martin, or his assistant. Queries arise from these last checks and those are brought back to me for a final decision before the entry is made.

Now, if time remains before the 12 noon deadline, they start phoning owners to tell them of our proposed entries in case they disagree. And, just in case we can't get hold of the owner, we subscribe to, and pay for, Weatherbys' text messaging service on behalf of all our owners so that they are informed of all entries and declarations that have been made for their horses. Maybe this adds to the impression that there are a lot of entries and that they are handled by automated systems.

One owner complained last year that he was getting too many phone calls from our office – one to tell him about yesterday's runners, one to tell him about declarations, one to tell him about entries – and a load of text messages repeating the same thing. 'Why', he said 'can't you just wait till it's all done and put it on one email?' Others, of course, want as much information as possible."

Declarations to run must be made by 10:00am two days before a Flat race. Within 15 minutes of the deadline closing Weatherbys are able to send electronic files (Texts) to data customers. This forms the list of runners and riders for each race which appears in the racecard or for example in the Racing Post App. Usually the stable makes the jockey booking. The draw for the stalls position is also made. Of course before the declaration stage the fields of runners where a horse has been entered in several races, can be studied.

It is an interesting exercise for an owner to go through the other entries and compare for example form (if there is any), breeding, the jockey, weight carried and trainer form, with one's own potential runner. Mark and Charlie would be doing the same of course. It is inevitable if the entries are spread out over the country eg Brighton, Newmarket and Beverley, people who live in the north might prefer purely on the basis of being easier to get to the last mentioned. However, not if there are *"hot shots"* or potential improvers running against your horse. There is no point in running at a convenient track if the horse is not likely to win. Mark and Charlie will declare when they think a horse has a good chance of winning or perhaps in the case of a Class 1 race, of coming in the first three to get *"Black Type"*.

There is now a transparent online declaration system so it can be seen exactly which other trainers' horses are going to be declared. This enables a decision to be made as to whether the horse should run. Having a potential choice, over a period of a few days, from several races and being able to study the potential participants provides a better chance of declaring in a race that the horse can win and equally important not declaring where the opposition is too strong.

Mark has summed up by saying *"I keep getting asked, at the moment, what the secret is to us training so many more winners than everybody else. This is it. We place the horses well, with their chance of winning, value, and future (handicap rating etc), always in mind."*

P J McDonald on Victory Command at Thirsk. *Adele Brown*

6.2 Victory Command's First Run

On 8th May 2018 at Thirsk Victory Command ran in his first race; the Wise Betting Racinguk. com Novice Auction Stakes (Class 5) (2-year-olds) over 5 furlongs. The ground was described as *"Good to Firm"*. He looked a picture in the paddock with his shiny coat and as ever he was well turned out. P J McDonald was on board. It was Bryan & Sue Russell's local track and one of their ambitions is to have a winner there.

It was good fast break over the minimum trip and Victory Command was soon prominent. Dragon Beat, trained by Tony Coyle led on the far rail with Bouncing Back, trained by Nigel Tinkler also prominent. At the half way point Victory Command looked fairly comfortable in third but was passed by Fastman, trained by David O'Meara on his way to win. We kept running on and were only beaten by a head into the third place by Dragon Beat. A most acceptable first run.

Sue, one of the more experienced horsewomen in KP 10, thought the horse *"was still very backward looking, as he was obviously still growing, which wasn't surprising as he still had 16 days till his official 2nd birthday. He showed lots of promise and finished third"*. The Racing Post's Steffan Edwards agreed that *"He shaped with promise on his debut."*

Mark was there to watch as was Paul Walker whose diary comment concurred with the *"very promising"* assessment by others.

David Hickin with Victory Command. *Nick Cowes*

Winning connections with Charlie Johnston, Jack Mitchell and Victory Command with David Hickin. *Nick Cowes*

6.3 Victory Command's Second Run

This was the Saint-Gobain Weber Novice Auction Stakes on 19th May at Doncaster. It was a Class 5 race over 5 furlongs and the going was Good to Firm. Colts and geldings carried 9st 2lb and fillies 8st 11lbs. However, being an *"Auction Stakes"*, for horses sold or bought in for £10,000 or less (Victory Command cost 6,000gns) there was a 4lb allowance. So he carried 8st 12lbs, whereas a large number of the colts carried 9st 2lb. Jack Mitchell was on board.

He broke well and led for the first half furlong. He was always in the front three in the company of Bungle Billy, trained by Les Eyre and Mazeo Lad, trained by Amy Murphy. At the two furlongs marker he was going smoothly in third. Oberon Martell, trained by Eve Johnson (a £28,000 yearling) came with a run down the inside and for a moment appeared to put in a challenge but Victory Command, under a good ride from Jack Mitchell, forged away in the final furlong to win by 1½ lengths and claim a 1st prize of £3,752.02.

Richard Young of the Racing Post thought that he would have no problems with 6 furlongs *"and is the type to win more races"*. Paul Walker's assessment was that he had won in the style of a good horse and was ridden well by Jack Mitchell.

In the winners' champagne reception watching the recording of the race, we were able to see again his surge forward in the final furlong and Charlie Johnston thought *"that it bodes well for the future"*. Indeed he was correct.

Of the three horses in KP 10 obviously Victory Command was up and running, but Dark Vision was taking a bit more time on the gallops to show some interest, in the task ahead of him. Seductive Moment was pleasing them with his work at home and entries were made for him in a 6 furlongs Class 4 Novice Stakes (Plus 10 Race) worth £7,400 at Ayr, and at Yarmouth in a 6 furlongs Class 3 Novice Stakes (Plus 10 Race) worth £15,000. He was also entered at Ripon in a 5 furlong Class 5 Novice Stakes, worth £6,000.

P J McDonald on Victory Command in the parade ring. *Mikaelle Lebreton*

Giovani Silva and Victory Command. *Mikaelle Lebreton*

6.4 Victory Command's Third Run

This was on Friday evening 25th May 2018 at Pontefract in the EBF Stallions Youngsters Conditions Stakes (Plus 10 Race) Class 2 for 2-year-olds over 6 furlongs. The going was Good. It was a big step up in class for Victory Command, but there were only five runners. He was treading the same path as Always Fruitful had done in 2006. The first three in the weights Kevin Ryan's Celebrity Dancer, Richard Fahey's Ninetythreetwenty and Victory Command had all won a race and therefore carried 9st 6lbs as a result of a 4lb penalty for their wins. Amy Murphy's Thegreatestshowman carried 9st 2lbs and the bottom weight Tony Coyle's Lincoln Park 8st 13lbs (a 3lbs allowance for first time out).

Pontefract's 6 furlongs is a stiff test as it is mostly uphill until the horses turn left handed into the short (2f) straight. An inside draw is preferable and we had that in stall (2). The betting showed that of the four that had had a run there was no clear resounding support for any of them, 9/4: Thegreatestshowman, 11/4: Ninetythreetwenty, with Celebrity Dancer and Victory Command at 100/30; Lincoln Park was the outsider at 16/1.

It was a good even break although Lincoln Park swerved to the right and dropped in to last place. In the early stages Victory Command was travelling well on the rail with Thegreatestshowman on his outside and Celebrity Dancer close by. Ninetythreetwenty was fourth at the 2f marker turning for home and Paul Hanagan was at work on him to pull him off the rail. He did so with great effect and stormed down the outside of Victory Command to win. The front two were well clear of the others. They had both won their last race at Doncaster and looked as though they had improved and would continue to do so.

A chilly evening at Pontefract, connections with Giovani Silva and Victory Command. *Mikaelle Lebreton*

Deirdre Johnston was in attendance and she reported that P J McDonald had said he ran a lovely race and did nothing wrong. He jumped well, sat on the rail with another horse (Thegreatestshowman) and he quickened out of the bend and tried to put the race to bed but was just caught by an improving horse with a turn of foot. P J went on to say of Victory Command: *"What a lovely horse and a pleasure to ride."*

It wasn't an exceptionally fast time but Adam Maidwent of the Racing Post thought the pace was *"sound"* and that Victory Command had improved. He thought the form was *"solid"*. As Paul Walker pointed out he did look as though he was going to pick up a *"nice prize for much of the home straight"*. £4,635 was not too bad for second; a present on his second birthday.

6.5 Seductive Moment Wins at Windsor

Making hay while the sun shone continued in the month of May 2018. I received a message that Catherine and Billy Ross were going to travel down to Windsor. I replied to say that I could not make it, and said that I hoped he is last into the stalls and the race commentator would announce *"we are just waiting for Mark Johnston's Seductive Moment"*. Well that came back to haunt me as sometimes during his career he was last into the stalls, uneasy at the start and often had to be pushed and shoved to go in, and on one occasion did not oblige at all.

The race was the Division 1 of the *"Sky Bet Fast Withdrawal Novice Auction Stakes (Class 5) (2-year-olds) over 6 furlongs"*. The going was Good. The jockey was William Buick. One could not make it up for a horse called Seductive Moment to run in such an aptly named race. John Scanlon wrote in the June 2018 edition of the Klarion –

William Buick takes Seductive Moment down to the start. *Francesca Altoft*

William Buick and Ratan Singh bring Seductive Moment back to the winning enclosure under the watchful eye of Mark Billingham. *Francesca Altoft*

Seductive Moment became the second Kingsley Park 10 winner of the month when making a successful debut under jockey William Buick at Windsor on May 28.

Tracking the leaders in fifth throughout the early stages of a six-furlong novice auction stakes, the Shamardal colt kept on strongly for continued cajoling by William and finished well on the stands' rail to defeat Oloroso by two lengths."

The assessment of Steffan Edwards of the Racing Post was that it was an ordinary Novice, and the slower of the two divisions by 0.8sec, but a nice performance from the winner (and) he looks a promising type.

William Buick said straight after the race that *"he is a nice straightforward colt with scope and he'll get further. I was always within striking distance, and once it opened up he picked up well."*

He was declared to run on 7th June at Carlisle in the Racing UK In HD Novice Auction Stakes, a Class 5 race over 6f on Good ground with Franny Norton on board. Jock Bennett sent out an update on the same day for the 3 horses with promising news about Dark Vision:

Dark Vision

He has had 4 gallops so far and is now cantering daily. He is heading in the right direction and hopefully should be on the track in July.

Seductive Moment

He is due to run tonight at Carlisle. He is currently favourite and he should have a very good chance.

Victory Command

He is due to run at Beverley on Saturday in the Brian Yeardley Condition Stakes. It is a race that we have a good record in and hopefully Victory Command will keep up the good work.

It was encouraging to note that Dark Vision had got over a few early teething problems and Jock thought hopefully he would run in July. So, soon it was hoped we would have all three horses in action.

Unfortunately Seductive Moment's first trip to Carlisle was not successful and although he pressed the leader and had a chance at around the 1 furlong marker he dropped away tamely to finish 7th of 12 with Nate the Great trained by Archie Watson the winner.

Victory Command in command under Joe Fanning at Beverley. *Hannah Ali*

Victory Command ran on Saturday 9th June at Beverley in the tough "Brian Yeardley" Class 2 Conditions Stakes with a drop in trip to 5 furlongs. The ground was Good and there was a 1st prize of £21,787.50.

He finished 3rd of 10 runners. He had led over 3 furlongs out but he could not quite sustain the effort. Deirdre Johnston reported *"that he jumped well and sat 1 off the rail with the horse on his inside just possibly taking him on a little bit more than we would have liked. He rallied well under pressure and was only beaten ½ length and 1½ lengths. He has run another very solid race in good company."*

Horses, especially young ones, are sometimes *"lit up"* as Joe Fanning once told me by the presence of another horse arriving upsides. This sudden burst of speed could result in too much energy being dissipated too soon. The most efficient use of the horse's energy store (and a human's too) is to run at a constant speed throughout a race. Also hopefully at one that is faster and sustained for longer than the other competitors.

Both horses were given a quick chance to redeem themselves as Seductive Moment was declared to run on 18th June again at Carlisle in a 5 furlongs Class 5 Novice Auction Stakes with Joe Fanning on board. Victory Command was declared to run the following evening in a Class 5 Novice Median Auction Stakes at Beverley also with Joe Fanning on board.

Seductive Moment had not read the script and came in 8th of 9 runners. Mark Billingham the Travelling Manager reported that he was beaten by 16 lengths. *"He travelled well in the race in second place; Joe was happy enough with him, but he didn't pick up when he wanted him to and he weakened from*

2 furlongs out. Joe was a bit disappointed." Early in July he was found to be lame after exercise and John Martin (vet) found after a prolonged investigation that he had fractured his right, hind hock. Box rest and then a period of rehabilitation was prescribed.

After Seductive Moment's disappointing runs anticipation and hopes were high for Victory Command on his return to Beverley.

6.6 We love Beverley: Victory Command wins twice in 7 days

Owners arriving at Beverley are met by Lorna and her team with a glass of chilled champagne readily available. I often joke and tell her that I will see her later; I should add that she also dispenses champagne to the winning owners at their reception, at the side of the weighing room.

On the evening of Tuesday 19th June the first race on the card was The Horse Comes First Novice Median Auction Stakes (Class 5). It was over 7½ furlongs and the going was Good. Victory Command was drawn 7 of 9 runners; an outside draw, which sometimes at Beverley may not be the best position to be in. The conditions of the race were:

"For novice two-year-olds, whose sire established one or more yearling sales in 2017 with a median price of not more than £55,000. The last sale to govern the price if sold more than once. Weights: Colts and geldings 9st 2lbs; fillies 8st 11lbs."

There was a 7lb penalty for each race won. Victory Command therefore carried 9st 9lbs, thus 7 pounds more than the 6 other colts in the race.

He broke smartly, straight out of the stalls like a bullet, and Joe was therefore able to come across from his outside draw to the rail, where he settled and led by 1½ lengths to 2 lengths from the grey Arden Warrior, trained by Archie Watson. At the bottom turn our horse and jockey looked to be travelling smoothly with jockeys behind hard at work and toiling in the two leaders' wake. Arden Warrior stuck to his task and stayed on well but 2 furlongs from home Joe gave Victory Command a squeeze and he quickened away to win by 2 lengths.

Joe was at his most relaxed and said that he was easy with him as he had run quite recently. I thought he was like a Class 2 horse in a field of average types and also thought he was a good 10lbs better. I predicted he would be rated by the handicapper in the mid 80's. To some extent it was like a stroll in the park. The time was reasonable and only slower by 2.40 secs than standard.

Dave Randall of the Racing Post pointed out that he:

"was carrying a 7lb penalty for a 5f Doncaster victory from a subsequent Sandown winner in May and finished third in a good 5f conditions contest here 10 days earlier. The War Command colt is a typically hardy horse for the yard who relishes quick ground and there were clearly no trip concerns stepping up to nearly 1m. He was sent straight to the front from a modest draw and completely dominated in tough fashion once asked to quicken towards the bottom of the incline.

Arden Warrior made it a one-two for his sire War Command. He clearly built on his promising Windsor debut, but couldn't get to grips with the penalised winner from some way out."

A week later (26th June) Victory Command returned to Beverley in the Racing UK In Glorious HD Novice Auction Stakes (Class 5) over 7½ furlongs. The course had been watered in view of the hot weather and lack of rain and the going was as Good to Firm. Joe Fanning again took the ride. There were only five runners, and he was drawn (4). The conditions for this Auction Stakes were that he was penalised 14lbs (2x7lbs) for 2 wins. But because of his relatively (now becoming a definite bargain) low purchase price we had a 6lbs allowance. As colts were to carry 9st 2lbs and fillies 8st 11lbs he carried 9st 10lbs; that was up to 13 lbs more than his rivals.

He went off as the odds-on favourite at 1/14!! Having learned my lesson with *"Crystal Gift"* some 30 years earlier I did not have a bet. I'm not sure about Bryan Russell who was also there, but I suspect he did not have a bet either. Charlie Johnston was on hand to give Joe the leg up.

Victory Command, Joe Fanning and Liam Conway return triumphant. *Hannah Ali*

Victory Command well clear of Biscuit Queen and wins by 9 lengths. Hannah Ali

He broke smartly as he had done in his previous race and took up a position again on the inside rail. It was a slow early pace, so Joe just got him to bowl along in front to lead by a length from Biscuit Queen, trained by Brian Ellison. At the foot of the hill and turning for home he gradually pulled away from his rivals and in the final furlong he was 5 lengths in front. It was a hands and heels ride and Joe asked the horse no questions. It was a very straightforward victory, which was never in doubt. I could see he was going to win from the bend, but was scolded by Liz Pescops, who thought my applause was premature. It wasn't, but maybe it was a bit cocky which is an unfortunate trait to reveal in this game.

Joe told us that he had worked harder that morning whilst riding out on the gallops at Kingsley Park. Charlie Johnston said that *"we hoped Victory Command would be able to win like that and we put him in the 'Spindrifter' at Pontefract next Monday so we will see what that race looks like. He was a good second to Ninetythreetwenty there earlier in the season."*

All in all a satisfactory end to a glorious June. Victory Command had run six times and was never out of the frame with 3 wins, a second place and 2 third places. Seductive Moment had won his first race and then faltered a little in his subsequent two starts. However, prize money accumulated in the pot for perhaps fancier entries to come. Dark Vision was on the mend and had put in some good work at home and was being entered up and hopefully would run his first race in July. Little did we know at this juncture what was in store.

Sue Russell walks in with Victory Command, Joe Fanning and Neil Hodgson. *Hannah Ali*

CHAPTER 7
JULY 2018: DARK VISION AT YARMOUTH, YORK AND GLORIOUS GOODWOOD; VICTORY COMMAND AT ASCOT

The month of July 2018 for the partnership was without question the highlight of the two years of Kingsley Park 10. There were a few small downs, as you will see, but these were far outweighed by the successes which kept coming thick and fast. Two of our horses took part in races, two of which were Class 1 events, at probably the best three racecourses in the United Kingdom. They ran with such enthusiasm and were ridden expertly by jockeys at the top of their game. Slowly away but coming with a final flourish became the hallmark of Dark Vision, whereas Silvestre de Sousa had a willing ally in Victory Command to win from start to finish at Ascot, with a virtuoso ride. Although I think most of us had perhaps not forgotten how little the Maestro of Middleham had paid for the horses we were, however, beginning to think ourselves equal to some of the very expensive purchases we were meeting at the track.

The fairytale month all began on 5th July at Yarmouth. Dark Vision who had remained fit for most of June and was entered in several races towards the end of June finally got his chance. He was obviously ready to run but had not been excelling at home, which sometimes is not necessarily a negative indicator. Double Trigger MJR's famous stayer was well known *"not to do much at home"*. The manner of his first win was a great surprise to his connections.

7.1 Dark Vision at Yarmouth

It was a warm sunny day and Paul Walker met Liz Pescops and Ruth Carty for lunch. Reg and Val Witheridge arrived soon after. All parties had a 400 mile round trip to get there and did not know what to expect. The race was the British Stallion Studs EBF Novice Stakes (Plus 10 Race) Class 4 over 6 furlongs. The going was Good to Firm. Franny Norton was on board.

There were only six runners and the expensively bought colt Alsimsaam, trained by Owen Burrows was the 5/4 favourite. The five colts were level weights at 9st 2lbs and the sole filly Rita's Folly carried 8st 11lbs. Reddiac and Sky Patrol were fancied whereas Dark Vision was the fourth favourite at 8/1.

They broke from the stalls with a fairly even break. Sky Patrol was away the best and ran down the middle of the track in front. The favourite Alsimsaam was positioned alongside Dark Vision near the inside rail. At the half way stage Sky Patrol and Rita's Folly were disputing the lead and Reddiac was making progress from the rear. Franny asked for an effort from Dark Vision who started to pick up but hung left. He was straightened out and he outpaced the others to win rather cleverly and was going away at the line with Sky Patrol staying on well to come second and Reddiac third.

Paul Walker commented that *"he arrived in the paddock looking like a 3-mile chaser. Clearly not fancied on the fast ground. He is a big bull of a horse and amazing he could win over 6f – finding a good turn of foot inside the last furlong. Great Yarmouth looked after us very well"*.

Franny after the race said *"he is a unit. He's got a monster neck on him, but just needed a bit of organising. He showed a bit of greenness, but was running through the line and for sure he can improve"*. Those who attended from KP 10 thought he looked a big horse but were impressed by his turn of foot from about 100 yards out. Reg and Val Witheridge told me that this *"debut win was memorable. It was a lovely summer's day and he absolutely outclassed the field. A very long trip for us but so worthwhile"*. A nice prize of £4,916.44 was picked up for the win.

Jock Bennett wrote to us and said *"Great result and did you notice he was the cheapest buy in the race?"* Mark added: *"One cost more than the whole budget for the partnership for the first year."* A good start.

Franny Norton on board Dark Vision with Ratan Singh. *Ruth Carty*

Happy connections with Katy Tyler and Ratan Singh. Ruth Carty.

Ruth Carty's collage of the Day

6th Race 4.50
The John Smith's
Median Auction Novice Stakes

Distance:	6f
Race Type:	Novice
Prize Money:	£15,000
Age:	2
Stalls:	Stands Side

No	Horse	st-lb	(kgs)	Draw

 1 Autumn Splendour (IRE) (15)   **9-8 (60.8) (4)**
B c Dandy Man (IRE) - Harvest Joy (IRE)
Jockey: Andrea Atzeni
Owner: Mr Saeed Manana
Form: 21 D
Trainer: James Tate, Newmarket
Breeder: John Hutchinson

Foaled 28 Feb. Half-brother to Andhesontherun, won twice at 5f and 6f. Won on his latest outing when 1-8fav at Yarmouth over 6f (good to firm) last month, beating Model Guest by 1 1/2l. Did it nicely last time and has claims despite the penalty for that success. Official BHA Rating -   **SP: 5-1**

2 Dark Vision (IRE) (9)   **9-8 (60.8) (10)**
B c Dream Ahead (USA) - Black Dahlia
Jockey: David Probert
Owner: KINGSLEY PARK 10
Form: 1 D
Trainer: Mark Johnston, Middleham
Breeder: S. F. Bloodstock LLC

Foaled 16 Feb. Half-brother to Al Hayyah, won twice at 7f and 1m. A winner at 8-1 at Yarmouth over 6f (good to firm) on his racecourse debut earlier this month, beating Sky Patrol by 1 1/4l. Finished his race well that day and could be a major player. Official BHA Rating -   **SP: 7-2**

 3 He'zanarab (IRE) (26)   **9-8 (60.8) (9)**
B c Footstepsinthesand - Ziggy's Secret
Jockey: Dane O'Neill
Owner: Douglas Pryde & James Fyffe
Form: 1
Trainer: Richard Hannon, Marlborough
Breeder: Mr Robert Norton

10 Foaled 17 Feb. Dam won twice at 5f and 7f. A winner at 8-1 at Windsor over 5f (good to firm) on his racecourse debut last month, beating Implicit by 11/2l. Shaped as though the extra furlong would suit last time and there should be more to come from him Official BHA Rating -   **SP: 3-1**

 4 Pearl of Qatar (60)   **9-3 (58.5) (3)**
Gr f Footstepsinthesand - Musical Molly (IRE)
Jockey: Ben Robinson (3)
Owner: Mrs J. A. Martin
Form: 1
Trainer: Brian Ellison, Malton
Breeder: Mrs Julie Anne Martin

Foaled 17 Apr. Dam won at 5f and 6f. A winner at 25-1 at Beverley over 5f (good to firm) on her racecourse debut in May, beating Ahlan Bil Emarati by 1l. Surprised almost everyone with that success on her first outing and could go close again. Official BHA Rating -   **SP: 7-1**

 5 Absolute Dream (IRE) (21)   **9-2 (58.1) (6)**
Ch c Dream Ahead (USA) - Absolute Diamond
Jockey: Jack Garritty
Owner: S & G Clayton
Form: 62
Trainer: Richard Fahey, Malton
Breeder: B. Kennedy & Mrs Ann Marie Kennedy

Foaled 6 Mar. Dam won at 7f. Placed once in two starts. Beaten a nose by Freed From Desire when second of 13 at 5-1 on his latest outing at Redcar over 6f (good to firm) last month. Produced a stirring finish to miss out narrowly that day and could go close. Official BHA Rating -   **SP: 10-1**

 6 Five Amarones (IRE) (50)   **9-2 (58.1) (7)**
B g Alhebayeb (IRE) - Mokama
Jockey: Alistair Rawlinson
Owner: The Famous Five Partnership
Form: 335
Trainer: Tom Dascombe, Malpas
Breeder: Kenneth Parkhill

Foaled 4 Mar. Placed twice in three starts. Finished 8l behind Arthur Kitt when fifth of 9 at 13-2 on his latest outing at Haydock over 6f (good) in May. Slightly disappointing latest, but placed on his previous starts at Bath and Pontefract and has been gelded recently. Official BHA Rating -   **SP: 12-1**

 7 Lincoln Park (28)   **9-2 (58.1) (2)**
B c Kyllachy - Twilight Pearl
Jockey: Paul Mulrennan
Owner: Craig Buckingham & Gary Dewhurst
Form: 54
Trainer: Tony Coyle, Norton
Breeder: Plantation Stud

Foaled 14 Feb. Dam won at 5f. Unplaced in both starts. Finished 2 1/2l behind Hesslewood when fourth of 10 at 33-1 on his latest outing over this course and distance (good to firm) last month. Showed considerable improvement from his debut last time and could be on the up. Official BHA Rating -   **SP: 10-1**

8 Self Assessment (IRE) (-)   **9-2 (58.1) (1)**
B c Elzaam (AUS) - Little Miss Diva (IRE)
Jockey: Clifford Lee (3)
Owner: Hold Your Horses Racing & Mrs E Burke
Form:
Trainer: K. R. Burke, Leyburn
Breeder: Joe Bishop Snr

Foaled 23 Feb. Half-brother to Princess Aloof, won six times between 6f and 1m 1f. His dam placed over a mile, suggesting that he may need further in time, so the betting market may prove the best clue to his chances on his racecourse bow. Official BHA Rating -   **SP: 20-1**

6

No	Horse	st-lb	(kgs)	Draw

9 Stronsay (IRE) (17) 9-2 (58.1) (8)
B c Gale Force Ten - Perfect Blossom
Jockey: Graham Lee
Owner: The Unscrupulous Judges **Form:** 5
Trainer: Bryan Smart, Hambleton **Breeder:** Mrs A. Morris

Foaled 23 Feb. Dam won eight times at 5f. Finished 7l behind The Mackem Bullet when fifth of 8 at 66-1 on his racecourse debut at Carlisle over 6f (good to firm) last month. Will need to have improved considerably to make an impact here. Official BHA Rating –
SP: 25-1

10 Top Cat (IRE) (16) 9-2 (58.1) (5)
B c Footstepsinthesand - Miss Mocca
Jockey: David Allan
Owner: Mrs Janis MacPherson **Form:** 3
Trainer: Tim Easterby, Malton **Breeder:** Minch Bloodstock & AV Bloodstock

Foaled 4 Mar. Dam a lightly raced maiden. Third of 11 behind Daafr beaten 3 1/2l at 50-1 on his racecourse debut at Newcastle over 6f last month. He was completely unfancied for his initial outing but he acquitted himself well. There should be more to come. Official BHA Rating –
SP: 8-1

NUMBER OF DECLARED RUNNERS 10...**(EXACTA)**
Running for the first time since Gelding No. 6.
STEWARDS NOTE
FIVE AMARONES: Following its run on 25/5/2018 it was reported that the horse hung badly left throughout.
PROBABLE S.P.'S
3-1 He'zanarab (IRE), 7-2 Dark Vision (IRE), 5-1 Autumn Splendour (IRE), 7-1 Pearl of Qatar, 8-1 Top Cat (IRE), 10-1 Absolute Dream (IRE), Lincoln Park, 12-1 Five Amarones (IRE), 20-1 Self Assessment (IRE), 25-1 Stronsay (IRE)

RESULT & PRIZE MONEY INFORMATION

1st	£9703	2nd	£2887	
3rd	£1443	4th	£721	
TIME		DISTANCES		

1. Autumn Splendour & **3. He'Zanarab** hold an entry in the Goffs UK Premier Yearling Stakes at the Welcome To Yorkshire Ebor Festival on Thursday 23rd August. There is no supplementary entry stage for this race.

3. He'Zanarab also holds an entry in the Al Basti Equiworld Gimcrack at the Welcome To Yorkshire Ebor Festival on Friday 24th August for which supplementary entries can be received by noon on Saturday 18th August for a stake of £15,000.

The connections of the winner, if qualified under the Rules of the Plus 10 bonus scheme, will share a prize of £10,000.

6

SIXTH RACE PRESENTATION & BEST TURNED OUT

The trophy for this race will be presented to the winning owner after the race by Caitlin McEachran, Assistant Brand Manager, Heineken UK Ltd.

John Smith's have generously given £50 and a case of John Smith's Smooth to the racing groom responsible for the best turned out horse in this race. They have also kindly provided a case of John Smith's for the stable of the winning horse.

85

7.2 Dark Vision at York 14th July 2018

Although Beverley and Hamilton Park are shooting up my leaderboard of favourite venues there can be no doubt in my mind that they still have some way to go to catch York. It is the place where I have spent a large part of my racing life, starting from humble beginnings on pub trips to the Tattersalls enclosure to being a member and now an owner. I had in fact been as an owner before this July 2018 race with Maid in Rio and Always Waining and the latter put in a great performance to come fourth in the Garrowby Lane.

Horses have raced at York since the days of Emperor Severus who died there (Eboracum) in 211 AD. Clifton Ings hosted the first organised events in the 16th century, but because this venue was prone to flooding the Knavesmire was drained to allow racing to continue from 1730.

It is a fair track, the viewing both of the parade ring and the course is unequalled in the UK and the Yorkshire hospitality at reasonable prices (the cheapest champagne, to wash down the fresh dressed North Sea crab on offer, on any UK racecourse) is much appreciated by the large crowds that flock there. However, to arrive on a hot summer's day in glorious sunshine with a horse that could only improve was a thrill indeed. Such was the weather that "Gentlemen" in the County Stand were allowed to attend without a jacket! *"Is it going to win"* I was asked as I mingled with my regular gang and *"what are you doing here on a Saturday"*. It was indeed unusual as John Smith's Cup day was usually very busy; the fact I was there was a tip in itself. *"It will be trying"* was my standard answer. The race card is produced above by the kind permission of Weatherbys.

There were four previous winners in the race and one of these, Richard Hannon's He'Zanarab was favourite at 7/2. We were joint second favourite at 9/2 with Richard Fahey's Absolute Dream.

The race was the John Smith's Novice Median Auction Stakes (Plus 10 Race) (Class 3) over 6 furlongs and on Good to Firm ground. David Probert was on board. He was moderately slow away from the stand rail draw (10) and was crossed by the favourite who broke from stall (9). Autumn Splendour led and looked to be keen to get on with things.

At the half way point Dark Vision cruised up into the race on the inside of the pack. He had *"travelled like a dream"*, the commentator said, and David Probert looked to his left to see where they all were. He just shot away from his rivals in great style with Absolute Dream 2¼ lengths behind. *"How good is this performance from Dark Vision? Now 2 out of 2"*, the commentator shouted.

David Probert told me that he gave him a bit of squeeze and off he went. I had been standing alongside Paul Walker, just outside the entrance to the Owners and Trainers' facility when Dark Vision cruised up to the pack apparently effortlessly.

We just looked at each other in stunned amazement. The hairs at the back of my head were bristling with electricity. We both knew at that moment that we had a good horse.

Richard Lowther in the Racing Post was also impressed and said:

*"**DARK VISION** didn't get away to the best of starts, not helped by being a little squeezed out leaving the stalls, but he made up his ground smoothly and bounded clear for an emphatic win. Unbeaten in two now, he had things go his way here to an extent, but he's a nice colt and it will be interesting to see how he gets on upped in class."*

Peter Naughton in the "Weekender" said *"Mark Johnston's juvenile deserves plenty of credit for travelling strongly into the race, having dwelt at the start. Soon in touch on the stands' rail David Probert was looking for dangers before asking his mount to quicken 2f out. This fine son of Dream Ahead easily brushed aside in-form rivals and saw off Absolute Dream in second by 2¼ lengths with more than 6 lengths back to He'Zanarab in third. Now unbeaten in two outings, the exciting colt is ready for a step up in class and Probert was very impressed with the performance."*

Dark Vision storms away at York. *Jeremy Phillips*

No stopping Dark Vision heading for the line. *Jeremy Phillips*

Walking in with Dark Vision, David Probert, Rhona Bagnall and Bhanwar Singh. *Jeremy Phillips*

Paul Walker summed up the day perfectly in his diary note:-

I enjoyed a lovely lunch in the York restaurant with 2 of the partners and we talk about Dark Vision's win at Yarmouth. Dark Vision looks on good form in the pre-parade but difficult to assess his chances without anyone from the stable here. Good to see David Probert riding. Despite a bump at the start, Dark Vision can be soon seen travelling smoothly and with 2 furlongs to go, I smile at Robin. He wins well. A Saturday winner at York. Aren't we lucky! Dark Vision looks a bargain.

We picked up £9,703.50 and were royally treated in the Winners' Reception, in the corner of the parade ring where the runners leave for the track. I spoke to William Haggas and he told us that he would like to have Dark Vision in his yard. Afterwards I headed to the Champagne lawns to relive the day and what a day it was. My first winner at York.

Well before Dark Vision's success an entry had been made for Victory Command for Thursday 12th July in the 2.25pm at Newmarket 6 furlongs – Class 1 Group 2 Arqana July Stakes, worth £80,000. On Saturday 7th July Paul Walker saw Charlie Johnston at Haydock and was told that they would be making the decision where Victory Command was to run next at Newmarket on the following Monday or Tuesday. Charlie felt *"that now he had won 3 races it might be worth going for something significant"*. He was pleased that they had found a winning opportunity for Dark Vision (namely his win at Yarmouth) over 6 furlongs and remarked that *"it may not have been the strongest race."* Obviously he was not armed with the result when he spoke to Paul of Dark Vision's win on 14th July at York.

Victory Command did not run at Newmarket in the "Arqana" but was entered to run on Saturday 14th July again at Newmarket in the bet 365 Superlative Stakes a Group 2, 7 furlong race. He did not run in that either. However, he was entered for Saturday 28th July at Ascot in the Wooldridge Group Pat Eddery Stakes. A Listed Race over 7 furlongs. Dark Vision was entered to run on Tuesday 31st July at Goodwood in the Group 2 Vintage Stakes. Two Class 1 entries.

Approaching the Winner's Enclosure. *Jeremy Phillips*

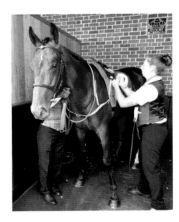

Very happy connections. Rhona Bagnall saddles up, Bhanwar Singh leads and Prize Presentation. *Carl Townsley*

These were hectic, happy days trying to second guess where they would run and to make plans for the required overnight accommodation, especially for those who lived in the North. Of course both horses were going up in the ratings (Victory Command's OR was 94) but the class of races in which they were now being entered meant they would, by and large, be off level weights.

In view of the fact that I had a golf tournament (booked in advance) on Saturday 28th July I decided to put all my eggs in the Goodwood basket and join Billy and Catherine Ross at the Old Thorns Manor Hotel at Liphook, just north of the South Downs. This was not the first time I had passed up the chance of attending Ascot on "King George Weekend." I did so when Always Waining won in 2003. If you buy a horse you have to go watch it run!!

In the end Victory Command was declared to run at Ascot. I understand that Mark and Charlie could see on the live declaration tracker screen that the Ascot race was cutting up (in other words horses were dropping out and not many were being declared). In fact the race was re-opened owing to a lack of runners so they popped him in.

7.3 Victory Command Makes All at Ascot Saturday 28th July 2018 on the King George VI and Queen Elizabeth Stakes Day

He ran in the 4.15pm The Wooldridge Group Pat Eddery Stakes (Class 1) over 7 furlongs. It was a Listed Race and had formerly been called The Winkfield Stakes. Pat Eddery was one of the finest jockeys of his generation, if not of any generation and I will always remember him for his many rides at York. Often in Prince Khalid Abdullah's colours setting sail for the line, positioned just off the far rail, soon after they turned for home. The battle in the 1998 Juddmonte International Stakes between Chester House, Faithful Son and One So Wonderful ridden by Pat Eddery to the line will go down as one of the best ever finishes. One So Wonderful getting home, having looked beaten, with the shortest of distances. Great riding.

Johnny Weatherby pointed out in the Chairman's welcome that Pat Eddery *"will always be remembered here for his exhilarating King George wins on Grundy and Dancing Brave."* The latter holds the accolade of being the second highest officially rated horse ever (138), only bettered by Frankel (140). It was another lovely sunny day and the warm, summer weather continued. It may well have been a factor as to why there was a relatively small field and the going was described as *"Good to Firm"*; right up Victory Command's street. They all carried 9st 3lbs. The race card is included with thanks to Weatherbys.

We were about to witness a start to finish win and a virtuoso performance from Silvestre de Sousa (SDS). Nate the Great, trained by Archie Watson, who had beaten Seductive Moment at Carlisle and had subsequently finished second in the Chesham at Royal Ascot went off as the 6/4 favourite with Victory Command third favourite at 9/2. He was drawn (6) so on the stand side of the others although the stalls were in centre of the straight 7 furlongs. With such a small field the draw was of no consequence.

There was a fairly even break into a headwind and a little coming together between Victory Command and Almurr, trained by Brian Meehan. However, Victory Command took an early lead of 2 lengths from Nate the Great. The others were in a group, one to two lengths behind him. By half way Victory Command had put a little break on them and as the commentator said *"stolen a bit of a march without appearing to have to work very hard"*. Nate the Great was shaken up in second, but did not make much of an impression and Victory Command still led by 2 lengths entering the final furlong. The race commentator asked the question: *"Can they reel in this leader as Victory Command is still in full command?* They couldn't and he went on to win by two lengths from Glorious Lover (10/1) with the favourite Nate the Great (6/4) in third. It was *an inspired ride by Silvestre de Sousa and Victory Command makes it all to land his hat-trick at 9/2.* Paul Walker noted that *"The 'splits' (sectional timing) showed that SDS had ridden perfect fractions, which into the headwind showed great skill."*

Bryan Russell walked in with the horse and was prominent on the TV coverage. He said to SDS that it was fantastic for a Thirsk boy; a town where SDS used to live and from where Bryan had many happy memories. Sue and Bryan Russell told me that: *"Ascot is the best day of racing that Bryan and I have ever had, it was amazing from start to finish with again beautiful weather, fantastic hospitality and a WINNER. SDS rode a wonderful race and Victory Command just kept galloping and won quite cleverly. Billy Ross commented that he could hear Bryan shouting from the other end of the grandstand!!"*

Catherine Ross continued her love affair with SDS and asked him whether Victory Command was better than Maid in Rio. *"Yes"* was the reply.

RACE 5

4.15PM
THE WOOLDRIDGE GROUP
PAT EDDERY STAKES (CLASS 1)
(LISTED RACE) (FORMERLY THE WINKFIELD STAKES)

Seven furlongs (7f) (1,400 metres)
for two yrs old

Total race value £30000. Owners Prize Money. Winner £13368; Second £5487;
Third £2745; Fourth £1371; Fifth £687; Sixth £342. (Penalty Value £17013) A SS
See page 79 for conditions of this race.

RACE FINISH | RACE START
STALLS: CENTRE

The Wooldridge Group has generously sponsored this race and will present a
memento to the winning owner, trainer & jockey and £100 to the stable employee
in charge of the best turned out horse in this race.

WOOLDRIDGE
GROUP

No	Horse		Draw	Jockey

1 ALMURR (IRE) (23)
B c Dandy Man (IRE) - Passion Planet (IRE) (Medicean)

			Draw 5	William Buick

Owner: ARAAM
Trainer: Brian Meehan, Manton
Breeder: Mr P. Turley
Form: 521

Horse Age: 2   Weight: 9   3
Colours: ROYAL BLUE, PURPLE chevron, PURPLE cap.

Foaled 12.4.2016. **BET WITH ASCOT VIEW**   Edged out a subsequent winner when striking at the third time of asking in 6f Newbury novice (good to firm) 23 days ago. Will need to leave that winning RPR of 80 well behind to follow up at this level but he is open to improvement up in trip.   Official BHA Rating 82

2 GLORIOUS LOVER (IRE) (19)
B c Tamayuz - Love Match (Danehill Dancer (IRE))

			Draw 3	Gerald Mosse

Owner: KIR (HK) Ltd & Dr Johnny Hon
Trainer: Ed Walker, Upper Lambourn
Breeder: Corrin Stud
Form: 31

Horse Age: 2   Weight: 9   3
Colours: PINK, ROYAL BLUE braces.

Foaled 2.2.2016. **BET WITH ASCOT VIEW**   Built on a promising 6.5f Newbury debut third (Almurr second) when justifying favouritism in 6f Windsor novice with a bit more in hand than the bare result implies. Up in trip. Definitely more to come.   Official BHA Rating -

3 HESSLEWOOD (IRE) (23)
B c Slade Power (IRE) - Rochitta (USA) (Arch (USA))

			Draw 4	James Doyle

Owner: Clarendon Thoroughbred Racing
Trainer: James Bethell, Middleham
Breeder: Nesco II
Form: 12

Horse Age: 2   Weight: 9   3
Colours: BLACK, WHITE chevrons on sleeves, WHITE cap.

Foaled 29.4.2016. **BET WITH ASCOT VIEW**   Sprung a 33-1 surprise in Class 3 maiden at York (6f, good to firm) and confirmed he's pretty useful when second under a penalty at Haydock (6f again) since. 7f should suit (half-brother to 1m2f winner) but he'll need to improve a fair bit for the extra yardage to go close.   Official BHA Rating -

4 MASTER BREWER (FR) (28)
B c Reliable Man - Quenching (IRE) (Street Cry (IRE))

			Draw 1	Ryan Moore

Owner: The Fitzrovians 2 and Fair Salinia Ltd
Trainer: Michael Bell, Newmarket
Breeder: Salinity Service AB
Form: 01   D

Horse Age: 2   Weight: 9   3
Colours: CERISE, ETON BLUE sleeves, hooped cap.

Foaled 29.2.2016. **BET WITH ASCOT VIEW**   Left Newbury debut well behind when landing 7f Newmarket novice (good to firm) a fortnight later. That was just a four-runner affair but he was by no means hard ridden to pull 2l clear and the second and fourth have both won since. Open to considerable improvement.   Official BHA Rating -

5 NATE THE GREAT (35)
B c Nathaniel (IRE) - Theladyinquestion (Dubawi (IRE))

			Draw 2	Daniel Tudhope

Owner: Mildmay Racing & D. H. Caslon
Trainer: Archie Watson, Upper Lambourn
Breeder: Mildmay Bloodstock & D. H. Caslon
Form: 12

Horse Age: 2   Weight: 9   3
Colours: DARK BLUE, LIGHT GREEN sash, WHITE cap.

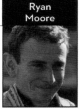

Foaled 2.2.2016. **BET WITH ASCOT VIEW**   Clearcut winner on 6f Carlisle debut. Left that bare form well behind when going down by only a neck to Arthur Kitt in Chesham over C&D (good to firm) at the Royal meeting. Stayed on strongly to pull over 3l clear of the third and he sets a clear standard here with further progress on the cards. Official BHA Rating -

6 VICTORY COMMAND (IRE) (32)

Draw 6

Silvestre De Sousa

B c War Command (USA) - Aguinaga (IRE) (Machiavellian (USA))

Owner: Kingsley Park 10
Trainer: Mark Johnston, Middleham
Breeder: Mr J. Higgins
Form: 312311 D

Horse Age: 2 **Weight:** 9 3
Colours: ROYAL BLUE, LIGHT GREEN epaulets.

Foaled 25.5.2016. **BET WITH ASCOT VIEW** Typical sort from this yard who is taking his racing well, making all in 7.4f Beverley novice auction events on his last two starts. This clearly harder but this uncomplicated sort can give it another good shot from the front under Silvestre De Sousa. Official BHA Rating 94

Record Time: 1 min 26.55 secs by Malabar age 2 wt 9-0 good to firm, 25/07/14
Median Time: 1 min 27.60 secs
2017: RAYDIANCE 2 9 3 Jim Crowley 7-1 (K R Burke) 7 ran

ASCOT RESULT

1ST	DISTANCE
2ND	
3RD	TIME
4TH	

BET WITH ASCOT

RACE PREDICTOR

BETTING FORECAST

11/8 Nate The Great, 3/1 Victory Command (IRE), 13/2 Almurr (IRE), Master Brewer (FR), 15/2 Glorious Lover (IRE), 12/1 Hesslewood (IRE)

Silvestre de Sousa maintains a two length lead on Victory Command. *Matthew Webb*

Winning connections. *Matthew Webb*

Savroop Singh leads SDS and Victory Command to the Winners' Enclosure. *Matthew Webb*

Ladies at Ascot

David Bellingham of the Racing Post put a more sobering tone on affairs: *An interesting Listed event that has been won by some decent sorts over the years, not least Toronado in 2012, but the form of this year's renewal has to be taken with a pinch of salt. Another reminder, were it needed, that if you allow a Mark Johnston runner a soft lead you are asking for trouble.*

VICTORY COMMAND a confirmed front-runner having his seventh start, was only going to be ridden one way and he had established a clear lead by halfway without having to do too much. That meant that when he needed a bit more to maintain his advantage, he had plenty left in the tank and at no stage did he ever look in any danger. Things are unlikely to always pan out so well, but this was a nice race to win.

At Goodwood I spoke to Brian Meehan the trainer of Almurr and his opinion was that the jockeys had been asleep to what was happening in front of them.

Charlie Johnston was quoted as saying:

"VICTORY COMMAND wasn't in the race at 10am, but they re-offered it and as he was the second top-rated we thought we would give it a go. He has a nursery entry at Goodwood next week and I wouldn't rule that out, although now he has won a Listed race we should probably start looking at Group races."

He picked up a first prize of £17,013 and a silver plate was presented to the ecstatic owners. The horse, of course, achieved the elusive accolade of *"Black Type"*. Charlie Johnston wrote to partners:

"Good evening I hope you are all well. Congratulations Victory Command ran at Ascot in the 4.15 and won. He jumped well, made all at a good tempo. He was 4 lengths clear at halfway and stayed on strongly to win comfortably. Fantastic win."

Paul Walker's diary note read:-

"Victory Command 28th July 2018

We are at Ascot on King George Day and a chance to enjoy a delicious lunch in the restaurant. Charlie joins us and says Dark Vision might go to Goodwood. There is a strong wind blowing up the straight and front runners aren't getting home but Charlie wants Silvestre to stick to the front running plan.

Viewing for owners at Ascot is not good but I find my usual position just beyond the winning post. At halfway Silvestre de Sousa pinches the race with a tactical masterstroke and Victory Command strides home to complete the hat-trick. Cue great celebrations. Another shrewd purchase and great placing."

7.4 An Offer for Victory Command

Perhaps the most precarious way of becoming an owner, or part owner, of a racehorse is to buy a yearling. The only more precarious route would be to buy a very expensive yearling. If you have got this far in the narrative you will have seen reports of many injuries and horses that have turned out to look beautiful, but were just no good at running fast or at least not as fast as the others. One way of trying to avoid these expensive disappointments is to buy a horse that is already up and running. In fact Johnston Racing have partnerships called "Ready to Run" and are usually stocked with 3-year-olds that Mark and Charlie have bought in at the Horses in Training sales. There are breeze-up sales where horses already at a fairly advanced stage are put through their paces on the race track. There are also Selling and Claiming races where the participants can be bought at auction or claimed straight after the race. Mostly, horses that run in the last mentioned class of race are not potential stars although there are some valuable "Claimers" eg Always Waining for example was claimed (sold) at Newmarket for £30,000.

Buying horses that have already run or are put up for sale during their careers for relatively modest sums are unlikely to win the most valuable races. Always in the back of my mind is the question why would somebody want to sell a racehorse if it is any good?

Of course sometimes a rich owner may make an offer for an up and coming youngster, who has already impressed on the track, and which the owners might be considered as foolish to turn down. In these instances colts and fillies (the latter with broodmare potential) can be sold for seven figure sums.

Some owners of *"horses with potential"* turn offers down as they believe (or hope and dream) that even better things are to come. Horse racing is littered with stories of lucrative offers being turned down and the horse did not train on or suffered a career ending injury. Mark has pointed out that he has had offers in the past for partnership horses which in hindsight he wishes he had accepted.

However, if you buy a yearling colt, he could win the Derby, or a filly could win the Oaks. This is the dream. It is a gamble as 50% of yearlings do not run never mind win a race, and when they do run very few win enough money to cover the cost of buying them and their training fees. In 2018 and 2019 less than 1% of horses that ran won more than £100,000 (see Table 1 in Chapter 14). But in the very beginning when reading the sales catalogues the dream is on.

A consequence of watching an animal grow and develop is that the owner(s) and also stable staff may become attached to it. I will never forget the broken hearted lass I met when we were making arrangements for Byres Road to be transported to Middleham having bought him at Tattersalls December Sales. If the horse tries hard, has ability and starts to win races the attachment grows. Framed photographs adorn walls. Sideboards and cabinets bulge with trophies.

Horses are beautiful animals and the well-mannered ones allow an owner to give them a pat and friendly word. I was close up to Byres Road once, in his box, when he just rested his head on my shoulder. Such an endearing moment, but he had to be sold as he had stopped winning (the handicapper had done his stuff). I also had to remember that he was a racehorse and the first four letters of the word were just as important as the last five.

So with all this in mind Mark's message to partners on the eve of Glorious Goodwood set out below was, for some a bombshell.

"Congratulations on Saturday's win and good luck tomorrow.

When two-year-olds win decent races, we inevitably get offers for them. In the past our partnership rules dictated that we needed a unanimous decision to sell a horse and this caused horrendous confusion when we did get good offers as unanimous decisions were never possible. I therefore changed the rules at the beginning of 2017 so that I would make the decisions and I have already turned down a couple of offers for other partnership horses which, in hindsight, I wish I had accepted. I have, however, decided that these partnerships are all about the fun and thrill of racing and I have been rejecting most offers.

I have already had to field enquiries about all three KP 10 horses and I have not been inclined to sell anything. However, an offer has now come in for Victory Command to go to Hong Kong which I feel it would be foolhardy to reject.

There are several things you must take on board about offers for horses, especially offers from HK: 1). Most horses – even sound, active, horses – fail the vet for Hong Kong, so do not count on this sale going through; 2). If the sale doesn't go through and we later sell him for a lot less, don't think that the sum offered was ever a true 'value'. It is the sum that someone is currently willing to pay for the potential and it can change daily. 3). While there is, of course, potential for this horse to win lots of prize-money and a dream of him having stallion potential, all but the top 1% of colts are eventually worth nothing. The aim is to get out at the top and, when the value starts going down, it goes down very rapidly.

So, in short, I am inclined to accept the offer and see what happens. I will, however, first offer him to my existing owners as this would, of course, be the best of both worlds for me but I would not have done this had we not received an unsolicited offer which I intend to accept. At no point have we actively sought to sell the horse."

I can't remember exactly where I was when I received Mark's e-mail but I must have been on the way to The Old Thorns Manor Hotel near Goodwood. Paul Walker, since we first met in December 2017, and I had had several conversations about either being a *"keeper"* or *"seller"* of horses. He always quoted the example of a horse called Unowhatimeanharry of which he had a share, which was sold *"to his great disappointment after it had won a race at the Cheltenham Festival. "To have this happen again is very difficult"* he said. He wrote to ask me if I had received Mark's e-mail and I wrote back with my thoughts:

"Yes I have. My first reaction was to be disappointed that Mark thinks we would be selling 'at the top' whereby Mark has implied that there might not be much more he can do with him rated at around 100.

Of course none of us can be certain but he will know more than many of us.

My feeling was that SDS stole that last race and as the Racing Post analyst said things might not go so well next time. So although a draw of 1/20 th of the sum offered is not attractive to me compared with visiting Grade 1 tracks, and running in stakes races, the novelty rubs off quickly on any track for that matter if the horse is beaten every time it runs.

At the moment some people in our almost unreal partnership may think we just have to turn up and win. We both know it is not like that. So apart from this correspondence, which we might keep to ourselves for now and a chat tonight with Catherine and Billy Ross, with whom I am staying I do not intend to discuss it until I see Mark and or Charlie.

Their judgement might persuade me to change my natural optimism to a more pragmatic or even realistic approach. It is softened by the fact that we might have other bullets to fire. See you tomorrow."

Liz Pescops has subsequently told me that:

"I will always remember Mark's email saying he was going to sell Victory Command. I was devastated as he had always been my favourite of all the horses… a talented, gentle, showy horse who loved an audience and being the centre of attention. He was very fit and gave 100%.

Still Mark was boss and we knew he had the final say. I emailed Mark expressing my concern about selling a good horse and received a polite reply explaining that you must not be sentimental over a racehorse."

At the back of my mind was what my mate Steve Youlden, who has spent his life riding horses, had advised when a good offer is made for a horse.

"What you should do when you meet somebody who has just bought your horse is to shake them by the hand and say I wish you all the best of luck. Thank them very much, smile, and hope they will buy the next one."

Discussions over dinner and a pint or two in the sports bar at the Old Thorns Manor with Billy and Catherine Ross did not get us much further and we retired to bed to dream of Dark Vision winning the Vintage Stakes.

To the north over Goodwood racecourse. *Mikaelle Lebreton*

7.5 Glorious Goodwood: Dark Vision wins the Group 2 Vintage Stakes

The South Downs are a range of chalk hills across the south eastern counties of England from the Itchen valley of Hampshire, in the west, to Beachy Head in the east. There is a steep escarpment on the northern side, at the foot of which is the South Downs Way, which runs from Winchester to Eastbourne. From the top of the escarpment there are commanding views to the north, towards Midhurst and to the south, towards Chichester, Selsey Bill and the English Channel. Goodwood racecourse is perched at the top of the northern slope on a wide ridge, "The Harroway".

The crowd in the grandstands look north onto the track, which falls away slightly down the contours of the escarpment. It is right handed and races over distances greater than 6 furlongs have their starts on a switchback part. The 7 furlong start (The Vintage) starts downhill but it is uphill until the bends to the straight. It is 4 furlongs from the lower bend to the finish. The ground on the straight falls slightly away from the stands rail.

It is a notoriously tricky course for jockeys to keep out of trouble and it can favour horses that have run at Goodwood previously. The programme notes ("*Course Characteristics*") explained:

"Goodwood's pronounced gradients and sharp bends favour the active, handy type of horse, the fluent mover rather than the big, long-striding, and this applies especially in short races when the going is fast. For the 7 furlong start the stalls are positioned on the inside rail".

Such daunting characteristics and descriptions were enough to give most owners qualms. Although we were confident Dark Vision was an *"active"* type we were not sure his size matched what was described as being needed. Deirdre Johnston pointed out it is the same for them all and he will make the best of it. The official going was *"Good"*.

"The Vintage" was the second race and that was a relief as the tension was mounting as we climbed the escarpment to one of the outer car parks. A shuttle bus brought us in to the Owners and Trainers' (O&T) entrance. Just inside to the right is the O&T bar and terrace, which overlooks the parade ring with the sea visible in the far distance. It was a lovely sunny day, with no wind. Some remarks were made about the proposed sale of Victory Command but the focus was on Dark Vision in the pre-parade ring. The race card is included with the kind permission of Weatherbys.

The betting showed that his odds were shortening towards favouritism. That was no surprise to me as I had watched the recordings of the opposition and although Cosmic Law (especially in the Woodcote), Confiding and Dunkerron had shaped up well none had put in the high level of performance and final speed that Dark Vision had done at York. Afterwards I found out that one of our York gang had had a bet of £5,000 to win at 4/1. I am still waiting for the Dom Perignon party he promised.

The Race Summary in the programme suggested he was an each way bet but they favoured Confiding. *"Confiding left a lasting impression after winning on debut at Newbury for Martyn Meade despite easy to back, and looks poised to build on that after a 47-day absence. The second, third, fourth, fifth, seventh, eighth and ninth from that race have all won since and he can account for Dark Vision, who has done it well the last twice for Mark Johnston, and Federal Law, who is going the right way for powerful connections."*

Richard Hoiles pointed out that:

"A race much under-rated in recent years is the Vintage Stakes - its recent roll of honour includes Group 1 winners Olympic Glory, Toormore and Highland Reel, while last year's victor Expert Eye could well add to the list in the Qatar Sussex Stakes on Wednesday.

Add in the small matter of the 2016 runner-up Thunder Snow winning this year's Dubai World Cup and it is a race that punches well above its weight.

This year it could throw up a good bet in: Dunkerron

Alan King does better than many realise with his juveniles but with a record of just 1/109 first time out it is well worth upgrading any that show promise on debut.

As such it was little surprise Dunkerron took a big step forward from his debut at this track and his fourth in the July Stakes last time is very solid form. The step up in trip to 7f looks highly likely to suit and his attitude looks spot on. He represents a decent each-way selection at the general 17-2 on offer."

All of the horses, except Mordred, trained by Richard Hannon, had won at least one race previously. Dark Vision and Blonde Warrior, trained by Hugo Palmer were on a hat-trick and Aiden O'Brien's Van Beethoven carried 3lbs more than the field under a penalty having won the Group 2 Railway Stakes at the Curragh. Cosmic Law trained by Richard Fahey had won the Woodcote Stakes on Derby Day in fine style and had showed great speed. Confiding trained by Martyn Meade had only previously run once (at Newbury). He burst away impressively to win there after having being ridden patiently in the early part of the race. *"Timeform"* rated Cosmic Law (116) and Dunkerron (113p) as the top two rated. Dark Vision scored 110p.

SECOND RACE 2.25PM

THE QATAR VINTAGE STAKES
(Group 2)

7F

Class 1. **About seven furlongs (abt 7f),** for two yrs old
Estimated Total Value: Total race value £200000. Penalty Value £113420.
Owners Prize Money: Winner £89120; Second £36580; Third £18300; Fourth £9140;
Fifth £4580; Sixth £2280. Distributed in accordance with Schedule (F)9.2.4

No	Horse	Weight	Draw
1	**VAN BEETHOVEN (CAN) (19)**	9-4	(11)

B c Scat Daddy (USA) - My Sister Sandy (USA) (Montbrook (USA))   Jockey: Ryan Moore
Owner: Mr D. Smith, Mrs J. Magnier, Mr M. Tabor   Colours: PURPLE, WHITE seams,
Trainer: Aidan O'Brien, Ireland   striped sleeves, PURPLE cap.
Breeder: Ballycroy Training Centre   Form: 312410

Foaled 19 Feb. Successful twice at 6f on good to firm and good to yielding ground. Beaten 9l behind
Advertise at 11-2 when seventh of 8 last time out in the Group 2 July Stakes at Newmarket over 6f
(good to firm) earlier this month. Disappointing there and more is required. Official BHA Rating 104

2	**BLONDE WARRIOR (IRE) (32)**	9-1	(3)

Ch c Zoffany (IRE) - Dame Blanche (IRE) (Be My Guest (USA))   Jockey: William Buick
Owner: Mrs Fiona Carmichael   Colours: PURPLE, LIGHT GREEN stars,
Trainer: Hugo Palmer, Newmarket   PURPLE cap, LIGHT GREEN star.
Breeder: Rockhart Trading Ltd   Form: 211   D
Sponsor: Alba Power Ltd

Foaled 8 Feb. Successful at 6f and 7f on good to firm ground. Won on his latest outing when 1-4fav at
Doncaster over 7f (good to firm) last month, beating Al Fajir Mukbile by 3 1/2l. Relished the step up
in trip there when beating a moderate field but wouldn't want rain. Official BHA Rating 94

3	**BURJ (21)**	9-1	(8)

B c Dansili - Dysphonia (AUS) (Lonhro (AUS))   Jockey: Edward Greatrex
Owner: Godolphin   Colours: ROYAL BLUE.
Trainer: Saeed bin Suroor, Newmarket   Form: 3101   D
Breeder: Godolphin
Sponsor: Emirates

Foaled 30 Apr. Successful at 6f and 7f on good to firm ground and on the all-weather. Won on his latest
outing when 1-12fav at Brighton over 7f (good to firm) earlier this month, beating Treasure Quest by
a neck. Didn't do that in the manner of an odds-on shot; opposed. Official BHA Rating 94

4	**CONFIDING (47)**	9-1	(10)

B c Iffraaj - Entre Nous (IRE) (Sadler's Wells (USA))   Jockey: Callum Shepherd
Owner: Manton Estate Racing   Colours: WHITE, BLACK disc, BLACK cap.
Trainer: Martyn Meade, Manton   Form: 1
Breeder: Brook Stud Bloodstock Ltd
Sponsor: Meyer Timber Ltd

Foaled 5 Mar. Half-brother to Royal Memory, won at 1m. A winner at 16-1 at Newbury over 6f (good
to firm) on his racecourse debut last month, beating Almurr by 1l. Burst away impressively there after
being held up and he looks set to build on it. Official BHA Rating -

40

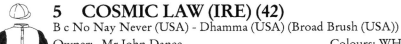

5   COSMIC LAW (IRE) (42)   9-1   (1)
B c No Nay Never (USA) - Dhamma (USA) (Broad Brush (USA))   Jockey: P. J. McDonald

Owner: Mr John Dance
Trainer: Richard Fahey, Malton
Breeder: Epona Bloodstock Ltd
Sponsor: Vertem Asset Management

Colours: WHITE, MAROON and PURPLE
         striped sleeves.
Form: 5110

Foaled 16 Mar. Successful at 5f and 6f on good to firm and soft ground. Beaten 7l behind Calyx at 11-1 when 9th of 23 on his latest outing in the Group 2 Coventry Stakes at Ascot over 6f (good to firm) last month. Woodcote winner who was far from disgraced last time out. Official BHA Rating 100

6   DARK VISION (IRE) (17)   9-1   (7)
B c Dream Ahead (USA) - Black Dahlia (Dansili)   Jockey: Silvestre De Sousa

Owner: KINGSLEY PARK 10
Trainer: Mark Johnston, Middleham
Breeder: S. F. Bloodstock LLC
Sponsor: Johnston Racing Ltd

Colours: ROYAL BLUE,
         LIGHT GREEN epaulets.
Form: 11

Foaled 16 Feb. Half-brother to Al Hayyah, won twice at 7f and 1m. Successful twice at 6f on good to firm ground. A winner at 9-2 at York over 6f (good to firm) on his latest outing earlier this month, beating Absolute Dream by 2 1/4l. Did that well despite a tardy start. Official BHA Rating 96

7   DROGON (IRE) (26)   9-1   (5)
B c Zoffany (IRE) - Flames To Dust (GER) (Oasis Dream)   Jockey: Richard Kingscote

Owner: APCC Limited
Trainer: Tom Dascombe, Malpas
Breeder: Graf Und Grafin Von Stauffenberg
Sponsor: APCC Limited

Colours: DARK BLUE, LIGHT BLUE hoop,
         LIGHT BLUE and DARK BLUE chevrons on
         sleeves, LIGHT BLUE cap, DARK BLUE diamond.
Form: 31   D

Foaled 19 Apr. Dam unraced. A winner at 7-1 at Haydock over 7f (good to firm) on his latest outing earlier this month, beating Hot Team by 3 1/2l. Took a big step forward there after a solid debut third and this son of Zoffany can continue to go forward for this team. Official BHA Rating -

8   DUNKERRON (19)   9-1   (6)
B g Kuroshio (AUS) - Triple Cee (IRE) (Cape Cross (IRE))   Jockey: Martin Harley

Owner: Ron Sullivan & Kingston Stud
Trainer: Alan King, Barbury Castle
Breeder: Barbury Castle Stud
Sponsor: Ultima Business Solutions

Colours: LIGHT BLUE, DARK BLUE Cross of
         Lorraine and armlets.
Form: 4114

Foaled 5 May. Successful twice at 6f on good to firm ground. Finished 3l behind Advertise when fourth of 8 at 20-1 on his latest outing in the Group 2 Arqana July Stakes at Newmarket over 6f (good to firm) earlier this month, and shaped there like 7f would suit him well. Official BHA Rating 103

9   FEDERAL LAW (CAN) (17)   9-1   (9)
B c Scat Daddy (USA) - Gravelly Bay (CAN) (Strong Hope (USA))   Jockey: Oisin Murphy

Owner: Qatar Racing Limited
Trainer: Archie Watson, Upper Lambourn
Breeder: Jim Dandy Stable
Sponsor: Tweenhills Farm & Stud

Colours: CLARET, GOLD braid, CLARET sleeves,
         CLARET cap, GOLD tassel.
Form: 21   D

Foaled 11 May. Dam unraced. A winner at 9-4 at Salisbury over 7f (firm) on his latest outing earlier this month, beating Duke Of Hazzard by a neck. Did that in a professional manner after a solid second over a shorter trip at Newcastle previously, and could go close here. Official BHA Rating -

10   GETCHAGETCHAGETCHA (42)   9-1   (4)
B c Champs Elysees - Paella (IRE) (Oasis Dream)   Jockey: Adam Kirby

Owner: Paul & Clare Rooney
Trainer: Clive Cox, Hungerford
Breeder: Mrs James Wigan
Sponsor: Clive Cox Racing Limited

Colours: DARK BLUE and YELLOW (quartered),
         striped sleeves.
Form: 10

Foaled 18 Apr. Dam unraced. A winner at 5f on good to soft ground. Beaten 8l behind Calyx at 66-1 when 11th of 23 on his latest outing in the Group 2 Coventry Stakes at Ascot over 6f (good to firm) last month. That was a solid run and he doesn't mind cut in the ground. Official BHA Rating -

41

11 JUNIUS BRUTUS (FR) (38)

Ch c Cockney Rebel (IRE) - Tricked (Beat Hollow)

9-1 (2)
Jockey: Harry Bentley

Owner: King Power Racing Co Ltd
Trainer: Ralph Beckett, Kimpton Down
Breeder: Larissa Kneip & Sandrine Grevet
Sponsor: King Power International Co Ltd

Colours: ROYAL BLUE, WHITE hoop, striped sleeves, WHITE cap, ROYAL BLUE star.
Form: 116

Foaled 31 Mar. Successful twice at 5f on good ground. Finished 3 1/2l behind Soldier's Call when sixth of 28 at 17-2 on his latest outing at Ascot over 5f (good to firm) last month. It will be interesting to see if he stays this far on his debut for a new stable. Official BHA Rating -

12 MORDRED (IRE) (17)

B c Camelot - Endure (IRE) (Green Desert (USA))

9-1 (12)
Jockey: Jim Crowley

Owner: Mr Martin Hughes
Trainer: Richard Hannon, Marlborough
Breeder: Lynn Lodge Stud
Sponsor: Old Oak Holdings Ltd

Colours: PURPLE and WHITE diamonds, PURPLE sleeves.
Form: 23

Foaled 23 Mar. Full brother to Camomile Lawn, won at 1m 2f. Placed once in two starts. Third of 6 behind Federal Law beaten 2 1/2l at 11-4 on his latest outing at Salisbury over 7f (firm) earlier this month. Held on that form and difficult to see him reversing the places. Official BHA Rating -

---

NUMBER OF DECLARED RUNNERS 12

Raceform Median Time: 1 min 27.00 secs Record Time: 1 min 24.99 secs

BETTING FORECAST 4-1 Confiding, 6-1 Dark Vision (IRE), 7-1 Dunkerron, 8-1 Van Beethoven (CAN), Blonde Warrior (IRE), Drogon (IRE), 10-1 Cosmic Law (IRE), Federal Law (CAN), Junius Brutus (FR), 14-1 Burj, 16-1 Getchagetchagetcha, 20-1 Mordred (IRE)

Race Result

1st: .... 2nd: .... 3rd: .... 4th: ....

Distances: 1-2 .... 2-3 .... 3-4 .... Time: Min . Secs

---

2017 WINNER: EXPERT EYE 2 9 1 Andrea Atzeni 7-4 (Sir Michael Stoute) 10 ran

STEWARDS NOTED:

VAN BEETHOVEN: Following its run on 12/7/2018 it was reported that the trainer could not explain the poor run.

RACE SUMMARY

CONFIDING left a lasting impression after winning on debut at Newbury for Martyn Meade despite being easy to back, and looks poised to build on that after a 47-day absence. The second, third, fourth, fifth, seventh, eighth and ninth from that race have all won since and he can account for Dark Vision, who has done it well the last twice for Mark Johnston, and Federal Law, who is going the right way for powerful connections.

Win: Confiding   *Each-Way: Dark Vision*

42

In the parade ring everybody was doing their best to look relaxed and calm. They were not. Francesca Cumani strode by our group purposefully eyeing up Dark Vision. I found out afterwards that she had been quite taken by Dark Vision's large, strong looking athletic frame. He did look a picture. She coined the nickname *"the Beast"*, which fortunately did not stick. Silvestre de Sousa came for his instructions from Mark. Contrary to what many people believe, trainers (or at least Mark) do not go into a detailed discussion of what the jockey might try to do. For example a lot of Kingsley Park horses lead from start to finish but I have never heard Mark advise a jockey to do that. I do remember him saying that he has been, in his previous two starts, (his only starts) a bit slowly away.

Of course Silvestre was the flavour of the moment after his wonderful ride on Victory Command just 3 days earlier to win a Listed race at Ascot. We wished him good fortune and a safe ride.

Nerves of the owners were jangling and the feeling of anticipation was palpable. Although I have no idea from where the large turnout of partners, their partners and friends watched the race it was definitely not together. Billy Ross always watches a race alone. I always try to watch from the part of the stands, which is designated for Owners and Trainers. Charlie Johnston, at Goodwood watches, on a big screen at the western end of the parade ring. This is where the horses after the race thread their way through to the winners' enclosure or turn off to the right to be dismounted and unsaddled in the area in front of this large screen. Mark watched it standing up at the very back of the seated area in the O&T stand. I sat with Deirdre on my right and Anna Lisa Balding on my left, just below Mark's position. I could see Liz Pescops and Ruth Carty a few rows back in the same area.

It was a fairly even break and although Dark Vision did not dwell in the stalls he did appear to miss the break as he did not start out like some of the others. It took him a while to stride out. By this time Dunkerron, Drogan, Cosmic Law and Burj had stolen a bit of a lead and Dark Vision was shuffled back a bit and at this stage, although not last he was at the rear of the field. Silvestre did not panic and he looked quite happy to be where he was. He later said that it was definitely not where he wanted to be. As they got to the turn Confiding, Cosmic Law, and Burj were prominent. Dark Vision was the back marker (Groans from Deirdre and myself). A quick, snatched look round and I saw Mark frowning.

Into the last 2 furlongs Burj came through strongly but Dunkerron swooped to take it up with Confiding close by. Cosmic Law was still in contention on the far running rail but Dark Vision was behind them all and also hemmed in on the rail.

Then, with one furlong to go Silvestre edged Dark Vision out (Jim Crowley on Mordred told me much later in Dubai that he had let him out!) and he had got into his long powerful stride. He powered down the centre gaining all the time to win emphatically by 1¾ lengths. Perhaps a little cosily. The crowd were on their feet (many of whom will have been on him in view of the fact he was the favourite). The noise was deafening.

I shot into the air and we were already on our feet with excitement- hugged Anna Lisa and then Deirdre or the other way round. Mark smiling calmly tucked away his binoculars. He came down the steps to make his way to the winners' enclosure. I joined him and our immediate thoughts were what an outstanding, breathtaking performance that was and that we had another valuable horse on our hands.

Silvestre arrived on Dark Vision to rapturous applause from the large throng of people that had somehow got there quite suddenly after the race. Perhaps some had not left the parade ring and like Charlie had watched it on the big screen.

Radio, Newspaper and Television reporters were everywhere. Radio Goodwood interviewed me but not surprisingly the main targets for the cameras were Mark and Silvestre. The ladies received the trophy during the presentation, which I missed as I was jabbering away into a microphone.

Dark Vision in the clear and heading for the line. *Stephen Davies*

Well clear and Dark Vision wins cosily. *Stephen Davies*

Silvestre de Sousa and Savroop Singh return with Dark Vision to the *Winners'* Enclosure. *Stephen Davies*

Happy connections with Savroop Singh. *Stephen Davies*

Delighted Dramatis Personae. *Ruth Carty*

There were partners from England, Scotland and Ireland and we all repaired to the winning owners' Reception to sample Goodwood's ("First Class") hospitality and to watch the race again.

I remember hugging Charlie and saying that this is just fantastic, but your Dad keeps telling me to keep my feet on the ground. He said "good advice, but if there is a moment to lift them off it is now." I shook hands with Martyn Meade who towered above me and who was magnanimous in defeat.

So the afternoon progressed. More champagne and smiles all round. The Johnston Racing owners, who make an annual pilgrimage to Glorious Goodwood, joined in. I particularly remember Dougie Livingston giving me a hug of congratulations. I was close to tears (the champagne). It was a while before I found out which horses finished where, although I did see Alan King (Dunkerron) and Martyn Meade (Confiding) in the champagne Reception. Their horses were second and third respectively. Paul Walker had a chat with Richard Hoiles who he knew from the Racegoers Club and he was very impressed. He had described the final stages of the race on the ITV coverage as follows: Here come the giant strides of Dark Vision galumphing down the outside, two strides to their one...what an imposing horse, vintage performance from Dark Vision. He added that "we might have some difficulty in keeping him."

I think we (the Ross's and I) went round to the local pub that evening for a relatively more subdued celebration and dinner. We were so excited and decided to have the following day off as it would have been "after the Lord Mayor's Show". I played golf at the Old Thorns Manor course.

7.6 Analysis of Dark Vision's Win

The immediate detailed reaction to the win in the winners' enclosure was from Mark and SDS. They were both interviewed. *Mark said: "That was quite incredible. I can hardly believe it myself.*

I was trying to keep everybody's feet on the ground today. The partnership (Kingsley Park 10) had a winner at Ascot on Saturday with a horse that cost £6,000 (Victory Command) and this one cost two and a half times as much at £15,000. I never really thought when I set him off at Yarmouth that he'd be coming to a Group 2 race and when he missed the break I thought it was all over. I was thinking I'd have to go home and teach this horse to come out of the stalls.

At that stage, if he'd come fourth I'd have thought I've got a really nice horse on my hands. I never thought until a furlong out that we had any chance of winning."

Betfair initially went 33-1 about Dark Vision for next year's Qipco 2000 Guineas, before cutting him to 20-1, the same price as RaceBets offered. On immediate plans, Johnston said *"I haven't thought beyond today"*.

SDS was asked *"what happened in the early part of the race and were you where you wanted to be?"*

"No not at all I just wanted to be with the leaders or just behind. They went a bit quick early on and he is such a big horse he was slowly into his stride and I was shuffled back. From four furlongs out he galloped really well and from then on I was always happy. In the straight he ate up the ground and would not be intimidated and put the race to bed very quickly. He never gave me a feel at all and never picked the bridle up. When I look at the size of him on a sharp track he needs a lot to go right. He is a lovely horse and I am sure he will improve."

SDS was given the *"ride of the day"* accolade by the Racing Post.

Their analyst Dave Bellingham wrote up the race as follows:-

Qatar Vintage Stakes (Group 2)

(Class 1) (2yo) 7f Good

1st £113,420; 2nd £43,000; 3rd £21,520; 4th £10,720; 5th £5,380; 6th £2,700

Race distance increased by 10yds. Since first run in 1975, three winners of the Vintage Stakes have gone on to win the Derby, namely Troy (1978), Dr Devious (1991) and Sir Percy (2005), while other subsequent

Classic winners/top class performers to have won this include Don't Forget Me, Shamardal, Olympic Glory, Highland Reel and Galileo Gold. With the winner and third coming into the race unbeaten and the runner-up already having made the frame at Group 2 level, there is every reason to believe that this year's renewal was well up to scratch and the winner especially looks exciting. They went a strong pace too, with none of the early leading group of five finishing in the frame and the pair that forced the early pace dropping right out.

DARK VISION> *whose stable has won this with a few good ones over the years, came into this 2-2- over 6f on fast ground. Slightly outpaced early, he then found himself even further back when meeting trouble after a quarter of a mile and was still last entering the final 2f, but once pulled out wide he produced a devastating turn of foot to run down the second and win going away. He is a big colt, so did well to handle this track and his pedigree suggests that he will have no problem getting another furlong at least. He was certainly a bargain at 15,000gns and must be a major candidate for some of the top 2yo races over 7f and 1m in the autumn. He was quoted a top-price 20-1 for next year's 2,000 Guineas afterwards.*

Dunkerron> *up a furlong after his fine fourth in the July Stakes, looked to have timed it right when switched left and sent to the front over a furlong from home, but he could do nothing about the winner's turn of speed. He can be given extra credit as he raced closer to the strong pace than the first and third and deserves to win a nice race. His rider was suspended for two days for using his whip above the permitted level inside the final 2f.*

Confiding> *Held up just ahead of the winner, he was also brought wide for his effort and although his late run wasn't so potent, he still finished off in pleasing style. He was the least experienced in this field and remains a decent prospect.*

Mark was quoted:*"I hadn't thought beyond today. We had Dark Vision and Victory Command in nurseries. I wasn't sure I was doing the right thing bypassing the handicap and coming to a Group 2 with this horse, but it has been the right decision."*

Charlie Johnston was caught on the TV cameras shouting the horse home (at a big screen) and ITV's Luke Harvey stuck a microphone in front of him minutes afterwards. *"Dark Vision had to be very, very good and quite lucky to win from where he was. Clearly he is a very, very good horse."*

Wednesday 1st August's 2018 Racing Post had *"Yesterday at Glorious Goodwood"* and Lee Mottershead reported:-

"Dark Vision surges home in the Group 2 Qatar Vintage Stakes under Silvestre de Sousa, whose mount came from last to first.

If you are going to have a problem, have a nice one. The lucky 19 people who own Dark Vision now have such a problem. Their trainer Mark Johnston will be the one who must decide how to solve it.

In Dark Vision, the striking last-to-first winner of the Qatar Vintage Stakes, the Kingsley Park 10 partnership is now in possession of a most valuable commodity, a colt quoted at just 20-1 for the Qipco 2,000 Guineas.

Each member of the syndicate paid a total of £7,000 to cover the purchase price and juvenile season training fees of three horses, described as at one point 'left on the shelf, unsold' by Johnston.

One of the three, Victory Command, landed an Ascot Listed race on Saturday, but the best appears to be Dark Vision, who could now be worth a seven-figure sum to a big owner with big pockets. To keep or to sell. Johnston must decide.

It's very difficult, said Johnston. A problem with inexperienced owners is sometimes that they get carried away with the dream. You have to be sensible.

They've now gone from gambling £7,000 to gambling hundreds of thousands of pounds – and it is a gamble. We had a real good horse last year who attracted a £750,000 offer after one run. He was beaten next time and that was hundreds of thousands lost.

A couple of years ago, when I first started doing these Kingsley Park partnerships, we had a big offer for a filly. At that stage the rules said there had to be a unanimous decision. Getting a unanimous decision from 19 people is impossible – so I changed the rules and now it's my decision.

The Kingsley's can take heart from the fact Johnston has yet to let them down. Two of his three previous Vintage winners, Mister Baileys and Shamardal, went on to Classic glory. The manner in which Dark Vision mowed down Dunkerron and Confiding under Silvestre De Sousa suggests he deserves to be at least talked of as a long-range Classic contender. The biggest problem Johnston will have now will be keeping everyone's feet on the ground."

After our day off on the Wednesday 1st August 2018 the Ross's and I set off again for the track. My game of golf had been excellent with three Insurance Brokers from London. One of them knew a bit about horseracing but the others were unaware that Glorious Goodwood, some 8 miles away, was taking place and had wondered why the hotel was so busy. We of course knew that on the Thursday Dark Vision and Victory Command had not been declared to run.

The topic of conversation amongst the Johnston Racing supporters, once we got there on the Thursday, centred around how much Dark Vision was going to go for. I felt that Mark would sell him after our short discussion about his value immediately after the race. He had also, unknown to others until much later, told Liz Pescops, who was not keen to sell Victory Command, in the first place that he would now not sell him after all.

I was slightly miffed with one part of Mark's quote in the Racing Post of the day before:

"A problem with inexperienced owners is sometimes that they get carried away with the dream. You have to be sensible."

I had certainly lived through the experiences of the ups and downs of owning a horse over many years to know how precarious, but also rewarding, the sport can be. Sometimes it appeared an injury was just lurking around every corner. Also some of my horses had been slow ones. Jane Knight who had Watersmeet running later in the week, an accomplished horsewoman herself said that *"he is correct they just don't know horses"*.

Mark was certainly correct about *"the dream"* and we were bombarded with mostly optimistic quotes about Dark Vision taking part in major 2-year-old races in the autumn and perhaps the following year in the 2000 Guineas. Would we ever get the chance again to be in this potential position? Some of us on "the back nine" of life, probably thought it was unlikely. It had taken me upwards of 30 years to get where I was so at 70 years of age to live for, although hopefully possible, another 30 years was an unlikely medical feat. However, Mark was also correct about being sensible but, of course, in the days before the sale was announced we had no real idea what sums were involved. However, a seven figure sum was openly debated. Adages abounded such as *"you always take the first offer in racing"* and it became obvious all the professionals that were involved in racing advised to sell.

Back in the hotel that evening Franny Norton joined Catherine and Billy Ross and I for a drink and left his awestruck audience in no doubt what to do next. *"SELL"* was his theme. *"SELL them both and spend the money."* I had the temerity to interrupt him in full flow and suggest that Dark Vision might win the 2000 Guineas. *"It is not easy to win the 2000 Guineas"* was the reply. *"Sell them and spend every January in Barbados"* he suggested. I quipped that in any event I spend every January in Gran Canaria. *"Go in February then"* was an immediate riposte. *"Mark Johnston knows more about horses than anybody I know."* So there we had it.

Knowledgeable, experienced pragmatists vs dreamers. The following day, although shattered but still elated, we headed north and home.

Ken Pitterson in the Weekender was impressed:

"Dark Vision

Winner, Vintage Stakes 7f (Group 2, Goodwood, Tuesday July 31)

This Group 2 attracted a competitive field which saw this son of Dream Ahead maintain his unbeaten record. I was impressed by the change of pace he showed which took him to the lead and enabled him to pull away near the line. Mark Johnston clearly has a talented juvenile on his hands and considering this yard has won this race with Mister Baileys, Lucky Story and Shamardal, this could bode well for the future."

On 6th August 2018 Mark wrote on his *"Bletherings"* page on the Johnston Racing website that:

"It is a ridiculous amount of time since I last blethered. There are of course no end of things to write about at this time of the year but I find it extremely difficult to set aside any time at all to allocate to this. One thing I have found time for is watching last week's Vintage Stakes over and over again. I really don't think I have watched a race so many times since Mister Baileys won the Guineas back in 1994. I still can't believe it. It was such an incredible performance.

In this morning's Racing Post, Simon Turner rates it 'the most taking juvenile performance' of the week but tempers his comments by saying that 'the pace of the Group 2 prize clearly favoured those coming from off the pace'. Did it? I'm not sure. The second placed horse hit the front with two furlongs to go; the third came from well back but started his run long before Dark Vision; and the fourth was in mid-field from the bend. I think it was just such an extraordinary performance that we are all looking for ways to explain it.

Only time will tell whether the field comes up to the usual standard for this Group 2 event but there is little doubt that the winner was far and away the best horse in the race. Our previous winners of the Vintage Stakes, Mister Baileys, Lucky Story and Shamardal all went on to be top class and Dark Vision was as impressive as any of them."

In the following days there was much analysis of what actually happened. SDS looked back on the following Sunday at the race:

"As riders, we all know Goodwood is a sharp track which doesn't suit all horses. You have to help some of them to do their best there and Dark Vision is a massive colt who didn't really act on the ground, so I had to ride him with that in mind.

A lot of people said he missed the break, but he jumped as good as the other horses, then he got a bit tight for room and I just wanted to let him find his feet. You're running downhill and straight away there's a bend coming up, so I looked for a bit of room because I didn't want to knock him around and get him unbalanced.

By that stage I was happy enough with my position because I knew they were going too fast, but as we turned for home we were still nearly last and not in the ideal place, so you have to sit, look at what's happening in front of you and weigh up your options. I didn't want to break his stride, so my thinking was that I couldn't afford to go to the inside, and have to wait for a run and use a turn of foot, I had to let him get rolling and do his stuff, and I started trying to angle out.

My decision was really made for me by the type of horse I was riding rather than the track, and I chose the safe option. Unfortunately the horse on my outside was going backwards and he wasn't doing me any favours as I tried to get into the clear. Dark Vision is still a bit of a baby and it's such a sharp track, a place that demands a lot from a horse, physically and mentally, so I had to help him, but once he got to the outside I was always happy we'd get there – in fact, although he had to overcome a lot to win, he didn't have that hard a race.

I know Mark often likes to see his runners rolling along near the front, but he knows we do that kind of thing day in and day out, so he never tells me how to ride, he just tells me what I want to know about the horse and then his faith in my ability to do the job.

It was great to win for him and such a lovely group of owners with a horse who cost so little. It's always easy to be happy after you win, but I felt pleased that I made the right calls and got the job done."

Pragmatic viewpoints were not lacking in the *"Expert Jury"* in Tuesday's 7th August 2018 Racing Post. They were asked *"How highly do you rate Dark Vision after Goodwood?"*

<u>*David Baxter – Reporter*</u>

Money makes the world go round and Dark Vision would certainly command some serious bids even though he has raced just three times. He is as short as 10-1 for the 2,000 Guineas, and Mark Johnston spoke in the aftermath of his last-to-first Vintage Stakes victory about whether to cash in or carry on with the his bargain. The cynic in me thinks if an offer too good to refuse came in for the colt, connections should take it. He is progressive, and I think he'd get a mile no problem, but I wouldn't consider him a Classic contender at this juncture.

<u>*James Hill – RPTipping*</u>

You can argue the sky's the limit for Dark Vision; equally, you could say the colt's stock will never be higher than now. It's difficult to gauge how good he is as his last-to-first victory in the Vintage Stakes at Goodwood owed as much to the crazy pace they went up front as anything and it played into his hands. He won nicely, but a future champion? I'd say he has the potential to land a Group 1 and wouldn't go further.

<u>*Mark Scully – Bloodstock editor*</u>

As problems go, the one facing the Kingsley Park 10 is as desirable as they come. Having put relatively little into the acquisition of Dark Vision, do they stick, retaining the colt in their ownership to discover how far he can take them, or twist, cashing in now but meaning any future success would not be their own? It is not hard to imagine him going on to be a force in some of the year's biggest remaining races, especially if he can continue to deploy that turn of foot over further. If he were mine though, he would be doing it in somebody else's colours if the right offer came in.

"In the same edition of The Racing Post David Carr picked up on the *"Bletherings"* article and quoted Mark:

Impressive two-year-old performances can sometimes turn out too good to be true and Johnston said: 'I don't make our geese into swans and that's why I keep looking at it again.

If you look at the way the horse passes the line, he's hardly turned a hair. He didn't look to have a hard race and he came from a completely impossible position. He lost 10kg, which is just average for a race, and he's already started putting it back on.

We put him in at the second entry stage for the National Stakes [at the Curragh] and I'd think you're most likely to see him next in that or the Dewhurst, or both.' Not all juveniles prove as good at three but Johnston is confident Dark Vision has the size and physical scope to train on saying: 'For sure, you'd say he's a big backward baby of a horse.'

Johnston has always maintained that Shamardal is the best colt he has trained to date, although he lost him to Godolphin and Saeed bin Suroor who subsequently won the French Guineas and Derby with him.

I wonder if he will be changing his mind come next May?"

Three very happy partners wrote to the Kingsley Klarion (August 2018) with their appreciation:

<u>*"The joy of partnerships*</u>

I just wanted to say thanks to Mark, Deirdre and Charlie and everyone at Kingsley Park for an extraordinary 12 months on the racecourse.

When I had my heart attack last May, I decided to increase my involvement in syndicates by adding to the shares that I already had. The fun for me is picking out likely prospects at an affordable price. Fortunately, I joined Kingsley Park 10 and with your help, Mark, and the team around you, it has been a great success with eight wins from three horses.

These experiences are so good to share and I am lucky enough to be involved in groups of like-minded racing people from Hampshire to Yorkshire and all places in between. As always, the horse coming back safe is all I ask, but the joy on people's faces when we share a winner is a wonder to behold.

Victory Command making all to win a Listed race at Ascot on July 28 for his fourth success and Dark Vision's Group 2 win at Goodwood on July 31 have been the highlights so far.

Here's looking forward to more fun and success in the months and years to come. Best wishes to all at Kingsley Park.

Paul Walker

Blakedown"

"*Over the moon!*

Congratulations to all at Kingsley Park on more fine winners for the KP10 partnership. Dark Vision won on his debut at Yarmouth July 5, and once he got the hang of what he was doing, he did it very well indeed.

Then he went on to win again at York on July 14, topping it all with his Group 2 win at Glorious Goodwood on July 31. And on July 28 another KP10 horse, Victory Command, had his fourth win, taking a Listed race at Ascot.

We are over the moon. KP10 have had eight winners this year!

Many thanks

Lorna and Lionel Beecroft

Midhurst, West Sussex"

7.7 The Sale of Dark Vision

On 7th August Mark wrote to the partners of KP 10 to tell us that if all went to plan the sale of Dark Vision would be completed by the end of the week. His message was as follows:

"I have been deliberately avoiding entering into debate, especially by email, on the possible sale of one of the horses as, as we saw with the offers for Victory Command, it quickly degenerates into disagreement.

However, there are, apparently, rumours circulating on social media and so I feel I must update you.

We had some discussion about the pros and cons of selling and keeping after Victory Command's Ascot win and I could see that I was going to have to make a decision that would be unpopular with some. However, in many ways, Dark Vision's win has made that decision much easier. Prior to his Vintage Stakes victory I could not have justified keeping Victory Command and taking what I know to be a very significant risk with a large amount of money but now, with two very valuable horses, I think I can justify keeping one and selling the other to ensure that, while you will still be taking a big gamble, you will have netted a very substantial profit whatever happens.

I do not want to go into the figures involved until I am certain that a deal is done as I know that these things have got a terrible habit of going wrong and I don't want anybody thinking that is what the horse is worth. The offers we have had are not based on future earning capacity but are simply down to what very rich people can afford to pay for the dream of having the best horse, in exactly the same way as they will pay vast sums for yearlings.

If all goes according to plan, the sale of Dark Vision will be completed by the end of the week and I am very confident that you will all be happy with the result and agree that I have made the right decision. He will be vetted on Thursday and has to pass that for the sale to go through. I never take that for granted and that is why I don't want anyone jumping to conclusions yet.

Please let's not have any debate on it. I am confident that I am making the right decision and I am confident that, if it goes through, you will be getting the best possible deal.

I will let you know as soon as I have something concrete.

Best regards.

Mark"

The news soon broke and David Milnes of the Racing Post had the following article on 10th August 2018 published in *"Bloodhorse"*.

"Impressive Qatar Vintage Stakes (G2) winner **Dark Vision**, *who earned quotes of 16-1 for next year's QIPCO Two Thousand Guineas (G1) after extending his unbeaten record to three, has been purchased by Godolphin but will remain in training with Mark Johnston."*

'*Dark Vision has been sold to Godolphin and will be staying with us,' Johnston said. 'He was vetted yesterday, and we are currently waiting on some blood tests, which should be known on Monday, but this is just routine.*

I'm not sure which colours he'll be racing in - whether it's the all-blue or those of Sheikh Mohammed's son (carried by Dee Ex Bee) – but we'll have a sit down and chat with the new owners about where the horse will run next.

Possible targets include the Group 1 National Stakes at the Curragh and the Group 1 Dewhurst Stakes at Newmarket, which is sponsored by Darley.'

On the same day Mark wrote again to partners:

"Although not formally concluded, news of the sale of Dark Vision has hit the press so, although I was trying to hold off until we had invoiced for the horse, I feel I must now tell you where we stand.

I have agreed a sale to Sheikh Mohammed. The horse *was vetted yesterday and passed but we are awaiting results of blood samples taken before we can invoice for the horse.*

When the dust has settled and we know exactly what your bank balance is I will also make a proposal to you to buy more horses for KP10 but, for that, I would need unanimous approval. If, even one person feels that they would prefer the partnership to end in October 2019, we shall stick to the original terms. I will let you know as soon as the sale is formally concluded.

Best regards, Mark"

Reg Witheridge told me that:

"After Dark Vision's magnificent triumph selling him for what was likely to be a seven figure sum and the bonus of retaining Victory Command seemed a superb deal. We reasoned that in a year's time we were having to sell anyway.

I thought he had a 5% chance of winning the 2000 Guineas and maybe a 10% chance of winning a Group 1. We were very happy when Godolphin paid what they did.

We still feel that Dark Vision is still partly ours and we cheer him on when he runs (except when running against Victory Command)."

The proposal to buy two more horses did not receive the required unanimous approval as some of the partners decided to take the money. I have not much of an idea what some of the partners felt at the time, as the majority have not expressed their views. In view of the events that were to follow, perhaps this topic should be "put to bed" in much the same way as Silvestre de Sousa and Dark Vision did in the last furlong of the race. As Mark and several reporters commented time will tell whether the correct decision was made and the perfect science of hindsight will allow, at a future date, a full and accurate analysis to take place.

CHAPTER 8
SUMMER TO AUTUMN 2018

The hard work did not stop and as they say, *"the show must go on"*. The work riders, yard managers, assistant trainers and Mark himself continued to watch and report on the performance of each horse on the gallops. Meanwhile news of Seductive Moment's progress from vet John Martin was encouraging when he reported on 10th of August.

"Seductive Moment was examined again this week having had two weeks box rest as planned. He was sound at led trot and I repeated the images of his right hind hock. These images showed no further progression of the new bone formation on the central tarsal bone. I felt given the radiographic appearance of the joint, the clinical picture and the time frame involved it was appropriate to start walking exercise again. My plan is for him to continue with walking exercise for 3 weeks and examine again at the end of the month with the aim of resuming ridden trotting exercise."

It was good to hear from John that things were looking hopeful for Seductive Moment. However, as any owner will tell you things don't always go to plan and a month later John further reported:

"Further to my last email Seductive Moment continues with ridden trotting exercise and remains sound. We feel that now would be an opportune time to geld the horse as he can recover from the procedure whilst continuing the rehabilitation for his hock injury. Our plan is to geld him tomorrow and he will continue with ridden trotting exercise from Thursday."

Paul Walker commented *"No more seductive moments for him then"*. However, true as this was, you will see later in this chapter he did make a comeback at the year end.

On 8th August early closing entries were made for both Dark Vision and Victory Command on 15th September in the 1 mile Golden Fleece Stakes (Group 2) at Leopardstown worth £132,000.

An entry was also made for Victory Command in the 1 mile Stonehenge Stakes (Listed Race), on Friday 24th August at Salisbury, worth £32,500. That was the same day as the third day of the Ebor Festival.

Victory Command and Dark Vision were kept in the Champion Juvenile Stakes (Leopardstown) at the forfeit stage. They were also entered in the Champagne Stakes (Group 2) to be run on 15th September at Doncaster.

Eventually, Victory Command was declared for Saturday 1st September in the 188 Bet Solario Stakes (Group 3) over 7 furlongs at Sandown Park and Dark Vision was destined to run at Doncaster in the Champagne Stakes.

8.1 Victory Command in the 188 Bet Solario Stakes

It was a sunny day and the going was Good.

There were six runners all carrying 9st 1lb. The even money favourite was Too Darn Hot (OR 104), trained by John Gosden. He and Arthur Kitt, the winner of the Listed Chesham Stakes at Royal Ascot trained by Tom Dascombe, provided Victory Command with by far his stiffest opposition to date. Not to mention the others which included Dunkerron (OR 108) and Confiding, 2nd and 3rd in the Vintage Stakes behind Dark Vision, respectively. Watan trained by Richard Hannon was runner-up in the Group 3 Acomb Stakes at York. Silvestre de Sousa was on board Victory Command.

Too Darn Hot broke very keenly but Arthur Kitt soon took up the race on the rail with Victory Command in second. It looked like a good pace. Arthur Kitt and Victory Command were having a right old battle at the head of affairs with Too Darn Hot in third. Dunkerron was being driven along and Confiding was on his inside. Suddenly Too Darn Hot took off and went well clear leaving some good horses in his wake. The commentator remarked *"Too Darn Hot was just Too Darn Good"*.

Victory Command with SDS on board in the parade ring with Savroop Singh at Sandown. *Ruth Carty*

It was a comfortable win. Arthur Kitt was four lengths behind and Victory Command just lost third place to Confiding who stayed on gamely. So the star potential that Timeform suggested had oozed out of Too Darn Hot on his first run and previous win at Sandown certainly showed itself in this race. It was a much deeper race and Too Darn Hot won it very impressively.

Charlie Johnston was there and reported:

"Victory Command ran at Sandown in the 3.35 and finished 4/6. He broke well and sat 2nd through the first half of the race travelling comfortably. He moved up to challenge 3f out going very well and looking like he would take a strong hand in the finish but from 2f out his run gradually weakened and he was caught for 3rd close to the line. He has run a solid race and shown he is up to Group level in what was a very strong renewal of this race. Silvestre felt that the combination of slower ground and a stiff finish meant he didn't see out this race quite as strongly as he has done previously. Judging on today's run either better ground or a slightly easier 7f would suit him better. All in all it was a solid run from him and he has shown he is up to this level."

Paul Walker reported:

"Hadn't expected Arthur Kitt to lead but SDS dropped in as you saw off a strong pace. SDS was convinced afterwards he didn't stay 7f on that ground at Sandown. The race was very quick for the conditions and you have to bear in mind that VC has been off for 35 days."

A few days later on 5th September Mark wrote to partners with his thoughts on the two horses which remained in KP 10 and the financial state of the partnership:

"I was a bit disappointed with Victory Command's run at Sandown although all that Charlie said about the ground and the competitiveness of the race is correct. We can only hope that he is a bit better than what we saw and that he will be competitive at that level, or above, next year. Not to say that we won't try again this year if conditions are right.

It was a lesson for all, however, about the value of two-year-olds and how they fluctuate dramatically with each run. We probably couldn't get the same offers for him now as we were getting immediately after Ascot.

I would have liked to be racing Seductive Moment now and to be in a better position to decide whether we should be keeping him for next year but the injury has forced our hand. We will keep him into next year but may sell him before October if he does not live up to original promise.

Nonetheless, the partnership is in a very healthy state. Of course there is nothing else to pay for keeping both horses for next year and, even allowing for this, and the fact that entry fees for Victory Command might even outstrip training fees, we have plenty to spare."

8.2 A record 4,194 Winners and Counting

Amongst the discussions and deliberations about the future of Dark Vision and Seductive Moment, and Victory Command's fourth place at Sandown, Mark Johnston on 23rd August at York became the trainer to have won the most races in the history of British Flat Racing.

Poet's Society (a Kingsley Park 9 "Ready to Run" horse) ridden by Frankie Dettori won the one mile Clipper Logistics Handicap on the Knavesmire. The win meant the previous record held by Richard Hannon Snr had been surpassed.

Frankie performed one of his trademark flying dismounts to the delight of Mark and the many well-wishers congratulating him in the winners' enclosure. Amongst those present was his good friend and fellow trainer Mick Easterby. Lord Grimthorpe was also there to present Mark with a framed, commemorative collage of his achievement.

John Scanlon's *"Off the bridle"* column in September's edition of the Kingsley Klarion paid the following well deserved tribute:

"The media response to Mark's surpassing Richard Hannon Senior's record for the number of British winners by a trainer was, in many ways, remarkable.

Frankie Dettori dismounts Poet's Society to the delight of the crowd and Mark Johnston. *Jeremy Phillips*

Mark Johnston with Poet's Society- Robynne Watton looking on. *Jeremy Phillips*

There's no doubt that Frankie Dettori's involvement in partnering the record-setting winner, in a race broadcast live on a mainstream terrestrial television channel, helped the 'theatre' of the moment. Frankie's flying dismount from Poet's Society was a very visible acknowledgement to everyone who witnessed it that Dettori recognised the magnitude of Mark's achievement. Dettori's cheerful disposition and larger-than-life personality made the post-race celebrations all the more enjoyable, and he was also very generous in his praise of Mark after the race.

ITV Racing, too, paid tribute to Mark before interviewing him live with Messrs Chamberlin, Weaver and Murtagh in the parade ring. Mark responded by being an excellent interviewee, enjoying some good-natured verbal jousting with the former jockeys, and letting the public see a more relaxed side to his nature.

However, I was particularly struck by two personal contributions to the media coverage that started me thinking about Mark's modus operandi. Sir Mark Prescott said that the only advantages with which Mark started out in his training career were 'a thoroughly good brain and complete self-belief.' In a lighter vein, his fellow Newmarket trainer, and former Kingsley Park vet, James Tate, confessed that he used to share a joke with the lads that 'a winner a day keeps MJ away', the implication being that if the horses weren't winning, a 'grumpy' Mark would be on the case and determined to find out why.

It seems to me that much of the secret of Mark's success lies in the fusion of these remarks. It's not that the 'complete self-belief' about which Sir Mark Prescott talks means that Mark thinks he always has the key to how his horses perform; rather it is his utter determination to find solutions when problems arise. He doesn't think he knows all the answers, but he appreciates that it is his job to leave no stone unturned in pursuit of those answers. 4,194 winners (and rising) suggest that he is better at finding those solutions than anyone else in the training ranks."

In the Kingsley Klarion's review of 2018 Mark was quoted as follows:

"When the record-breaking winner came along," recalls Mark, 'it was as much a relief to finally get there as anything else. Of course, Frankie Dettori's involvement was tremendous, and he was fantastic on the day.'

What the record underlined for me most of all was the consistency we have been able to achieve across the years. Where other yards hit purple patches of form, or shut down in bad times complaining about the [equine] virus, we keep going, leaving no stone unturned in the pursuit of training winners for our owners.

So to train another century of British winners, our 25th in a row and this time achieved before the end of June, was very satisfactory. It was even better to turn that century into 200 winners, and better still to set a new personal best for our yearly score." By the end of October 2020 the tally had risen to 4646 winners.

After Mark's milestone we all hoped that the KP 10 horses could continue the onwards and upwards trend. As such, two entries were made for Victory Command: Thursday 27th September at Newmarket in the Tattersalls Stakes, Group 3 over 7 furlongs and also at Newmarket on Saturday 29th September in the Juddmonte Royal Lodge Stakes (Group 2) over 1 mile. Dark Vision remained in the Champagne Stakes but he did not add to the winning statistics.

8.3 Dark Vision finishes last in the Champagne Stakes

The Group 2 Howcroft Industrial Supplies Champagne Stakes (Group 2) over 7 furlongs 15th September at Doncaster was keenly anticipated by Kingsley Park 10 partners. Obviously as erstwhile owners of Dark Vision, who was now running in Godolphin's colours. Silvestre de Sousa took the ride and he was up against Too Darn Hot, trained by John Gosden and ridden by Frankie Dettori, as he was when he thrashed the opposition last time out on 1st September in the Solario Stakes at Sandown Park. Van Beethoven trained by Aiden O'Brien (beaten by Dark Vision in the 2018 Vintage Stakes) and ridden by Ryan Moore was one of two Ballydoyle runners. Cardini ridden by Seamie Heffernan was the other. Charlie Hills's Phoenix of Spain and Bye Bye Hong Kong trained by Andrew Balding completed the six runner field. The official going was Good.

It was an even break and Dark Vision broke well this time. Bye Bye Hong Kong ran freely in the lead with Cardini second in pursuit. Van Beethoven was at the back and Dark Vision was alongside

Too Darn Hot about 2 lengths to 3 lengths behind the leaders. At half way Dark Vision was off the bridle and struggling whereas Too Darn Hot cruised up to the leaders and went away with Cardini and Phoenix of Spain staying on to be 2ⁿᵈ and 3ʳᵈ. A race which will be remembered for Too Darn Hot's scintillating performance.

Ron Wood of the Racing Post reported that:

"With Dark Vision not travelling from an early stage, a couple of those who were following him soon got well behind in a surprisingly strung-out field, including the winner. But John Gosden's colt produced another really smart performance, getting there readily and matching the time of the preceding older-horse Group 2 Park Stakes.

Dark Vision came into this 3-3, purchased by Godolphin after winning the Group 2 Vintage at Goodwood, but he was a total flop this time. The jockey said he found the ground quite loose."

Mark said that: "Dark Vision's performance was diabolical. He was under pressure almost immediately and wasn't going to be involved from a long way out. The jockey said the ground was very loose, but I've never been someone who looks to blame the ground especially with a horse only having had three races before today."

Just over one week later Mark was reported to have *"revealed"* that Dark Vision sustained a suspected pelvis injury in the Champagne Stakes. He had been unsound since the race and was sent to the Newmarket Equine Hospital for a bone scan. *"It looks like he's got a stress fracture of his pelvis"* said Mark.

Another horse who had been on the injury list was Seductive Moment. He continued to recover from his hock injury and on 28ᵗʰ September John Martin sent the following message to partners:

"Seductive Moment has completed 4 weeks ridden trotting exercise and was examined today. He was sound at led trot and has recovered from his gelding operation. I repeated the radiographs of his right hind hock and the changes present here have settled further over the last month.

I feel based on the clinical examination, the radiographs and the length of rehabilitation he has completed that he is now fit to resume cantering exercise. We will start him cantering and trotting on alternate days for two weeks as we find this a good reintroduction to fast work after a prolonged period of reduced exercise. Providing he remains sound during this period we will then increase his exercise further."

8.4 Victory Command finishes fourth in the Juddmonte Royal Lodge Stakes at Newmarket

It was a gorgeous day at Headquarters. There had been selective watering after racing the previous day.

The Juddmonte Royal Lodge Stakes (Class 1) (Group 2) was over one mile on the Rowley Mile. It was one of the seven races to feature as part of the *"European Road to the Kentucky Derby"* a qualification series of one mile races throughout Europe.

The winner of the Juddmonte Royal Lodge received 10 points in the series. The horse scoring the most points from the seven races secured a place in the Kentucky Derby.

Silvestre de Sousa was on board Victory Command, who faced six other runners. It was a strong field. Arthur Kitt trained by Tom Dascombe had already beaten us in the Solario at Sandown. Aiden O'Brien fielded three contenders, Cape of Good Hope, Mohawk (both Galileo colts) and Sydney Opera House by Australia. John Gosden who had won the race the previous year with Roaring Lion fielded Beatboxer. Paul Cole had the Lope de Vega colt Duke of Hazard in and was one of the few to have run as often as Victory Command had. It looked a very competitive race.

Timeform's analysis in the race card suggested Beatboxer had created a very good impression in winning his previous two starts and was expected to take this step up in class in his stride. Arthur Kitt who had chased home Too Darn Hot in the Solario, the latter having gone on to win the

Champagne Stakes at Doncaster *"may again play second fiddle, while Cape of Good Hope merits respect"*. Charlie Johnston told me that he had seen Mohawk run at the Curragh and thought he was very good.

Victory Command prior to the Juddmonte Royal Lodge Stakes at Newmarket, with Paddy Trainor. *Nick Cowes*

Beatboxer, Timeform's selection, was indeed the 7/4 favourite with Arthur Kitt the 11/4 second favourite and Cape of Good Hope 9/2 by far the best backed of the three Irish raiders. Victory Command was 16/1.

The break was even. Victory Command and Sydney Opera House disputed the early lead. Mohawk was tracking Sydney Opera House. Duke of Hazard, Beatboxer and Arthur Kitt were at the rear. In the final half mile the pace lifted and Victory Command had a narrow lead. Frankie was hard at work on Beatboxer. Mohawk challenged on the far side and took the race from his two stablemates with Victory Command in fourth.

Victory Command reversed the placings in the Solario on Arthur Kitt something Silvestre commented upon afterwards with a smile.

The Racing Post analyst, Ron Wood thought Victory Command's run *"was respectable without proving he was up to this standard."* We assembled in 4th spot in the winners enclosure and Mark gave his thoughts on the performance. Although he much preferred to be in the parade ring in the winners' area after a race rather than where the jockeys dismounted from the unplaced horses he wondered, however, whether this type of race, a Group 2, was perhaps a step too far for Victory Command. He pointed out the financial consequences, owing to the high entry fees in these races, are substantial if the horse does not win. Even though fourth place paid £7,169 most of that would be accounted for with various deductions including the cost to enter the race.

Victory Command with Paddy Trainor and the Author after the Juddmonte Royal Lodge. *Robynne Watton*

Aquarium with a 2 length lead in the closing stages at York. *Jeremy Phillips*

Mark thought the horse:

"will be difficult to place now and to keep going down the Group 2 route in this country would not be cost effective bearing in mind what we have to pay to enter." Off the cuff he thought that it would be his last race this year and the Dubai Carnival, the German 2000 Guineas, a £100k race at Newcastle, the Craven and the Free Handicap were mentioned as options for next year. Charlie had mentioned the Racing Post Trophy at Doncaster but Mark pointed out *"it would be too wet by then."*

We all thought that he had been beaten by some good O'Brien horses. He did run well and fourth place was probably his best form. Liz Pescops accepted the fourth prize, a silver goblet and a bottle of Woodford Whiskey (now on my sideboard) – oh and also one point towards a potential run in the Kentucky Derby. The day itself was just great and we all were invited up to the unoccupied Royal Box for a glass of champagne. Thank you Newmarket.

This proved to be Victory Command's last race in 2018 and although several entries were made, a foot abscess prevented him from running. He was to rest and recover awaiting what turned out to be a trip for some Winter Sun (Chapter 9) .

8.5 Aquarium Wins at York

Bryan and Sue Russell and I decided to take full advantage of the Kingsley Park Owners Group to follow Aquarium on 13th October 2018. Kingsley Park partners are entitled to be a member of the Group. Jock Bennett was in attendance and I asked him about Seductive Moment and Dark Vision. The former was back cantering and things were going well. *"It shouldn't take long to get him fit"* Jock said. No timescale was available. Dark Vision had been checked over at Newmarket and nothing new or definite was found. He was being treated cautiously with box rest before he returned to walking and trotting exercise.

On Saturday 13th October the 2.05 race was the Download The Coral App Stakes over 1 mile 2½ furlongs and was for 3-year-olds and upwards. It was a 96-110 rated Handicap and the going was Soft. Aquarium rated 100 was drawn (4) and Franny Norton was on board. There were 15 runners and he went off at 16/1. Mountain Angel trained by Roger Varian was the 4/1 favourite.

Drawn (4) was a real advantage and Aquarium broke well although in the first couple of hundred yards he was shuffled back a bit. He then made up some ground and the front five at half way were clear of the struggling pack, left behind on the soft ground. Taking the turn they came down the centre of the home straight and fanned out across the track. About 1½ furlongs out Franny made his move to challenge and the horse responded to take a two length lead.

It was tough work on the testing ground and My Lord And Master trained by William Haggas and ridden by Cieren Fallon came with a strong late run but Aquarium held on to win by a neck. Dave Randall of the Racing Post wrote:

"He looked well beforehand and 3-year-olds have a strong recent record in this race. He tanked through the contest in about fifth on the rail from a low draw and found much more than the other prominent runners from halfway up the straight. A late closer nearly spoiled the party but he just held on."

Jock told Dave Randall that *"Aquarium was very game, that was a long last furlong but he held on. He's been very consistent, he started off on the all-weather and now he's won off a mark of 100."*

After we had collected and posed with the trophy we all repaired to the Winner's Reception to have a glass of champagne and watch the replay. That was my second visit to this facility (the first was of course in July after Dark Vision's win) and after 30 years of trying to have a winner at York, they were coming thick and fast – well at least two wins and in the same year is not too bad.

Winning connections with Franny Norton, Jock Bennett, Barry Lusted and Tristan Burton-pye. *Jeremy Phillips*

8.6 Party Time

On the horizon was a party. After such a year it did feel as though the Kingsley Park 10 partnership should celebrate. We were invited to much bigger events as coinciding with our first year's successes was, of course, the momentous achievement of Mark and Johnston Racing to break the record for the most wins ever in British racing to record 4194!! Invitations were sent out for celebrations to be held on the weekend of 10th/11th November at Kingsley Park. Such was the number of invited entries and declared runners there were two divisions, one each on the Saturday and Sunday nights. These turned out to be a parties to remember.

The Kingsley Klarion reported (December 2018):

*"**Doubling up means twice the fun***

When the achievement you want to celebrate is the remarkable record set by Mark in August, when he became Britain's "winningmost" trainer of all time, the problem you face is how to have a party to mark the occasion that is special enough to do it justice. Mark and Deirdre came up with the perfect solution to this dilemma: why throw one party, when it's possible to throw two?

Masterminded by Deirdre, the parties were hosted in two massive marquees at Kingsley Park. The attention to detail which is so evident in all that Johnston Racing does in its racing activities was brought to bear on the arrangements for the parties. The marquees were decorated in the stable's colours, with the tables dressed in blue and the carpets green. Dozens of floral arrangements were flecked with gold, mirroring the 'Winged Spur' on the stable (and Johnston clan) crest. The marquees were transformed into what one guest described as a 'fantastic Disney wonderland style setting'.

Guests were welcomed on the approach to the party site by huge, illuminated numbers spelling out the record tally (4,194) and by cardboard cut-outs of first winner Hinari Video, and the record-breaker Poet's Society.

Contributions

Saturday evening began with a drinks reception for guests who included long-standing owners and friends such as Paul and Adrienne Venner, Ron and Norma Huggins and Markus and Irene Graff. Jockeys who have made significant contributions to our winning tally over the years were also there to celebrate including Jason Weaver with his wife, Fiona, Kevin Darley and his wife, Debbie, PJ McDonald and his wife Abby, and Joe Fanning with his wife Sarah.

There were even Olympic medallists in attendance, in the shape of diver Jack Laugher MBE, a friend of Angus Johnston since school days at Ripon Grammar, and Nicola Wilson, who won an Equestrian team silver at the Olympics in 2012.

They were joined by triathlete and dualathlete Jane Holmes, sister of vet Simon Stirk, who has been dubbed 'the fastest granny in the world!'

One of the marquees was set for dinner, and the partygoers enjoyed a fantastic meal provided by the caterers, Foodamour of Newmarket. The facilities in that marquee included a live link to the dance-floor of the other marquee.

Immediately after the meal, the guests were treated to a commemorative video produced by Equine Productions, whose visual director Nathan Horrocks used to ride out at Kingsley Park. The video, which included contributions from Charlie and Angus as well as lengthy reflections by their parents, was greeted with a standing ovation by guests.

Musical entertainment was provided by Party Band, The Nightjars, and during the break between the first and second parts of their set the Scottish ceilidh band, The Bahookies, put partygoers through their paces.

As guests danced the night away, the evening seemed to pass by in a flash, and Mark and Deirdre enjoyed the company of so many people who have played such a huge part in the success story of Johnston Racing.

The following evening saw some 220 guests, split between owners and staff, descend on the party campus for more of the same. Sunday's guests were treated to a set from Angus Johnston's band, The Soundtrax, and responded energetically to the ceilidh capers of The Bahookies.

Again, partygoers thoroughly enjoyed the video and were treated to a sumptuous meal provided by local caterer Guy Fairhurst and his team.

In recognition of Mark's achievement, Goodwood Racecourse had been kind enough to donate 30 cases of beer and 30 cases of lager to Mark and the team and this all helped to make the party go with a swing!

All too soon, the celebrations had to come to an end. It all amounted to two fantastic evenings of celebration, doing full credit to Mark's wonderful record!

The Author with P J McDonald.

Touched

Since the parties, Mark and Deirdre received so many cards and letters from guests expressing thanks for the parties and saying what a wonderful time was had by all. They were genuinely thrilled and touched by the warmth of the response they received and wanted to thank everyone for taking the trouble to make contact afterwards and also for any gifts received.

They also extended their heartfelt thanks to all their guests for making the occasion so memorable, and also to those whose efforts and generosity made the whole weekend so special. Particular thanks were extended to

Equine Productions Limited, to the caterers, to Hawes Creamery, who had donated cheese in recognition of Mark's achievement and to Goodwood Racecourse.

Deirdre wanted particularly to thank Wendy Millbank, for all her help in organising the layout of the marquees, Gilly Guthrie and her team for the magnificent floral displays, Mikaelle Lebreton and Kristy Kettlewell for all their help in assisting with the invitations and accommodation arrangements, and anyone who played any part in making the parties such a roaring success."

8.7 Partners' Meeting

The following weekend, Sunday 18th November, the early winter partners' meeting was held at Kingsley Park. Several horses had been bought at the Sales and new partnerships KPs 11, 12, 13 and 14 had been announced. It was a chance to see the new horses, to try to spot the potential superstars, of which it turned out there were to be some, view the ones already running (or recovering from injury) and of course meet partners and relive the exploits of the past year. Mark and Charlie also gave a summary of the current state of each partnership and the possible plans and aims for the horses. The names of the horses, their breeding, sex and cost of KPs 11,13 and 14 are included in the table.

Table: Horses in KPs 11,13 and 14.

Partnership	Sire	Dam	Name	Sex	Cost
KP 11	Dream Ahead	Petits Potins	Bavardages	Colt	10000gns
	Gleneagles	Crossover	Auchterarder	Filly	€18000
	Fountain of Youth	Art of Gold	Golden Fountain	Colt	£18000
KP 13					
	New Approach	Karen's Caper	King's Caper	Colt	11000 gns
	Slade Power	Shirley Blake	Blake's Vision	Colt	€11000
	Dawn Approach	Shannooan	Quantum Dawn	Colt	€20000
KP 14					
	Brazen Beau	Malpas Missile	Artillery	Colt	€8000
	Planteur	Croisiere		Colt	
	Casamento	Mambo Rhythem	Mesmeric	Colt	€11000
	Make Believe	Cruck Realta	Rose of Kildare	Filly	€3000

At the time of the meeting the plan was not to include Rose of Kildare in KP 14 but in February 2019 the Planteur colt suffered a setback so the inexpensively bought filly was added to this partnership.

Rose of Kildare proved to be a resounding success for KP 14 and together with Auchterarder, of KP 11 and King's Caper, of KP 13 they continued to provide many happy days for the partnerships. Their best results are included in Chapter 14 and a description of their major exploits in Chapter 15.

Such was the turnout (around 70) after coffee, on arrival, and a viewing of the horses, lunch was taken in the Key Centre in Middleham. A glass of champagne followed by a buffet lunch was a prelude to Mark's address to the partners. He pointed out that KP 10 had fared so well financially that he felt the need to remind new partners that it would be wise to regard this performance was the exception rather than the rule. He told the audience that it is possible that KP 10's Victory Command may travel to Dubai in the New Year for the Carnival. The possibility of a run in the United Arab Emirates 2000 Guineas was mentioned.

8.8 Seductive Moment's Return and Plans for Victory Command

Also during the first few weeks of December, entries were made for Seductive Moment's return to the track. He was declared to run on 19th December at Lingfield in a nursery handicap, for horses rated 0-85, over 7 furlongs. Franny Norton took the ride.

Ruth Carty attended and reported:

"Seductive Moment ran at Lingfield this afternoon in a nursery handicap (7 furlongs 1 yd) against 4 other contenders. He was rated as the 16/1 outsider. Seductive Moment bunny hopped out of the stalls (jockey Franny Norton's words) and was slow to find his stride. After keeping pace with the field but with no way through it, Franny switched him to the outside on the final straight and then began to run on strongly. Franny said he could have got third if the race had been a little longer or he hadn't been slow to start. He ran on well and had worked hard, judging by his heavy breathing in the ring after the race. Well done Seductive Moment."

Seductive Moment at Lingfield 19th December, Franny Norton on board, with Tim Jarvis and Gianni Masala.
Ruth Carty

Charlie reported:

"Seductive Moment ran at Lingfield this afternoon and finished 4th of 5 beaten 2½ lengths. He broke a little sluggishly and as a result found himself at the back of the field. As the pace began to quicken he was caught slightly flat footed but once balanced in the straight, he was beginning to stay on when he was slightly short of room. But for this I think he would have been a length closer.

Although disappointing to only finish 4th of 5 I thought this was a solid return to action as he looked a little rusty on his first start back for 6 months and I also think he will improve when stepped up to a mile."

Victory Command was accepted to run at the Dubai Carnival and Charlie wrote with a plan of attack. *"The plan at the moment is for Victory Command to fly to Dubai on January 15th. There are four possible races for him during the Carnival;*

31st Jan – Meydan Classic Trial 7f Turf $100k

14th Feb –Meydan Trophy 9 1/2f Turf $100k

28th Feb – Meydan Classic 8f Turf $175k

9th March – Al Bastakiya 9 1/2f Dirt $300k

He will run in a minimum of two races, quite possibly more, but it is hard to say exactly what his passage through these options will be this far out, particularly as they are over quite a wide range of trips. As soon as we have any more detailed plans we will let you know.

Best of luck with Seductive Moment this afternoon."

Seductive Moment had been declared to run on New Year's Eve at Lingfield in a 0-75 (Class 5) Handicap. On the same day an entry was made for Victory Command to run in the UAE Derby (Group 2), on World Cup night, March 20th 2019. It is a 9.5 furlong (1,900m) race on dirt. The prize money was $2,500,000. Whoops of delight was the response from some of the partners. E-mails flowed. Charlie (with his feet on the ground) explained soon after this entry:

"This was a free entry and purely made to keep all options open during his time in Dubai. But with this possible race in mind, it is now likely that his first start, all being well, will be on the 24th of January over the course and distance of this race.

How he handles the dirt will obviously dictate his future plans in Dubai with the option of coming back to turf for the previously mentioned races on 14th of February and 28th February.

There are subsequent options on dirt on 7th February and 9th March should he show a liking for the surface."

Mark also wrote to tell us all not to rush out and book flights as participation in the UAE Derby would depend on how Victory Command performed at the Carnival.

It was also confirmed that Aquarium who had won recently at York, Love Dreams owned by Mick Doyle (Crone Stud) and Ventura Night, a Middleham Park Racing Club horse, would accompany Victory Command to Dubai.

8.9 Seductive Moment at Lingfield on New Year's Eve and Newcastle 8th January 2019

After an encouraging performance on 19th December at Lingfield, Mark had found a very winnable race at the same track, hopefully to follow up his first promising run after his long break. He was by far the highest rated (OR 73) horse in the race and was the 5/4 favourite. He carried 9st 7lbs, 4lbs more than the second favourite Aleeka at 2/1, trained by David O'Meara. Um Shama trained by David Loughnane was the third favourite at 3/1 and carried 8st 8lbs. The outsider at 14/1 Warrior Display trained by J S Moore carried 8st 6lbs.

The race was the Ladbrokes Nursery Handicap (Class 5) (0-75) over 1 mile on New Year's Eve. The going was standard, Richard Kingscote was on board. Seductive Moment was slowly away and Aleeka went into the lead. However, Richard got him into his stride and he moved up towards the outside of Aleeka, who still led. Past half way Seductive Moment appeared to be cruising and Um Shama moved up on the outside. However, round the final bend and into the straight Seductive Moment powered into the lead and showed no signs of stopping and won easily by 2¼ lengths from Um Shama. He won and was a Class above his opponents. He just needed to get his starting prowess a bit sharper. But as Richard Kingscote remarked he did (does) *"get a bit worked up at the start."*

Seductive Moment powers away from his rivals at Lingfield on New Year's Eve 2018. *Ian Headington*

In fact he did the same at the start 8 days later on 8th January at Newcastle. The race was the Ladbrokes Home of The Odds Boost Handicap over a shorter trip of 7 furlongs. It was a Class 3 (0-90) and the going was standard. He was rated 79 up 6lbs after his win at Lingfield on New Year's Eve. He was third favourite at 9/2 with Mardle trained by Karl Burke and Zip trained by Richard Fahey 15/8 favourite and 9/4 second favourite respectively. Joe Fanning was on board Seductive Moment.

Robynne Watton reported:

"We hope you are well. Seductive Moment ran at Newcastle in the 4.45 and finished 5/5. He got restless down at the start and a bit upset in the stalls, he jumped slow, coming out he went left and then he got up with the pace and was travelling well until about 1½ furlongs out where he started to fade and Joe said he didn't find anymore to give. Charlie said we are going to do some stalls work with him at home."

John Martin advised the next day that he had pulled up slightly lame with a superficial graze on his cannon bone after his run. Two reports from John Martin might have gone some way to explain Seductive Moment's relatively poor run at Newcastle.

"Further to our post race report for Seductive Moment he resumed ridden trotting exercise as normal on Thursday and looked to be moving well. He was then noted to be trotting lame on his right foreleg over the weekend and on examination he had an abscess in his right fore foot. His shoe was removed and a poultice was applied to the foot. He was on walker exercise only for the last two days. I saw him this morning where he is much improved but there was still some discharge from the abscess tract. On this basis I poulticed the foot again this morning but if we have continued improvement over the next few days I expect he will be

reshod and back to ridden exercise by the end of the week. Further to my email earlier in the week I am pleased to report that Seductive Moment was sound at trot this morning. He will be shod and ridden tomorrow and providing he remains sound he will resume cantering exercise at the beginning of next week."

Paul Walker who was at Newcastle spoke to Robynne Watton and she told him that she was to fly out to Dubai on 14th January to await the arrival of Victory Command and the other three horses. Travel plans were afoot. I was already out of the country but made immediate plans to travel even further afield to Dubai.

Seductive Moment and Richard Kingscote led in by Keith Watson. *Ian Headington*

CHAPTER 9
WINTER SUN, MEYDAN: UNITED ARAB EMIRATES
9.1 The Journey

Every year many hundreds of horses are flown all over the world. The distance from the UK to Dubai is a relatively short trip when compared with, for example, a journey to Australia. Johnston Racing's horses, destined for the Dubai Carnival, were transported to Chelmsford to stay overnight before they were loaded onto a large plane, where the interior had been specially adapted to house horses in stalls or small boxes. The horses are not sedated but are fed and looked after by vets and grooms who ensure that the horses remain fully hydrated. On arrival in Dubai, after a 7 hour to 8 hour flight they make the short journey to the quarantine barn at Meydan where amongst other stables there is a yard set aside for International Arrivals. The riders and visiting stable staff often stay in accommodation provided at the same location. The facilities are top notch for the horses and staff. Locally employed grooms are hired to help with the upkeep at the stables and the handling at the track, which is less than two miles away.

One of the attractions of taking a horse to Dubai for the Carnival, apart from the weather and the eye-watering prize money, is that if a horse runs at least twice all expenses are paid for by the Emirates Racing Authorities. My local contacts told me that at one time owners also had their expenses reimbursed but owing to large groups often turning up in abuse of the hospitality afforded, this luxury was stopped.

Wonderful Meydan at Night.

So we; Catherine and Billy Ross and their daughter Elaine and I, arrived in Dubai on the evening of Monday 21st January 2019 off the daily, Emirates Airlines morning flight from Manchester. Paul Walker and Adele Brown were to arrive the following day also from Manchester. We stayed in the

Jumeirah Beach area which nowadays resembles Manhattan, a far cry from 40 years previously when my maritime investigation work took me there for the first of many visits to Dubai. Paul and Adele had booked into the Meydan Hotel which is part of the racecourse complex.

For Paul Walker it was his first visit to Meydan and Dubai and he enthused about the whole experience as his description of events showed. He wrote:-

"Racing in Dubai – January 2019

For racing fans everywhere, Meydan Racecourse should be on your list of places to visit. At first, I needed some persuasion but I cannot speak too highly of the whole experience.

Of course, it helps to have a runner to focus the mind and give shape and purpose to the week, but the racecourse itself is quite magnificent and the turf track an excellent test of the thoroughbred.

It is well over 10 years that I had flown anywhere long-haul so all I can say is that the 2019 flight with Emirates was a pleasure. Attentive cabin service and a wide range of in-flight entertainment means that time passes reasonably quickly for the economy traveller. A prearranged transfer to your hotel is highly recommended but there are public transport links and taxis readily available.

Since we were going for the racing, our booking was in the Meydan Hotel which overlooks the racecourse and merges seamlessly into the racecourse grandstand. For early risers, this affords the pleasure of watching track work from your balcony as the desert sun appears above the horizon.

Many of the hotels (including the Meydan) provide an executive club facility which offers significant benefits to residents. They are well worth investigating prior to booking.

During the Carnival season, there is racing every Thursday and sometimes on Saturday too. There is no betting and online UK betting websites are blocked. For those keen to have an interest there are competitions on each of the races with bets similar to our jackpot and tricast bets.

Kingsley Park 10 had enjoyed remarkable success in 2018 with 9 wins from 17 runs from our 3 horses. Victory Command was a late May foal and improved throughout his 2-year-old season winning 4 times including a valuable listed race at Ascot in July and then finished 4th in 2 pattern races up against some of the best."

9.2 A Visit to the International Stables and Jet lag

Six of us decided to go and we all met on the Wednesday morning to visit the International Stables to see Victory Command and the other Johnston Racing horses. Robynne Watton and Emma Bedford were on hand to show us round and to discuss tomorrow's prospects.

It was clear that he was on great terms with himself, eating and drinking well and having taken the flight out all in his stride. He looked fit and ready to do himself justice."

In fact Paul and Adele also looked remarkably fit considering that their morning take off from Manchester had been delayed and they arrived late to allow only a few hours' sleep before setting off to the stables. We were all suffering a bit from the four hour time difference between the UK and Dubai. Jet lag was certainly one of the topics of conversation. We wondered if the horses were suffering a bit like we were.

Neil Mechie, one of Johnston Racing's vets had written in the Kingsley Klarion on the subject with regard to humans and horses and how it can improve a horse's performance. He explained:

International travel across time zones may leave us humans as underperforming shells of our normal selves as we struggle to recover from the phenomenon known as 'jet lag'.

We have previously discussed the circadian rhythm of a horse in the Klarion when discussing the introduction of our full spectrum, daylight-mimicking lighting system at the yard. That is used to enhance the wellbeing of horses by affecting natural daylight so that we can effectively lengthen actual summertime and reduce the depths of winter.

The circadian rhythm is a roughly 24-hour cycle of wakefulness and rest periods driven by biological chemicals and hormones within the body. In humans this rhythm is so strong that even when placed in constant complete darkness, periods of activity and sleep will correspond to those of previous day and night-time hours.

This is what leads to the impairment caused by jet lag, which occurs when travelling to and from different time zones, for the inherent circadian rhythm conflicts with the new hours of light and darkness, causing the body to take time to adjust to its new environment. In humans this is approximately an hour's alteration towards alignment of circadian and daylight hours per day. In horses, their rhythm of activity is entirely related to light exposure. Once light cues are removed from horses for a prolonged period of time, their activity becomes random throughout a 24-hour period. Unlike humans, once exposed to a new daylight routine a horse will immediately alter its rhythm of activity.

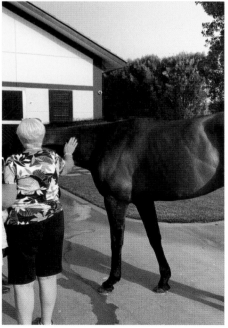

The International Stables with Victory Command

An interesting study has been carried out by Bristol University, in which horses were placed in an environment where daylight hours could be manipulated and they were acclimatised to treadmill exercise. While exposed to normal daylight hours a standard exercise test was performed to assess the athletic ability of each individual horse. The light in the horses' environment was artificially altered to mimic a seven-hour advancement in the onset of daylight.

The horses then undertook another exercise test and the results were compared to the baseline results prior to the time shift. Surprisingly, unlike humans in whom performance is dramatically reduced both physically and mentally, the horses displayed a significant improvement in athletic performance. The most notable parameter was that the experimental horses were able to gallop for 25 seconds longer before fatigue started to show. In a racing scenario this would translate into a significant advantage. The positive effect slowly faded over two weeks in the new time zone.

In reality, international travel has negative effects physiologically on the horse related to decreased feed and water intake and limited movement, so the full benefits of the time shift on performance may not be seen. This has led to two schools of thought among trainers with international runners. Either their horses run shortly after making a journey so they have the beneficial effects of the time zone shift; or they allow their horses several weeks to acclimatise, which means they lose the benefits of the time zone shift, but they can recuperate fully after travelling.

However as displayed in the Bristol study, travel is not necessary to achieve performance enhancement. It can be done through adjusting lighting, and this may in time be used to enhance racehorse performance. This may in turn reduce injury rates as, statistically, more injuries occur towards the end of exercise or a race as the body tires.

There is no doubt the light was bright and in sharp contrast to the drizzle and the dreich, murky, middle of winter days back home.

9.3 The First Race

As Paul has described, the horses are exercised early in the mornings at the track itself. Steve Youlden was on hand to help supervise and organise the various groups/strings cantering and thought Victory Command was going well. The jockey booked to ride him, Royston Ffrench, had already ridden him and liked him. Robynne is shown aboard in the photograph with the imposing grandstand in the background.

Paul described the scene on the morning of the race:

"Race day dawned bright and clear and Victory Command could be seen stretching his legs on the dirt at his usual time of 0655 hrs. It's a strange feeling being the only spectator to your horse cantering at Meydan in complete silence."

We met in the foyer of the Meydan Hotel which afforded from its Reception Bar terrace a brilliant view of the racecourse. Unlike the World Cup night at the end of March, the number attending was not high. A seamless transition from the hotel to the owners' facilities therefore ensued. These are on the first floor of the main stand and provided a view of the finishing line and the parade ring below. Attempts were made to fill out their version of the *"placepot"*, *"jackpot"* and *"tricast"* while trying to remember to write from right to left. One of Mark's owners had in fact won the "jackpot" many years ago on World Cup night. I was a non trier as concentration on anything other than the opposition in our race and on my immediate surroundings was not possible.

The horses are saddled and paraded first at the rear of the main stand and brought through a walkway under the stand to the parade ring. Excitement was building. Fortunately we were the second race which was the Al Bastakiya Trial sponsored by Emirates Global Aluminium over 1900 metres (9½ furlongs) on dirt. As southern Hemisphere horses were older they carried more weight than those from the northern Hemisphere. Fillies had a 2kg allowance. Winners of two races or more carried a 2.5kg penalty. Victory Command was equal second top weight, Royston Ffrench was the jockey. The talking horse was Grecko (9/2), trained by Kenneth McPeck from Argentina. Estihdaaf, trained by Saeed bin Suroor was the favourite and had run 14 days ago here to come second. Manguzi trained by Arai Rayi had also run well two weeks ago at Meydan and he was at 5/1. Victory Command was 14/1. Art Du Val trained by Charlie Appleby was a non-runner and James Doyle, who rode Aquarium in the 4th race, told me his outside draw (15) did not encourage the connections to run him. *"We are to wait for another day."* We were drawn on the outside in stall 13.

Robynne Watton on Victory Command at Morning Exercise at Meydan

The dirt track was indeed very tight. It was almost a symmetrical oval shape with two shoots to the back straight for the 1600m and 1500m starts. The 1900m start was in front of the stands, which meant the horses had to go round the entire oval with a tight bend, soon after the start, and a second which led to the home straight. Shane Ryan the official starter told me that an outside draw was a definite disadvantage, unless the horse broke very smartly. He said that is what they all try to do here in order to get a clear run without suffering kick back from the surface. It felt as though the saying should be changed to the *"bad luck of the draw."*

The Pre-Parade Ring and Saddling Area behind the Main Stand

The Parade Ring

There were also several horses in the field with *"no official rating"* (NOR). They were obviously deemed good enough to take their chance but I understand they had a tendency to break well, go off like the clappers and often fade beyond half way when they had run out of steam. This is another reason why a good break with daylight in front rather than a cloud of dirt was essential.

The montage shows Emma Bedford with Catherine and Elaine Ross and the Author with Royston Ffrench. It also shows that Jock Bennett was on hand to give Royston the leg up after which we all went our different ways to find a spot from where to watch the race.

It was indeed a fast break and although Victory Command in stall (13) shot out of the stalls, as normal, he had 12 other horses drawn inside of him. Al Seel Legacy's (10), Superior (4), Tone Broke (8), Manguzi (3) and Grecko (6) led on the inside, round the first bend. Victory Command was on the outside of the pack, where Royston chose to stay to avoid the considerable cloud of kickback. Down the back straight Manguzi had the rail with Superior close by. Victory Command was at the rear keeping a wide berth.

A Dirty/Dusty Victory Command back in the Unsaddling Enclosure

Happy Connections under the "Third Marker." *Elaine Ross*

Rounding the final bend Manguzi forged clear by 4 lengths to 5 lengths and was increasing his lead with every stride. Well inside the final furlong the wide gap was eaten into by the fast finishing Estihdaaf. Victory Command now in the clear picked up pace and passed tired horses to run and finish in third place, running strongly to the line. Manguzi held on to win by ½ a length.

The jockey and trainer were delighted with Victory Command's run as were the connections. All had looked lost down the back straight but his trademark gutsy performance and no mean ability was just a thrill to watch. He was led back to the winner's enclosure.

The horse and Royston had been plastered with dirt/dust and none of us liked to see the thick layer of kickback on the horses face. Royston explained that the horse had acted on the track and in the back straight he chose not to try to thread his way through the horses that were coming back to him, but to stay wide. This paid off as he passed, apart from the two who were well clear, all the other horses. He ran 24 metres further than the winner. He may not have won with a better draw but he would have been closer to the winner at the end. He had just earned the small matter of $10,000 for third place.

A delighted group posed for a photograph under the 3rd place sign. We all went first to the owners' facilities to celebrate. Aquarium ridden by James Doyle ran in the 4th race on the card: The EGA Jebel Ali Trophy over 10 furlongs worth $81,000 to the winner. He broke slowly, was always at the rear and finished last of 9 runners.

9.4 Party Time Again

We then left for our own *"private party"* back at Paul's hotel next door. I'm not sure what the bill was but we were all floating on air or his account was. A fantastic evening, a wonderful experience sitting outside in the balmy desert evening in the confines of what must be one of the most spectacular racecourses in the world –our very own Victory Command ran his heart out.

Celebrating on the Terrace of the Meydan Hotel

Robynne and Emma at the Westin Hotel

The party season was in full flow as Dougie Livingston was out with Jock and others for the Desert Classic Golf tournament at the Emirates Golf Club. We were invited to his legendary Friday Brunch party at the Westin Hotel. Robynne and Emma, Catherine, Billy Ross and Elaine and I joined Dougie and as always thoroughly enjoyed ourselves and Dougie's hospitality was much appreciated.

9.5 Struggles on Turf

Victory Command ran twice more at Meydan on February 14th in the Meydan Trophy a conditions contest over 9½ furlongs worth $100,000 and on February 28th in the Meydan Classic sponsored by Mohammed Bin Rashid Al Maktoum City-District One (A Listed race). It was over a mile worth $175,000.

Both races were on Turf, which was a relief as after his race at the end of January it took two hours for a vet, using drops, to remove dust/dirt particles from Victory Command's eyes.

In the Meydan Trophy, on February 14th he broke and travelled well but *"stopped"* when it came to push on time at the last bend. We were all a bit bemused and Billy Ross pointed out that *"it was his worst performance to date."* Art Du Val trained by Charlie Appleby like a good thing at odds-on (4/5) went on to win by 4 lengths. No wonder he was *"saved"* for this race. Victory Command finished a well beaten 9th of 12.

The Meydan Trophy- John Martin and the Author flank Emma, Billy Ross gives Royston instructions and Steve Youlden looks on from Chico, his 25-year-old gelding

I played golf with Steve Youlden and others, one of the many delights of mixing with racing connections also out for some winter sun. Steve had told me that the draw this time would not have been a factor. He was just up against better horses on the day.

His third and final race (in Listed company) in the Meydan Classic was a disastrous run and he came 12th of 13. Again he tracked the leader but weakened 2½ furlongs out. Sporting Chance, trained by Simon Crisford and ridden by Pat Cosgrove won by a neck from Golden Jaguar, trained by A bin Harmash and ridden by Connor Beasley. It was difficult to find credible reasons for his uncharacteristic poor performance, but perhaps, even though he had been out in Dubai for four weeks, Neil Mechie's observation that: *In reality, international travel has negative effects physiologically on the horse* came into play.

Arrangements had been made for Victory Command to return home as his form did not justify an extension of his stay. The UAE Derby on World Cup night remained a dream. My return flight seemed to take much longer than it had on previous visits. Both Robynne Watton and Emma Bedford had looked after the horses superbly during their Winter Sun *"holiday"* and both had advised the warmth and light will have done him good. Jock Bennett had earlier told me something similar. It was indeed a welcome break from the frost and snows of Yorkshire and an experience I will always remember.

Dinner at The Qube, Meydan Golf Club after the Al Basti sponsored Tournament. Clockwise- Liz Youlden, Steve Youlden, the Author, Jim Crowley, Kieren Fallon, Richard Mullen, Larry Coleman and his daughter Louise

CHAPTER 10

VICTORY COMMAND'S TOUGH TIMES IN THE MOST PRESTIGIOUS HANDICAPS

If anybody had told me that a horse which cost £6,000 as a yearling would, as a 3-year-old, over a period of 4 months run at Newmarket in the European Free Handicap (Listed Race), at Haydock in the Amix Silver Bowl, run at Epsom on Derby Day in the Investec Private Banking Handicap, at Royal Ascot in the Britannia, win at Hamilton in the Almada Mile, run at Glorious Goodwood in the United Handicap, win at Chelmsford in the Bet totescoop 6 Handicap, run at York on Ebor day and at Beverley in the William Hill Silver Cup it would be met with disbelief and maybe even some amusement. Victory Command did all of the above and more.

Throughout his campaign the weight he carried, and indeed the weights some of the opposition carried, I believe played a crucial and often decisive rôle in the chances he had of winning. The draw also played a part. The ground conditions maybe did not as the weather throughout the summer of 2019 was fairly consistent, apart from a very soggy Royal Ascot. By and large his attitude was to try his heart out but there may have been, here and there, a few slight quirks in the way a race panned out to have an influence on his finishing position. He was also up against very good horses and on the day they may have been better than him.

He returned from Dubai with an official handicap mark of 103, which as it turned out was the highest he ever achieved, or to be burdened with depending on one's point of view. He was soon put through his paces at Kingsley Park. Robynne Watton was on 19th March 2019, again on board.

VICTORY COMMAND 19.03.19

Victory Command

Victory Command and Robynne Watton. *Mikaelle Lebreton*

The idea of a handicap mark and how it is determined has been explained in Chapter 3, but in short, and to repeat, it is to make a race more competitive as the range of weights is designed to make all the horses equal as to their chance of winning. Some horses, however, turn out to be more equal than others. There are too many variables associated with a race and its runners and indeed imponderables to allow the system to achieve fully and consistently its stated aims. Of the two extremes in the range of weights in a Handicap, the horse carrying the lowest weight, if it is a slow one, will not win, whereas a very good horse with the highest weight to carry might. In other words a poor horse will not benefit from a low weight whereas a good horse will be burdened by extra weight on its back. It still may win but its chances of doing so are reduced. Is there any wonder then that layers like Handicaps?

10.1 European Free Handicap

The first race in the long sequence was on 16th April 2019 in the bet 365 European Free Handicap, a Listed race at Newmarket Rowley, over 7 furlongs. The going was Good to Firm. He was drawn (7) of 7 runners which was considered not to be an advantage or disadvantage. Ryan Moore was on board.

Shine So Bright (OR 106) trained by Andrew Balding broke well and took a keen hold in the lead. Victory Command chased after him and stayed in the van but was unable to match Shine So Bright's pace when he quickened away. Space Traveller trained by Richard Fahey was second, Azano trained by John Gosden third and Victory Command was fourth well clear of his stablemate Arctic Sound in fifth. Perhaps the shorter trip meant the pace was a bit too quick for him.

The report from Claire Short, the newly appointed secretary to the Kingsley Park partnerships read:

"Victory Command jumped well holding second position on the stand side rail in the 2.25pm race at Newmarket this afternoon. A generous pace was set and he travelled well throughout the race. Once asked he stayed prominent but was unable to match the pace of the winner finishing 4/7. Ryan Moore was happy

after the race and suggested to look at some big handicap races over 1m such as The Britannia Stakes at Royal Ascot."

We both agreed I should not be rushing out to Oliver Brown's just yet. Charlie Johnston's reaction was to say *"OK we'll work back from there then."*

On 23rd April 2019 a decision was made to scratch Victory Command from both the 2000 Guineas at Newmarket and the Italian 2000 Guineas in Rome. After winning a race a horse's handicap can go up quite a few pounds, depending on the horse's performance. On losing a race often only a couple of pounds or less may be deducted.

The European Free Handicap, Newmarket Rowley. Ryan Moore and Savroop Singh

However, the handicapper saw in the Free Handicap, what perhaps had been coming since his second race in Dubai namely that Victory Command's handicap mark was too high. He was dropped 7lbs to (OR 96). The handicap mark is not just important in weight calculations but also as to whether a horse can get in a particular race. Some eyes were being kept for example on the Britannia with regard to whether we would we get in. Paul Walker pointed out that an Official

Rating of 90 in 2018 was good enough to get in, *"but 91 or 92 would be safer"*. Another snippet of news around this time was that Seductive Moment was now sound and had started ridden walking and trotting exercise.

10.2 Another Try at Newmarket

With this unusual and generous reduction, optimism was high when on 5th May he returned to Newmarket to contest the Quatar Racing Welfare Handicap (Class 2) (0-105) over 1 mile on the Rowley Mile with Joe Fanning on board. The going was Good. He was still the highest rated horse in the race save for Certain Lad trained by Mick Channon.

Victory Command finished 8th out of 10 runners and Joe Fanning reported that the horse was off the bridle too early to blame the trip and he always felt the horse was out of his comfort zone. He was beaten before distance became an issue. Mark added that *"the field looked too quick for him. Back to the drawing board and the team will discuss where to go from here."*

On the day before Dark Vision came 12th of 19 in the 2000 Guineas. He showed on the basis of that performance he may not be Group 1 material. Both races did not go to plan and it did appear that Victory Command was run off his feet. Not the best day at the office. My instinct was that Victory Command was still too high in the handicap and perhaps should be tried over further.

Victory Command at Haydock with Connor Beasley, Tristan Burton-pye and Paul Walker

10.3 A Comeback (well almost) at Haydock

We had been dropped another 4 pounds down to an OR of 92 for the Amix Silver Bowl Handicap (Class 2) for 3-year-olds over 1 mile at Haydock. The going was still Good to Firm and a £50,000 first prize was on offer.

As well as Victory Command carrying 8st 8lbs and ridden by Connor Beasley, Johnston Racing had two others in the race, the second favourite Oasis Prince ridden by Franny Norton and Octave ridden by Royston Ffrench who was over from Dubai. Two of the horses which were beaten by Victory Command in the Juddmonte Royal Lodge Stakes, Beatboxer (wearing head gear) trained by John Gosden who had cost $650,000 as a yearling and Duke of Hazard (who had run well in the French 2000 Guineas) trained by Paul Cole were present. Also Certain Lad trained by Mick Channon had run in Victory Command's last race at Newmarket. Awe (tipped to keep improving) trained by William Haggas was the 4/1 favourite and we were out with the washing at 25/1 and it was suggested he had yet to find his stride. Each way bets for myself and Nick Cowes, who also attended. A technical glitch meant that the time had to be recorded by hand.

The mile distance at Haydock involves a start just before the left hand bend into the straight. It was an even break but what happened next was not so smooth. Oasis Prince with Franny on board got into no end of trouble and for a moment it looked as though there was going to be a pile up. Connor Beasley on Victory Command saw this happening and steered a wide berth round the bend as did Beatboxer. Hall of Champ trained by Ivan Furtado, drawn (1), was able to get a clear run down the inside into the lead. He increased his lead in the straight to 2 lengths. He was just caught on the line by the fast finishing Beatboxer with Victory Command also in hot pursuit running on in third. My immediate impression was that the finish line had come too soon for Victory Command and over further, although he may not have beaten the winner, he would have caught Hall of Champ in second. Beatboxer was back, his second run after a wind operation and the Racing Post reported that Victory Command had taken *a belated step back in the right direction back up in trip.*

Claire Short reported from the stable that Charlie Johnston had said: *"He was very happy with the run and it was good to see him back, close to his best. Charlie added that we will look more seriously to the Britannia at Royal Ascot."*

In the next 5 races Victory Command sequentially ran his 15th to 19th races. However, each of the winning horses had only run either 3 or 4 times. Beatboxer was the first in this sequence although there was a completely good reason for his lack of races. He had undergone a wind operation, which almost certainly meant he had an enforced 274 days break between the end of his 2-year-old campaign, at the end of September 2018, to the start of his 3-year-old campaign on 4th May 2019 at Newmarket. A theme of whether horses could have a handicap commensurate with their ability after such a small number of appearances is a topic I have already discussed in an article: *"a case for changing the conditions of entry for the most prestigious handicaps"* (Kingsley Klarion, Issue 294, March 2020). More discussions will follow here as the sequence of prestigious Handicaps progressed.

10.4 Investec Derby Day

Perhaps buoyed by Victory Command's willingness to stay on at the finish of his last race at Haydock he was stepped up in trip from a mile to 1 mile and two furlongs. We were in the first race The Investec Private Banking Handicap Stakes (Class 2), £50,000. Joe Fanning was on board. A selection of *"The Dramatis Personae"* descended on the Epsom Downs in their best bib and tucker on a super sunny day and the going was Good.

The course at Epsom can be tricky and one has to walk the track to appreciate not only the early switchback but the downhill section to Tattenham Corner and the camber in the straight. The ground falls away dramatically from the stand side rail to the far rail. The programme notes set the scene.

Derby Day 2019. Victory Command in the Investec Private Banking Handicap with Joe Fanning and Barry Lusted

"Today's 240ᵗʰ running the Derby is not only one of the most significant events in the racing calendar, but it is also one which is full of history and remarkable stories.

The race was named after the 12ᵗʰ Earl of Derby and the first horse to win it was Diomed on the 4ᵗʰ May 1780. Lord Derby claimed his only triumph of his race just seven years later courtesy of a horse called Sir Peter Teazle.

The Derby has been run at Epsom Downs every year except during both World Wars when the race was run at Newmarket, known to many as the 'New Derby'. Two notable horses that won this prestigious race during those years were Gainsborough and Dante. The former won the Triple Crown – the 2000 Guineas, Derby and St Leger in 1918 – whilst Dante, who was trained in Middleham by Matthew Peacock, won eight of his 9 starts, and the Dante Stakes at York, a key trial for the race, is named in his honour."

I understand the transmission of beliefs which are passed on from generation to generation to hold the Derby at Epsom, but I can't help but think that a flatter and more even terrain would be a better location. However, the uneven track is all part and parcel of this great race. Not only has a horse to be very quick and be able to stay 1 mile 4 furlongs, it also has to be balanced to cope with the camber and of course to have a good jockey on board to steer it home. Anthony Van Dyck, trained by Aiden O'Brien and ridden by Seamie Hefferman won the 2019 edition.

Anyway sadly we were not in the Derby, we were in the first race on the card. There were nine runners and three of these were trained by Mark Johnston: Nayef Road ridden by Ryan Moore, The Trader ridden by Silvestre de Sousa and Victory Command ridden by Joe Fanning. Nayef Road had in fact run in the Group 2 Dante at York and on his return to Handicap company his official rating of 105 guaranteed top weight of 9st 7lbs. The Trader (OR 92) carried 8st 8lbs and Victory Command (OR 93) one pound more at 8st 9lbs.

Amongst the lighter weights was Le Don De Vie (OR 86) at 8st 2lbs who had already won at Epsom over a shorter distance. He broke well from stall (4) and soon led. Victory Command also broke well and was second with The Trader on his outside. Kheros was also handy. Nayef Road was buffeted and a bit behind the leaders. Le Don De Vie had the rail and made smooth progress round the slight left hand bend, Kheros and Victory Command were in touch.

On the descent towards Tattenham Corner The Trader moved up on the outside of the leader who was going well. Victory Command was fourth with Kheros third.

In the final two furlongs Martin Dwyer on Le Don De Vie asserted and went clear of Victory Command and Kheros but The Trader hung onto him. Alkaamel was making good progress from the back. Under pressure The Trader hung right and Le Don De Vie surged ahead to win, eased down by 4½ lengths from The Trader. Victory Command was just passed in the last 20 yards by the improving Alkaamel. A thrilling race and yet another tremendous performance from Victory Command who was giving the winner 7lbs.

The Racing Post "*live*" analyst thought that Le Don De Vie had a lot of attributes and can track along. He also thought Andrew Balding "*often sneaks a horse in an attractive Handicap on a fairly lenient mark.*" This was indeed a masterly piece of placing by the trainer of Le Don De Vie who was probably running off a handicap mark which was too low for his ability. It is not an indubitable fact that the apparent wrong rating made the difference but it would have been a help. Soon after the race he was sold for £460,000 to be trained by Hughie Morrison. He went up 10lbs in the weights. Without wanting to sound like a broken record that was only his 5th run. It was Victory Command's 15th - who plugged on at the end but could not quicken in the final furlong. I am not sure he improved over the longer distance. The Johnston team was fairly pleased with his performance.

10.5 Royal Ascot: The Britannia

The programme notes included a welcome note on the first page from The Queen. Although Weatherbys have given me permission to quote from their racecards (thank you) rather than risk a breach of protocol I can say that Her Majesty, wished everybody an enjoyable time. It was in fact another monarch, Queen Anne, who in 1711 when riding out from Windsor Castle saw the potential of the land for horse racing we now know to be Ascot Racecourse. The inaugural event "*Her Majesty's Plate*" was held that same year. Some 100 years later it was the English dandy Beau Brummell, a friend of the Prince Regent, who suggested a special dress code, which has morphed into the top hat and tails of today.

The prize money has certainly changed over the years and in 2018 the total prize money topped £7million for the first time, with no race run for less than £90,000. Group 1 prize money started at £500,000. Not the stratospheric purses found in the Middle East or the United States but everybody wants to win here and most of the best horses in the world now do battle. To have a runner at Royal Ascot is one of the pinnacles of an owner's career. To have a winner well that would be something. The Britannia Stakes is a Heritage Handicap. It was first run in 1928. It has a similar profile to the Royal Hunt Cup but is only for three-year-old colts and geldings. An outstanding name on the roll of honour is Teleprompter, who won in 1983. Irish based trainer Joanna Morgan, the first woman to ride at Royal Ascot in 1975, saddled her only winner at the meeting when Roca Tumu won in 2013.

The weather was unsettled and there was definitely Soft in the ground description. The pre-meeting news was also dominated by a rail strike by South Western Railway, and the plans for extra car parks. Bright and early on Thursday 20th June I set off from York Railway station to arrive in plenty of time.

The only car park I was interested in was the Owners and Trainers one opposite the main entrance where Johnston Racing was holding their annual party. Deirdre and her team know how to throw a party. I met Paul Walker first, where the badges are allocated and off we went for a glass of champagne and canapés. Catherine and Billy Ross, Reg and Val Witheridge, Lionel and Lorna Beecroft and Liz Pescops and Ruth were there. Claire was mucking in behind the bar. It was indeed a reunion as the originals (David White and Ron Huggins) were also there as they had Summer Moon in the King George V Stakes, a race Juste Pour Nous ran in a few years previously.

The Britannia at Royal Ascot

Victory Command leaving the paddock with Franny Norton and Savroop Singh. *Mikaelle Lebreton*

Thursday was the third day of racing and as we sheltered under the gazebo canopy and umbrellas the first topic of discussion was the going. Charlie was very worried about our draw (3) which was on the far side of the track. The races for the first couple of days over the straight track had been won by horses with high draws ie on the stands rail. In fact only 2 horses have been successful in the last 11 runnings (2011-2021) of this race from a far side stalls position; a low draw. Some people in racing tend to shrug their shoulders when an unfavourable draw is allotted to their horse. *"That's racing" "Ah well we'll have to make the best of it"* and so on. I don't go along with this and it should not be beyond the wit of man on a straight track to have no draw bias. Round a bend I can understand, but on straight track sorry but I can't.

After another glass of champagne a certain philosophy sets in where *"it is what it is"* creeps into the conversation and resignation to the fact any amount of moaning will not change anything.

There were 28 runners which were spread out across the entire track at the 1 mile start. The official going was Good to Soft, there was drizzle in the air. The first prize was £74,700 so not surprisingly the race had attracted the best 3-year-olds rated (0-105) of that season. It was a star-studded field. Beatboxer trained by John Gosden and Pogo trained by Charlie Hills had both beaten us. Dark Vision had the worst draw (1) of all and met Dunkerron again, trained by Alan King. Certain Lad trained by Mick Channon we had already beaten.

The first three in the betting were Turgenev at 7/2 trained by John Gosden and ridden by Frankie Dettori. The price was probably much shorter than the form of the horse warranted, but Frankie was on a roll and the bookies with accumulator bet liabilities were squealing after he had had a succession of earlier winners. Second favourite was Velorum at 6/1 trained by Charlie Appleby and third favourite at 7/1 was Migration trained by David Menuisier. Victory Command, ridden by Franny Norton was not fancied at 50/1. Dark Vision was 18/1 but was giving weight to everybody.

They broke in a decent line and split into 2 groups. Certain Lad led the group of about 8 horses on the far rail with Victory Command and Dark Vision at the rear of that group. Turgenev was prominent and then led on the stands side and it looked as though that group had a slight lead. At the 2 furlongs from home marker the far group with Victory Command now prominent started to tack over to the near side where Turgenev, with Frankie hard at work opened up a two length lead. The crowd were going mad, the bookies were probably apoplectic.

Biometric however, was having none of it and overhauled Turgenev just before the line to put daylight between him and the gallant Turgenev to win by 1¼ lengths. Victory Command was 6th, 7¾ lengths behind and Dark Vision 8th 2 lengths further back. We had beaten Beatboxer and Pogo, who for once had to give us weight.

So what appeared to be a hopeless task from the outset turned into a race where hopes increased as the race unfolded. If only we had been given a better draw, but our horse had shown his true guts and determination under a very good ride from Franny Norton. Mark was delighted with the performance and thought, like the rest of us, the draw had beaten him. I was amazed to find that for 6th place the prize was £1,404. We returned to the party in the car park.

Nigel Tinkler was there and we had a long chat about the race and he was quite open about the Heritage Handicaps being won by potential Group Class horses. Such Handicaps were, in fact, often more valuable than some Class 1 events. Biometric had run only 3 times prior to the Britannia (a not unusual occurrence if one looked at the winners over the last few years).

Victory Command was having his 16th run. We were off level weights of 8st 8lbs, an equal rating of 92. It was fairly obvious to me which of the two had a rating which described the horse's ability more accurately. Mark came across from Dark Vision's connections to tell us that he thought Victory Command ran a fantastic race from an impossible draw. The official word on the effects of the draw was that there wasn't a bias – it was just that the fastest horses were drawn on the stand side.

10.6 Victory Command at Hamilton Park

Whenever I travel to Hamilton Park racecourse I am always reminded of New Year's Day 1990 when I travelled from Yorkshire to Glasgow to open a new office for my company. I had just been awarded partner status in Dr J H Burgoyne and Partners (on the understanding I would emigrate) and was heading for an apartment located over the old Fire Station in Ingram Street and an office in the adjacent Queen Street at the corner of George Square. I stopped at the Hamilton "*Services*", it was lashing it down with rain (I picked up the language quite quickly), to have a coffee and a final look at the map to make sure I could find my way to the City Centre.

Almost 30 years later on Tuesday 2nd July 2019 I turned off the M74 just before the Hamilton "Services" and headed to the racecourse. After Victory Command's striking performance in the Britannia he had been dropped only 1lb in the weights.

The Almada Mile Handicap (for the Watson Memorial Cup) a Class 2 (0-100) handicap was run over 1 mile and ½ furlong for 3-year-olds and upwards. The going was Good and P J McDonald was to ride.

There was a valuable first prize of £18,675 and a newly commissioned silver cup was awarded to the winners as the programme notes explained:-

"The winning Owner of today's feature race, the Almada Mile Handicap Stakes, will be presented with the newly unveiled Watson Memorial Cup for the first time.

Sir Julian Somerled Watson, 7th Baronet of Earnock, was a shareholder, loyal supporter and regular visitor to Hamilton Park. Following the passing of Sir Julian in May 2016, the Watson Baronetcy became extinct and since then the team at Hamilton Park have been working closely with the Watson estate to ensure a lasting legacy.

Since it was founded in c1895, The Watson Baronetcy of Earnock contributed considerably to the local Hamilton community. Sir John Watson, 1st Baronet of Earnock, owned several collieries in the area including the Neilsland and Earnock colliery on the Neilsland Estate which covered over 2,000 acres. The Watson family also gifted the elaborate Watson Fountain to the town of Hamilton, which still stands proudly at the triangular merging of Cadzow Street and Muir Street.

Sulekha Varma, Racing Manager at Hamilton Park Racecourse, said The £30,000 Almada Mile Handicap is rapidly becoming one of the most popular races in the Hamilton Park calendar. To honour the memory of the Watson Baronetcy, and their contribution to the local area, is something we are very proud to do and associating the family with this particular race is of great significance for the racecourse and the people of Hamilton."

The track is not straightforward. It is right-handed, sharp and undulating. Just over 3 furlongs from home there is a hollow with steep gradients into it from the loop (used for distances over 6 furlongs) and out of it to the finish line. Our start was in the loop and involved the negotiation of a sharp right hand bend soon after the start, which led onto the straight 5 furlongs from home. In soft conditions it is a tough uphill finish. Thankfully the ground was Good. The racecard is shown below courtesy of Weatherbys.

Club Wexford was a non-runner. We had a reasonable handicap mark and there were four above us in the weights. The draw (2) gave Victory Command a chance, if he broke quickly as usual, to grab the rail, which he did. The two Tim Easterby horses Brother McGonagall ridden by David Allan and Mikmak ridden by Jason Hart also broke well and the former took up position on the rail about 1½ lengths ahead of Victory Command and the latter on the outside of them.

They stayed in these positions until they entered the hollow and hit the rising ground in the straight with Nonios also joining them. Nicholas T, trained by Jim Goldie was going well and held up behind the leaders. About 2 furlongs from home PJ edged Victory Command out, off the rail and a gap opened up, which he burst through. Nicholas T came with a late surging run down the

The Almada Mile Handicap Stakes (Class 2) (For The Watson Memorial Trophy)

The Watson Estate

ONE MILE about 68 YARDS (8f abt 68yds) (1600m)
for three yrs old and upwards
TOTAL RACE VALUE £30000 (FOR CONDITIONS OF THIS RACE SEE PAGE 46)

HAMILTON PARK RACECOURSE EXECUTIVE will present a memento to the winning Owner, Trainer and Jockey. The Winning Owner will be presented with the Watson Memorial Trophy which will be retained by the racecourse. In addition, they will present a cash prize to the person in charge of the horse judged to be the best turned out. The Race Incentive Fund, supported by the Horserace Betting Levy Board, provides for the inclusion of £2200 towards the prize money for this race. Owners Prize Money, Winner £14568; Second £4869; Third £2433; Fourth £1218; Fifth £609; Sixth £303. (Penalty Value £16675)

Betting Forecast: 11-4 Coolagh Forest (IRE), 11-2 Never Be Enough, 6-1 Club Wexford (IRE), 13-2 Victory Command (IRE), 7-1 Nonios (IRE), 9-1 Nicholas T, 12-1 Mikmak, 14-1 Brother McGonagall

Race Summary: COOLAGH FOREST has been hit hard by the handicapper, but he's clearly on a sharp upward curve and is fancied to complete the hat-trick with further improvement on the cards. This is a competitive race though, with Never Be Enough and fellow 3-y-o Victory Command others to take seriously.

1-2-3: 1.COOLAGH FOREST (IRE) 2.NEVER BE ENOUGH 3.VICTORY COMMAND (IRE)

2018: VENTURA KNIGHT (IRE) 3 9 0 P J McDonald 9-2 (Mark Johnston) 8 ran

Raceform Median Time: 1 min 48.40 secs

Stewards Note: MIKMAK: Following its run on 26/6/2019 it was reported that the horse was denied a clear run.

NUMBER OF DECLARED RUNNERS 8

Race Description

This is a valuable 1 mile 68yds (1669.87m) race worth £30,000. For horses rated up to 100, the start is part of the way around the loop section of the track and the horses will climb steadily uphill for the first third of the race which should help them to settle and find a good tactical position. Once they turn into the straight, they will run downhill initially and then there is a steady climb up towards the winning line. The jockeys have to ensure they have encouraged their mounts to save enough energy to see the race out right to the Winning Line.

No	Horse	Age	st-lb	Draw

1 **Club Wexford (IRE)** (6) B g Lawman (FR) - Masnada (IRE) — **8** **9-8** **(4)**
Owner: Mr C. Varley — Jockey: Ben Curtis
Breeder: J. S. Bolger — Trainer: Roger Fell, Nawton
Probable S.P.: 6-1
Form: 0-45115 D BF
TIMEFORM VIEW 2 wins from 5 runs this year. Latest win at Ayr in June. 9/2, shaped as if still in good form when fifth of 16 in handicap at Carlisle (7.8f, good) 6 days ago. TF Rating ★★★☆☆ BHA 88

2 **Coolagh Forest (IRE)** (60) B c Elzaam (AUS) - Ekagra — **3** **9-7** **(6)**
Owner: Mr Alan Harte — Jockey: Sean Davis (3)
Breeder: Leaf Stud — Trainer: Richard Fahey, Malton
Probable S.P.: 11-4
Form: 41-3311 D
TIMEFORM VIEW 2 wins from 4 runs this year. Career best when winning 6-runner handicap at Musselburgh (9f, good, 8/11) 60 days ago, easily. Open to further progress and hat-trick possible. TF Rating ★★★★★ BHA 96

3 **Nonios (IRE)** (12) B g Oasis Dream - Young and Daring (USA) — **7** **9-5** **(7)**
Owner: Millingbrook Racing — Jockey: Dylan Hogan (5)
Breeder: Sheikh Sultan Bin Khalifa Al Nayhan — Trainer: David Simcock, Newmarket
Probable S.P.: 7-1 — Headgear: Hood — Sponsor: Al Basti Equiworld
Form: 412463
TIMEFORM VIEW Latest win at Chelmsford City in April. Returned to form when third of 10 in handicap at Chelmsford City (10f, 14/1) 12 days ago, closing all way to line. TF Rating ★★★☆☆ BHA 85

4 **Brother McGonagall** (6) B r Equiano (FR) - Anatase — **5** **9-3** **(5)**
Owner: Reality Partnerships VI — Jockey: David Allan
Breeder: J. P. Coggan — Trainer: Tim Easterby, Malton
Probable S.P.: 14-1 — Sponsor: Easthorpe Hall Stud
Form: 0-06610 CD
TIMEFORM VIEW C&D winner. Cashed in on a reduced mark at Beverley in June, but wasn't in the same form from 10lb higher at Carlisle last week. TF Rating ★★★☆☆ BHA 83

5 **Never Be Enough** (5) Ch f Sir Percy - Camp Fire (IRE) — **4** **9-3** **(1)**
Owner: Straightline Bloodstock — Jockey: Tom Eaves (in 5lb ex)
Breeder: Mr J. L. Skinner — Trainer: Keith Dalgleish, Carluke
Probable S.P.: 11-2 — Sponsor: Straightline (NE) Ltd
Form: 012021 CD
TIMEFORM VIEW Impressive winner of 8-runner handicap at this C&D (firm, 5/2) 5 days ago, keeping on well. Well respected under a penalty. TF Rating ★★★★☆ BHA 78

6 **Victory Command (IRE)** (12) B c War Command (USA) - Aguinaga (IRE) — **3** **9-2** **(2)**
Owner: Kingsley Park 10 — Jockey: P. J. McDonald
Breeder: Mr J. Higgins — Trainer: Mark Johnston, Middleham
Probable S.P.: 13-2 — Sponsor: Johnston Racing Ltd
Form: 040346
TIMEFORM VIEW Very respectable sixth of 28 in Britannia Handicap at Royal Ascot (8f, good to soft, 50/1) 12 days ago, faring second best of those who raced in disadvantaged centre of track. Merits consideration. TF Rating ★★★☆☆ BHA 91

hamilton-park.co.uk

7 Mikmak (6) B g Makfi - Rakata (USA)   **6 9-2 (8)**
Owner: K J Racing
Breeder: Mr H. & Mrs C. Robinson
Probable S.P.: 12-1   **Headgear:** Cheek Pieces
Jockey: Jason Hart
Trainer: Tim Easterby, Malton
Sponsor: Easthorpe Hall Stud

Form: 30-0450 D

TIMEFORM VIEW Not seen to best effect when eighth of 16 in handicap (8/1) at Carlisle (7.8f, good) 6 days ago, running on. Remains one to keep an eye on.   **TF Rating ★★★☆☆ BHA** 82

8 Nicholas T (10) B g Rail Link - Thorntoun Piccolo   **7 9-1 (3)**
Owner: Mr James Callow & Mr J. S. Goldie
Breeder: W. M. Johnstone
Probable S.P.: 9-1
Jockey: Ben Robinson (3)
Trainer: Jim Goldie, Glasgow
Sponsor: Crawton Ltd

Form: 0-53046 D

TIMEFORM VIEW Twenty four runs since last win in 2017. 7/1, respectable 4 3/4 lengths sixth of 11 to Club Wexford in handicap at Ayr (8f, good to firm) 10 days ago, needing stronger gallop. Enters calculations. **TF Rating ★★☆☆☆ BHA** 81

Result

1ST ....
2ND ....
3RD ....
4TH ....

Time/Distance

....
....
....
....

No.	Last 6 Runs	Horse	Career Wins	Places	Total Runs	Career Winnings	Winning Distance Range	Winning Going Range	Runs Since Wins
1	9-45115	CLUB WEXFORD	8	14	54	71259	7-8F	G-GF	1
2	41-3311	COOLAGH FOREST	3	1	6	28270	7-9F	G-ST	0
3	412463	NONIOS	6	12	37	65754	9-10F	ST	4
4	9-06619	BROTHER MCGONAGALL	7	2	32	28789	8-9F	G-S	1
5	812721	NEVER BE ENOUGH	2	4	10	12162	8F	GF	0
6	048346	VICTORY COMMAND	4	5	17	28830	5-7F	G-GF	10
7	38-8458	MIKMAK	3	11	39	29146	7-10F	G-HV	9
8	0-53046	NICHOLAS T	4	8	37	32098	8F	G-GF	24

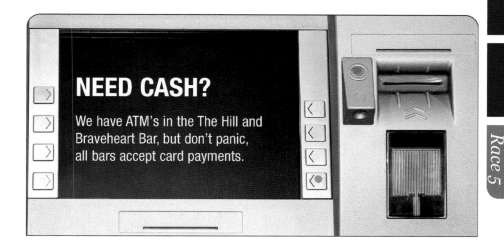

tote
Please note that the tote windows will close **30 minutes** after the last race.

Lost Property
For enquiries please contact the Racecourse Office on 01698 283806

Levy Board
The Horserace Betting Levy Board prize money schemes provides for the inclusion of £294,855 at this Racecourse in 2019.

centre but Victory Command held on to win by ¾ of a length. He had won the best turned out prize for groom Rima Ram so the superstition that such horses can't win was certainly completely false. He won really well. Thankfully, touch wood, I am not superstitious and enjoyed my trip to the Tote window to collect.

PJ told us in the winner's enclosure that he thought the *"Easterby horses"* had a plan namely Brother McGonagall to go off in the lead and Mikmak to box Victory Command in on the rail. The plan was working until the home straight and PJ seemingly unruffled, held his nerve and found a gap. The horse just appeared to hesitate for a moment (to give his supporters a few jitters) and then forged through the gap to win fairly cosily. Nicholas T came down the centre with a head of steam on the outside, but we had flown. Horse and jockey were all class.

Connections enjoying Hamilton

Victory Command Storming to the Line with Nicholas T (red and blue colours)
Gaining with Every Stride on the Stand side. *John Grossick*

Happy Connections with P J McDonald, Rima Ram and John Scanlon. *John Grossick*

A Representative of The Watson Family Presents the Watson Memorial Cup and Prizes. *John Grossick*

The Watson Memorial Cup

Sue and Bryan Russell, Catherine and Billy Ross and myself were on hand to receive the prizes, which indeed included a solid silver cup. Mark Billingham and the prize winning groom Rima Ram looked after the horse. John Scanlon of the Klarion who lived locally, and whose reporting has contributed greatly to this book was also there to help us celebrate. Hamilton Racecourse looks after owners well and we had already had a splendid lunch so now we were treated to a glass or two of champagne and a recording of the race. The cup was passed around for photo opportunities.

I had decided to stay in Glasgow for the night in the Babbity Bowster hotel in Blackfriars Street near to where I had lived when I first moved to Glasgow. I would have loved to have taken the cup to show everybody but the instantaneous development of photos on smart 'phones had to suffice. Lapsing into the vernacular *"a sore heed"* somehow developed the next day.

When I eventually decided I was fit enough to drive home, a warm feeling and smile presented themselves as I passed Hamilton Park and the *"Services"* on my way back south.

10.7 Newmarket (July) Two Runs Within Eight Days for Victory Command

Victory Command was put up 6lbs to an OR of 97 for his win at Hamilton. There were four other runners on 13th July 2019 in his next race, at Newmarket (July) the Bet 365 Mile Handicap (Class 2) (0-100) for 3-year-olds on Good to Firm ground with Ryan Moore on board. We were 5/2 favourite and along with Bayroot trained by Roger Varian carried top weight of 9st 7lbs. There wasn't much in the betting *"the outsider"* being Motakhayyel trained by Richard Hannon at 5/1.

Victory Command led until headed by Motakhayyel 3 furlongs out. He went away in fine style to win by 2¼ lengths from Flashcard trained by Andrew Balding. Ryan Moore thought *"it was a tough ask to give 6lbs to less exposed rivals"* and Charlie saw some positives in the race. He was pleased that Victory Command rallied in the last few yards and would be happy to step him back up in trip. Some of the partners were disappointed that more use had not been made of Victory Command and Paul Walker noticed he looked full of running at the finish.

It was an impressive performance by the winner and Mark Brown of the Racing Post pointed out he had covered the last 3 furlongs in 34.65 seconds. He went on to say:

"How much of an advantage he was at in racing more central is unclear, and there's no doubt he was well positioned in the race, but either way he's a progressive and already smart handicapper with a big pot in him. Connections will no doubt be hoping he can make it at Listed/Group 3 level down the line." In fact as a 4-year-old he ran in Group 3 races.

Angus Gold, Hamdan Al Maktoum's Racing Manager said:

"Motakhayyel is an improving horse with a lovely attitude. Chris Hayes gave him a lovely ride, he was in the right place off a slow pace."

He had run only three times prior to this easy victory (OR 92) and was already being touted as being Listed or Group 3 material. Fourth from five runners for Victory Command wasn't so much of a disappointment as he had carried 5lbs more than the winner, a potential Class 1 horse. I wondered whether one of the conditions of such races should be level weights. This would be fairer as perhaps the best horse would win rather than the one which was "well handicapped". Motakhayyel was lauded *inter alia* as "less exposed", "progressive and already smart" and "an improving horse". All of which were used euphemistically to describe a horse with the wrong handicap.

The following Saturday 20th July 2019 I returned to the July course to watch the AFH Management Handicap (Class 2) (0-105) for 3-year-olds and upwards run over 1 mile. The going was Good and C Y Ho, who was having only his second ride in the UK was on board and was over from Hong Kong. I was the only partner there (I believe) and I half joked with Paul Walker prior to the race, *"that he (C Y Ho) was hopefully a spy over from Hong Kong and might be advising people back home to make us a better offer."*

It was beginning to cross my mind perhaps that we should have sold him, after his Listed win in 2018 at Ascot, although the enjoyment he had already given us in 2019 was probably, for me anyway, sufficient compensation for the alternative monetary gain.

Newmarket July. Victory Command, C Y Ho, Tim Jarvis, Savroop Singh and the Author

With the power of hindsight, a pattern emerged where he did not appear to have much chance of winning these prestigious Handicaps off a handicap mark of much greater than 95. I could see the emergence of this pattern towards the end of July 2019. I had said, which I do not regret, when a year earlier we had an offer (from Hong Kong) of a six figure sum for him that, although he would probably take us (if we kept him) to the Grade 1 tracks, (which he did) it would be no fun watching him being *"beaten"* every time. Franny Norton's advice at that time of "sell" was still ringing in my ears. However we would not have had the wonderful experience of the win at Hamilton, or the trip to Dubai.

Anyway back to the race. A four-year-old Indeed, trained by Dominic Ffrench was favourite and carried top weight to win comfortably. We were in touch and made an effort 3 furlongs out but were outpaced in the final furlong. He did not run as well as he had done the previous week. Vincent Ho reported the horse wasn't able to pick up when under pressure, as quickly as he would have liked, but was pleased at the way he stayed on in the closing stages. Dominic Ffrench said his horse is *"probably a Group horse and we were going to run him in the Listed Steventon Stakes at Newbury but he was a few pounds wrong."*

Victory Command had certainly been working hard since his return from Dubai and although in the next chapter, the return of Seductive Moment is described the former still had some miles left to clock up and a description of his exploits will be continued in Chapter 12.

CHAPTER 11
THE RE-EMERGENCE OF SEDUCTIVE MOMENT
11.1 A Return to Windsor

Prior to Seductive Moment's last run on 8th of January 2019 at Newcastle he had been lightly raced and had run only 5 times, winning twice. However, several injuries had afflicted him over the winter and spring but with patient and expert handling he was back racing on Monday 22nd July 2019 at Windsor in the Visit Jamaica Handicap (Class 5) for 3-year-olds and above over 1 mile. Silvestre de Sousa was on board. It was only his seventh career run having had a break of 195 days.

He was fractious at the start as he had been in his previous runs and seemed not to have forgotten how to be his usual slightly temperamental self. However, when the stalls opened it was a fairly even break. Casement trained by Michael Appleby went into the lead with Seductive Moment close by in second and Data Protection trained by William Muir in third. These were the three that led round the bend at the far side loop and at the 3 furlong marker Casement still was in front.

Happy Connections with Seductive Moment, Silvestre de Sousa, Ferenc Balogh
and Tristan Burton-pye. *Ruth Carty*

SEVENTH RACE 5.40

1m

THE HEATH COURT HOTEL bestwestern.co.uk
HANDICAP STAKES (CLASS 5)

for three yrs old and upwards | Total race value £8200

Owners Prize Money. 1st £3545, 2nd £1175, 3rd £587, 4th £293, 5th £240, 6th £240, 7th £240, 8th £240.
(Penalty Value £4528.30) Weights lowered 2lb.

FORM ANALYSIS - A CLOSER LOOK | FACTS | FANCIES | FORM | STATS |

Leading course trainer (14-19): M Johnston (48 wins from 234 runners, 21%) runs **SEDUCTIVE MOMENT**
Trainer-in-form (last 14 days): M Johnston (22 wins from 102 runners, 22%) runs **SEDUCTIVE MOMENT**
Longest Traveller: SEDUCTIVE MOMENT trained by M Johnston, Middleham, 200 miles.

Br Breeding   O Owner   B Breeder   J Jockey   T Trainer   S Sponsor   **RacingTV**   **toteexacta**

colours	no	horse	age	st-lb	Draw
	1	**PINNATA (IRE) (140)** 211-130 D BF	**5**	**10-0**	**(1)**

Br B g Shamardal (USA) - Lavande Violet (GER) (Hurricane Run (IRE))   **Adam Kirby** J
O Mr David N Reynolds & Mr C D Watkins   Stuart Williams, Newmarket T
B Ammerland Verwaltung GmbH & Co.KG
TIMEFORM VIEW Five wins from 17 Flat runs. 1 win from 3 runs this year. Latest win at Newcastle in January. 7/2, ninth of 13 in handicap at Wolverhampton (8.6f). Off 140 days. Others more appealing.   TFR★★☆☆☆ BHA77

| | **2** | **ALGAFFAAL (USA) (14)** 0-51033 | **4** | **10-0** | **(5)** |

Br Ch g Speightstown (USA) - Rockcide (USA) (Personal Flag (USA))   **Stefano Cherchi (7)** J
O MR IAN & TOM PALLAS & MRS D F ROBE   Brian Ellison, Malton T
B WinStar Farm LLC   Brian Ellison Racing Limited S
TIMEFORM VIEW Winner at Newcastle in April. 8/1, creditable third of 10 in handicap at Ascot (7f, firm) 14 days ago.   TFR★★★★★ BHA77

| | **3** | **SEDUCTIVE MOMENT (GER) (5)** 0041-51 D | **3** | **9-12** (in 6lb ex) | **(6)** |

Br Ch g Shamardal (USA) - Sexy Lady (GER) (Danehill Dancer (IRE))   **Joe Fanning** J
O KINGSLEY PARK 10   Mark Johnston, Middleham T
B Gestut Hof Ittlingen   Johnston Racing Ltd S
TIMEFORM VIEW Career best when winning 6-runner handicap at Windsor (8.1f, good to firm, 13/2) 5 days ago, well on top finish. Carries penalty. Expected to be bang there.   TFR★★★★☆ BHA77

| | **4** | **MY DEAR FRIEND (16)** 430-210 D | **3** | **9-5** | **(9)** |

Br B g Kodiac - Time Honoured (Sadler's Wells (USA))   **Harry Bentley** J
O King Power Racing Co Ltd   Ralph Beckett, Kimpton Down T
B W. & R. Barnett Ltd   King Power International Co Ltd S
TIMEFORM VIEW 1 win from 3 runs this year. Winner at Kempton in February. 12/1, ninth of 10 in handicap at Newbury (10f, good to firm) 16 days ago. Something to find on form.   TFR★★☆☆☆ BHA76

| | **5** | **ASSEMBLED (14)** 3410 D | **3** | **9-5** | **(7)** |

Br Gr c Iffraaj - Bezique (Cape Cross (IRE))   **Pat Cosgrave** J
O Mr V I Araci & Partners   Hugo Palmer, Newmarket T
B Aston House Stud   Vefa Stud S
TIMEFORM VIEW Lightly-raced winner. Winner at Windsor in June. 5/1, ninth of 10 in handicap at Ascot (7f, firm) 14 days ago.   TFR★★★☆☆ BHA76

| | **6** | **FITZROVIA (23)** 05/-0110 | **4** | **9-5** | **(4)** |

Br Br g Poet's Voice - Pompey Girl (Rainbow Quest (USA))   **Barry McHugh** J
O Simon Treacher & Clarissa Casdagali   Ed de Giles, Ledbury T
B Mrs Fiona Denniff   Ed de Giles Racing S
TIMEFORM VIEW 2 wins from 4 runs this year. Latest win at Nottingham in June. Tenth of 12 in handicap at Haydock (7.2f, good to firm, 8/1) 23 days ago. Ideally suited by softer ground.   TFR★★★☆☆ BHA68

| | **7** | **CRIMEWAVE (IRE) (16)** 52-0543 | **3** | **9-4** | **(3)** |

Br B g Teofilo (IRE) - Crossover (Cape Cross (IRE))   **David Egan** J
O The Rogues Gallery Two   Tom Clover, Newmarket T
B Newstead Breeding Llc   Tom Clover Racing Llp S
TIMEFORM VIEW 7/1, creditable third of 12 in handicap at Newbury (8f, good to firm) 16 days ago, running on. Blinkers on 1st time.   TFR★★★☆☆ BHA75

| | **8** | **GREEK KODIAC (IRE) (29)** 3-64205 | **3** | **9-4** | **(2)** |

Br B c Kodiac - Greek Easter (IRE) (Namid)   **Robert Winston** J
O Mr Kenny Bruce   Mick Quinn, Newmarket T
B J. Hanly   Purple Bricks S
TIMEFORM VIEW Cheekpieces on for 1st time, fifth of 8 in handicap (33/1) at this course (7f, good) 29 days ago. Can make presence felt.   TFR★★☆☆☆ BHA75

Silvestre started to shake up Seductive Moment, who responded immediately, and approaching the final furlong he opened up a clear gap of about 2 lengths to 3 lengths. He won by 2¼ lengths from Data Protection in second and Casement in third. He was back.

Silvestre de Sousa said that *"the horse travelled well throughout the race and when asked, he picked up well. He pulled away from the field nicely."*

Mark Brown of the Racing Post thought *"it may not have been the deepest race …. but he surely has more to offer."*

A first prize of £3,428.57 was added to the winnings.

As the race was on a Monday he was allowed to run off his old mark (OR 77) up to and including Friday 2nd August. He would, of course, have to carry a 6lb penalty for his win. However, the handicapper on the following Tuesday may have put him up more than 6lbs, so it was odds-on Mark would find another suitable race for him as soon as possible, assuming he had come out of the Windsor race well.

11.2 Newmarket [July]

He did and Seductive Moment was entered to run on Saturday 27th July, 5 days later in the Heath Court Hotel Handicap at Newmarket (July) (Class 5) over 1 mile for 3-year-olds and upwards. He was declared and Joe Fanning took the ride.

The race card is included above courtesy of Weatherbys. It was a damp afternoon with brollies to the fore. Liz Pescops, Ruth Carty, Reg and Val Witheridge, Paul Walker and Adele Brown and I attended. Deirdre Johnston represented the stable. She made sure that the starter knew the stalls handlers were not to use a hood to blindfold the horse if he would not go into the stalls. He had played up in the past, when this tactic was attempted.

Seductive Moment with Joe Fanning winning eased down at Newmarket July Course. *John Hoy*

Seductive Moment walking back to the Winners' Enclosure with Joe Fanning, Tim Jarvis, Nain Singh and Paul Walker looking on. *John Hoy*

"Timeform" thought Seductive Moment was *"an obvious player"* based on his performance at Windsor. Algaffaal trained by Brian Ellison, with Stefano Cherchi on board claiming 7lbs also had a chance. I liked the look of Crimewave trained by Tom Clover. Maybe some subconscious word association with my Home Office days or more likely it was because he was out of the same dam as the beautiful filly Auchterarder in KP 11. However, the nascent qualities of our horse were on show at Windsor and even with a 6lb penalty, which had put us 2lbs off top weight we were in with a chance.

He was not too badly behaved going into the stalls but managed to place his head over the side of the gate just as the stalls opened. He, therefore, missed the kick and was soon on the back foot, 2 lengths behind the pack where Pinnata led and Crimewave, running in blinkers for the first time, was keen to get on with things in second. At half way Seductive Moment was still at the rear but very much closer and Joe came up on the outside of the closely formed pack. At 2½ furlongs to go he swept by them and across to the far side rail. He shot away from the pack by about 5 lengths. The excited commentator exclaimed he was *"pouring it on and this is a huge moment for Seductive Moment."*

"Wow Seductive Moment has blown this lot apart" was the analyst's immediate comment and noted that the race had some unexposed 3-year-olds, Seductive Moment under a penalty being one of them. He won very easily by 3¾ lengths being eased down slightly towards the finish.

The drizzle seemed to disappear and the whole place took on a sunny demeanour. He had annihilated a field of reasonable class horses and picked up a first prize of £4,528.30. Paul Walker wrote in his diary:

"Seductive Moment 27th July 2019

Newmarket (July course). A 6lb penalty for the Windsor win and a very quick turn round.

A happy day at Newmarket July winning the Heath Court Hotel Handicap

Excellent buffet in the marquee; the Kingsley Park 10 owners keep pinching themselves about our good fortune. Seductive Moment manages to trap his head over the stalls and completely misses the break but he is soon eating up the ground on the outside and has the race in the bag a long way out. A lovely way to end the day celebrating a win on a historic racecourse with Deirdre, Joe and his proud owners. What a journey, what a story.

I am so pleased to have kept a diary – otherwise they would never believe us."

Keith McHugh of the Racing Post thought the race *"was torn to pieces by the easy winner who will surely go on to better things"*. He went on to comment:-

"SEDUCTIVE MOMENT, who returned from a break to win at Windsor five days earlier, was turned out under a 6lb penalty. His supporters must have been concerned when he fluffed his lines leaving the stalls, but he made up his ground easily and the race was all over as a contest once he swept to the front. He has three more entries next week and it would be no surprise to see him out again before the handicapper has his say."

Joe joined us at the Winners' Champagne Reception. He told me that Seductive Moment *"was well handicapped"* as Keith McHugh had alluded to in his report. It is difficult to handicap horses effectively if they don't run. On this occasion we took full advantage of this imperfect, and sometimes unfair system.

11.3 Beverley

Not surprisingly Claire reported the next day that following Seductive Moment's impressive win he had been declared to run again on Tuesday 30th July at Beverley in the 4.20pm race with Joe Fanning on board. The race was the Wilford Watts Memorial Handicap Stakes (Class 4) over 1 mile and we carried 12lbs extra for his two recent wins.

After his devastating turn of foot last time out at Newmarket I felt that if he behaved himself at the start he just had to turn up to win. My overconfidence was not put to the test as he just would not go into the stalls. He dug his heels in and no amount of cajoling would get him to go in. They went without him. The inevitable announcement came over the loudspeaker system for a representative of Johnston Racing to report to the weighing room (Stewards). A stalls test beckoned. Some disappointed owners trudged away from the track.

The good news was that Seductive Moment was back at the races, he had shown some promise for the future and one could only look forward to his next race.

CHAPTER 12
LATE SUMMER AND AUTUMN 2019
12.1 The Return to Glorious Goodwood

Towards the end of July 2019 the Golden Partnership embarked on the final fling of races. The two remaining horses, Victory Command and Seductive Moment were now running well and of course both were to be sold in the upcoming Tattersalls Horses in Training Sales in October at Newmarket. Entries were made for both horses to race in early August at Goodwood and for Seductive Moment at Thirsk. Ultimately, Victory Command was declared to run first at Goodwood's Unibet Handicap on 1st August. This was a Class 2 race over 1 mile 2 furlongs worth £46,687.20 to the winner. The going was Good and Franny Norton took the ride. He was off an official mark of 96 but carried *"only"* 8st 7lbs as Walkinthesand trained by Richard Hannon was rated at 110 and carried 9st 7lbs. The return to the happy hunting ground of Glorious Goodwood did not quite go to plan apart from the fact the horse ran very well and probably showed his best form. Mark said that he had run very well from a less than desirable draw and that Franny Norton was forced to go wide for the majority of the race.

Glorious Goodwood, Franny Norton on Victory Command, Savroop Singh and Joe Fanning on The Trader, Ratan Singh. *Adele Brown.*

My disappointment shone through in my e-mail reply to Paul Walker's message, who thought the *"horse had run another amazing race."* I replied that I thought he had indeed run a good race and it was probably up to his best form. However, although it was good to pick up a decent cheque he had come 4th to the winner Forest of Dean. I pointed out, yet again, that he was in the *"grip of the handicapper"* with only one victory in 2019 so far from 12 runs. I hoped that the "Maestro of Middleham" could find him a race and I thought the distance 1 mile 2 furlongs was the way forward.

Paul reported Franny Norton had said afterwards *"that he possibly had to get racing soon enough to keep his position and he just felt he was tiring just before the end. "*Paul added that: *"Goodwood are producing sectional times which are available on the Racing TV website. These bear out what Franny says. Victory Command is clearly not a slow horse as for the 4 furlongs between the 5f and the 1f the times are all below 12 secs."*

The Racing Post's analyst, Mark Brown thought *"it was a good quality 3yo handicap, the right horses came to the fore and the form looks rock solid."* He considered that on this evidence Forest of Dean is bordering on a Listed Class. John Gosden was quoted as agreeing: *"We'll either go for another three-year old handicap against older horses or try Listed Company."*

Happy Connections at Chelmsford with P J McDonald, Savroop Singh and Tim Jarvis. *Ruth Carty*

12.2 Victory Command Wins at Chelmsford

Our handicap mark was not adjusted and remained at 96. One way of taking an advantage of a weight adjustment is to run against older horses where there is a weight-for-age allowance and in our next race we did just that. The Maestro of Middleham, as I started to call him, dropped Victory Command in class and on 16th August we ran in a 3-year-old + race at Chelmsford. Paul Walker and I exchanged thoughts about a long trip to Chelmsford in deteriorating weather conditions. Paul was not keen on making the difficult journey, as he had already been twice to Chelmsford in 2019 and could not face it *"Even for Victory Command."* He also pointed out that both the Racing Post and Timeform fancied him. I agreed with all that Paul had said and also thought it was the type of race he could win.

It was the Bet totescoop6 At totesport.com Class 3 Handicap (0-95) for 3-year-olds + over 1 mile 2 furlongs with a first prize of £9,703.50. PJ McDonald was the jockey.

In fact we were the only three-year-old in the race. Victory Command broke well from stall 2. Lexington Empire trained by David Lanigan also broke well. Three Weeks trained by David O'Meara moved up towards Victory Command and Lexington Empire took up third position on the rail. Victory Command cruised round the bend to the back straight and was going very smoothly under a comfortable PJ. In the final straight they came down the centre of the track with Victory Command still going well. He and Lexington Empire forged clear of the rest. Our horse was always doing enough to win comfortably with the expert P J McDonald on board.

It was a very sound run and 1mile 2 furlongs appeared not to be problem now. He just galloped them all into the ground apart from the second which also ran well. The Racing Post liked the run and pointed out he was 5lbs higher in the weights than he had been at Hamilton. I thought he would probably be put up 4lbs or 5 lbs which would give us a chance to get in the forthcoming Class 2 handicaps including a valuable 1 mile 2 furlongs Class 2 on Ebor Day at York.

12.3 Three Runners at York's Ebor Meeting

Entries continued to be made after Chelmsford and one notification from the Racing Post's Horse Tracker system (shown on page 210) was a sight for sore eyes. The three partnership horses were entered in the same race on 23rd August at York's Ebor meeting. Strictly speaking, of course, Dark Vision was no longer part of Kingsley Park 10 as he had been sold to Godolphin, but I and I suspect many of our group still had a soft spot for him and were keen to follow his progress. To have all three horses entered to run at one's favourite track in a high class Handicap, and at the most prestigious Ebor meeting, was just wonderful.

Victory Command was also entered in the Sky Bet Handicap for the following day, on Saturday 24th August, again a Class 2 handicap.

On 19th August Seductive Moment passed his stalls test. He was declared to run at York on Friday 23rd August in the Nationwide Accident Repair Services Handicap (Class 2) (0-105) for 3-year-olds over 1 mile. The first prize was £43,575 and Joe Fanning was on board. Dark Vision was also declared.

The total prize money was £70,000 so it was indeed a big Handicap and had attracted some very good horses. In particular Dark Vision (OR 103) Drawn (4): ridden by James Doyle was top weight (9st 7lbs), Biometric (OR 101) (Drawn 16) the winner of the Britannia at Royal Ascot trained by Ralph Beckett and ridden by Harry Bentley was second top weight (9st 5lbs). Fanaar (OR 100) (Drawn 7) third in the Britannia, trained by William Haggas and ridden by Jim Crowley was third top weight (9st 4lbs), and Pogo (OR 99) (Drawn 3) trained by Charlie Hills and ridden by Kieran Shoemark was next on 9st 3lbs. Seductive Moment (OR 94) (Drawn 13) had gone up 17lbs since his comeback win on 22nd July at Windsor and his subsequent win at Newmarket (July).

Dark Vision went off as the 4/1 Favourite with Biometric and Fanaar both at 8/1. Seductive

The Golden Partnership horses entered in the same race at York

Moment was 14/1. The going was Good to Firm.

It was a good break and Charlie Hills' Pogo from Draw (4) got away to a good start on the inner rail. Seductive Moment drawn unfavourably on the outside made up a lot of ground and was second at the turn into the straight. Biometric was there as they came down the centre of the track with Dark Vision on his own towards the inner rail. At the 2 furlong marker Karl Burke's Vitralite took a slight lead with all the jockeys working hard. Pogo was still there with Fanaar switched by Jim Crowley and staying on. Towards the line it was a battle between Vitralite (Ben Curtis) and Pogo (Kieran Shoemark) with Pogo just getting up to win by a neck. Fanaar was a length back with Seductive Moment digging in for fourth beating Biometric in 5th and Dark Vision and Boston George who were in a dead heat for 6th.

I was in the Owners and Trainers' stand with Mark and my sister. We were urging Seductive Moment on and we were completely delighted with the runs of the two Johnston Racing horses. Seductive Moment had taken the scalp of Biometric and indeed Dark Vision. They both gave him weight of course. The top six finishers save for Boston George trained by Keith Dalgleish were in the top 7 in the weights. The Racing Post's analyst Mark Brown was correct in saying *"it paid to race prominently."* It did us no favours to be drawn (13) and the horse will have used early energy to get where he needed to be, up with the leaders. Mark Brown thought he performed *"most creditably considering the weights and class rise."*

I was reminded of when Always Waining finished 4th in 2004 in the Garrowby Lane and the *"Always Trying II"* partners milked the presence at the 4th spot in the parade ring. The same applied here as the photograph collage shows connections with the horse and Assistant Yard Manager Hari Singh Bhati.

Sadly, Hari suffered a fatal heart attack in February 2020 during his annual visit home to India to spend time with his wife and two children. He had been a much loved member of the close knit Johnston Racing team and highly respected by all. Charlie Johnston paid this tribute: *"Hari was one of our most experienced lead-up people, and his would have been one of the first names down to be leading up some of our high profile runners at major meetings."*

The following day a large number of partners were in attendance for Ebor Day to swell the already packed house for the fourth day of the festival. The Sky Bet Ebor attracted 22 runners which was not surprising with prize money of £1,000,000 up for grabs. Yes one million pounds. The Irish raider Mustajeer, trained by G M Lyons and ridden by Colin Keane won it at 16/1. Victory Command's race was also a valuable one with prize money of £70,000.

It was the Sky Bet Stakes for 3-year-olds and upwards (rated 0-105) over 1 mile and 2 furlongs. P J McDonald was on board. All the "*talk*" was about Forest of Dean trained by John Gosden. He had beaten us at Glorious Goodwood and his trainer had speculated he might be Listed Class. He had only been raised 7lbs (OR 100 and Drawn (1)) for this win and, as the programme notes suggested, he would take some stopping. Punters thought the same way and he was the 6/4 favourite. We were the same weight (OR 100) and drawn favourably in Stall 4. Punters were not so enthusiastic for our chances, which were reflected in the odds of 14/1. The horses above us in the weights were all older than 3 years and our stable had a four- year-old Ventura Knight (OR 94) Drawn (2) running. Rise Hall (OR 99) Drawn (6) trained by Martyn Meade and Johnny Drama trained by Andrew Balding were also above us. The going was still Good to Firm.

Connections in 4th position with Seductive Moment and Hari Singh Bhati. *Mayla Holleyhead*

Victory Command

Connections after the race with Victory Command and grooms Keith Watson and Savroop Singh. *Ruth Carty*

Victory Command got away well and led, positioned towards the inner (far) rail. That was the place to be. Johnny Drama and Society Red were nearby. Forest of Dean and Ventura Knight were close behind. At the half way point Johnny Drama was in the lead by about ½ a length and remained so when they swung left into the home straight to come down the centre of the track. They were side by side. Frankie Dettori then got to work on Forest of Dean who swooped by at the furlong marker to open a clear gap and won easily from the chasing pack. Victory Command tired in the closing stages but hung on to finish 5th. Johnny Drama stayed on to be second and Ventura Knight was third. We managed to pick up £1,681from the pot of £70,000.

Forest of Dean had won easily with *"plenty in hand"* according to Ron Wood of the Racing Post. He went on to say he *"ended up hitting the front sooner than was probably ideal, as he got there so comfortably."* Our stable's report quoted P J McDonald:

"P J McDonald said that Victory Command was up there with the pace for the majority of the race but didn't have the legs to go with the field in the final stages. Mark was happy with the horse's performance and said

213

that he thought he ran extremely well. Victory Command was only beaten by 3½ lengths."

Many years ago Mark had asked me what I considered to be the race I would like to win and I did mention the Ebor, but there are many more now which have been elevated above this race in my dreams. Nevertheless I had had a runner on Ebor day and one before it.

12.4 End of Season Runs

After Victory Command's run at York Charlie had told Paul Walker that he would keep running him. A week later on 31st August he turned up at Beverley in the William Hill Silver Cup. It was one of their main meetings of the year with the William Hill Beverley Bullet also on the card. Our race was a Class 2 over 1 mile 1 furlong for 3-year-olds with a total race value of £52,000. We had an official rating of 100 (9st 5lbs) and were only surpassed by Dark Vision off a mark of 102, (9st 7lbs). Good Birthday trained by Andrew Balding (OR 95) carried 9st; as did Desert Icon trained by William Haggas. Three Comets trained by Roger Varian (OR 92) carried 8st 11lbs and the bottom weight was Artic Fox (OR 87) trained by Richard Fahey. Desert Icon was favourite at 15/8.

Victory Command and Cesar Dayaca at Beverley. Also Neil Hodgson with Dark Vision wearing headgear

Victory Command with Connor Beasley in the Duty Free Handicap at Newbury. *Ruth Carty*

Victory Command got away well from a favourable inside draw but was soon joined by Dark Vision who appeared either to run freely or was determined to get on with it. Down the hill to the home straight right hand bend Dark Vision was 5 lengths clear of Victory Command with Desert Icon ¾ of a length back in third. Other than Dark Vision they were all close together in the uphill straight where he took it up 1½ furlongs from the line. He could not sustain the move though and Dark Vision dropped away and Desert Icon and Three Comets came down his outside. Good Birthday eased passed on his inside to win by half a length. Desert Icon was second and Three Comets third. Victory Command was fourth only just over one length behind the winner.

The handicapper would have been pleased perhaps with the blanket finish. Maybe Dark Vision going off like a train *"lit up"* Victory Command too much and allowed the others in the final stretch to come from behind with a late run. A nice 4th prize of £2,111 was gratefully received.

Andrew Balding suggested that the Cambridgeshire was a possibility for Good Birthday.

Victory Command on 12th October in the pre- parade ring at York

Victory Command (on the left of view) with Katie Williams and Seductive Moment with Andrew Shaw at Park Farm, 23rd October. *Ruth Carty*

On 9th September Victory Command and Seductive Moment were entered in the Tattersalls Autumn Horses in Training Sales to take place on the 28th to 31st of October. Before that, however, Victory Command was entered for Saturday 14th September in the P J Towey Construction Ltd Handicap (Class 2) over 1 mile at Doncaster and was declared to run 5 days later. This was St Leger Day. This meant if he made it to Doncaster he would have run on 2000 Guineas day at Newmarket, Derby Day at Epsom, Ascot Gold Cup Day, Glorious Goodwood, Ebor Day at York and finally, St Leger day at Doncaster.

The horse had other ideas and vet John Martin wrote to us on 13th September to explain that Victory Command had pulled up lame on the gallops. He diagnosed a subcutaneous infection and thought it would be highly unlikely that he would run at Doncaster. He did not make it to St Leger Day.

After Victory Command's enforced absence from Doncaster through a slight injury he recovered quickly and several entries were made, one of which was for Saturday 21st September at Newbury in the Dubai Duty Free Handicap Class 2 over 1 mile 2 furlongs. He took part that day with Connor Beasley on board. We were never prominent enough to land a blow at the finish and came 9th beaten by Caradoc trained by Ed Walker by 10 lengths.

It was an open age race and one of the three-year-olds, Forest of Dean, who had won so well at Goodwood and York was well down the field with us. A run to forget.

Victory Command's final race for the Golden Partnership was on 12th October 2019 at York. It was the Smart Money's Coral Stakes a 96-110 handicap over 1 mile 2 furlongs for 3-year-olds and older horses. Jason Hart took the ride. Total prize money was £30,000. We were opposed by some familiar names on the racecard. Dark Vision, Johnny Drama trained by Andrew Balding and Coolagh Forest trained by Richard Fahey.

The last mentioned since our beating of him earlier in the summer at Hamilton had come down in the weights and carried only 8st 6lbs. We, on the other hand were off a higher mark (OR 99) and carried 8st 9lbs with a weight-for-age allowance. Richard Fahey had another in the race (Forest Ranger) a five-year-old with a rating of 110. He had to lump 9st 10lbs round the distance in ground at York which was described as Soft.

My experience over the years of the conditions of Soft ground at York meant that we were in for a difficult time as any mention of Soft in the description of the ground usually meant it was very testing.

It wasn't raining but autumn had definitely arrived as I watched Victory Command walk slowly away from me in the pre-parade ring. My *"close bosom friend of the maturing sun"*. I felt sad as I suspected that it would be the last time I saw him, and I was also worried that with an official mark of 99, and in the testing conditions, it would be too much for him. Like all owners, thoughts such as *"I hope he comes back in one piece"* are never far away.

He ran well and led on the inner, far side rail for most of the race into the home straight. He was however, headed over one furlong from the finish and faded to come 6th of the seven runners. Coolagh Forest off a much lower mark than he was when we last ran against him turned the tables this time and beat Johnny Drama by 3 lengths to win. Dark Vision was a further 4 lengths behind in third. The ground had really taken its toll. The following day Victory Command was reported as being fine so it was onward to the sales. I felt a bit empty.

I had watched the race from my usual position about 100 yards before the finish line and after the race turned away to leave the track. I could not bear to go to any debrief where the horse was unsaddled and in any event it was likely that I knew, more or less, what would be said. Paul Walker wrote to me and said that he did go to see him being washed down and gave him a final pat and watched him go back across the Knavesmire for the last time.

My reply to his message was also tinged with sadness and included the valedictory comments that he had been an outstanding servant and I hoped he would do well with presumably new owners. A combination of poor ground and too much weight had blighted some of his last few runs but that will not be how I remember him. My visits to the track to watch him run and the large number of race winning photographs and trophies will not let me forget what a wonderful servant he had been.

Ruth Carty visited the stables on the 23rd October and captured Victory Command and Seductive Moment at Kingsley Park. Six days later on 29TH October 2019 they were both sold at Tattersalls Horses in Training sales to BBA Ireland.

12.5 Bavardages Breaks the Number of Winners in a Calendar Year Record at Kempton Park

Early in October 2019 there was an increase of excitement for the imminent prospect of Mark breaking another record, this time for the number of wins in a calendar year. The record of 235 wins had stood since 2013 claimed by Richard Hannon Snr in his final season. Richard Fahey had won the same number of races in 2015 but try as he may he could not get the extra win before the year was out.

A similar frustrating period was experienced by Johnston Racing as 30 or so runners suffered from the very soft conditions during October 2019. However, on 28th October 2019 the ground posed no such problems on Kempton Park's All-Weather surface. Bavardages, by the same sire as Dark Vision, (Dream Ahead), and one of the three horses in the Kingsley Park 11 partnership, ran in the Magical Fireworks Spectacular Here On Saturday Nursery Handicap (Class 6) (0-60) for 2-year-olds over 7 furlongs. The going was Standard to Slow. Joe Fanning was on board.

Thirteen runners went to the post and it was a fairly even break. Joe got Bavardages into a handy position near the front. Flashy Flyer was keen at the front and just led to the right hand turn. At the bend Bavardages took a lead of just under one length and was going well within himself in a position just off the rail. At the 3 furlong marker he looked to be going well but in the home straight wandered off a true line towards the finish and a pack of horses looked poised to pounce. They couldn't pass him and he went past the post all out to win by ¾ of a length under a driving finish by Joe Fanning. Kuwaity trained by Mohamed Moubarak just got up to claim second from Bryn Du trained by William Haggas.

The record was broken. That win recorded the 236th of the season for Johnston Racing.

Bavardages with Joe Fanning breaking the number of wins in a calendar year at Kempton Park,
28th October 2019. *John Hoy*

CHAPTER 13
DARK VISION'S COMEBACK

The sale of a horse is often accompanied with emotion. I have already discussed in a previous chapter how owners can become attached to their charges. A further emotion is to hope that the horse does well for its new owners and that they have continued success with their purchase. I am sure this was the most prevalent feeling of the KP 10 partners when Dark Vision was in August 2018 sold to Godolphin. His run six weeks later in the Champagne Stakes at Doncaster was a disappointment for all associated with him past and present.

He was sidelined for most of the winter of 2018/19 before re-emerging on the track on 11 April 2019 at Chelmsford in a Class 2 race, where he came third. This was a pipe opener for the 2000 Guineas on 4th May 2019 at Newmarket. Again he was a disappointment, Magna Grecia won the race and Dark Vision came 12th of 19 runners. By the time he ran on 20 June 2019 in the Britannia at Royal Ascot his rating had dropped from 113, awarded just after his win in the Vintage at Goodwood to 105. He competed against Victory Command that day and both horses had almost impossible chances of winning from their low draws. Dark Vision had the worst draw of the entire field. The race was won by the underexposed Biometric from a high draw. Dark Vision came eighth and showed signs of having recovered some of his zest for racing. He still had not returned to the scintillating form he had shown during his wins at York and Goodwood of the previous year. However, by the end of the season his mark was down to 97. I had two further emotions, the first of these was that I especially wanted him to do well as he had been my favourite in the Golden Partnership and the second I knew that to write about success was easier and far more enjoyable than to explain failure. Dark Vision's 2020 career is summarised in Table 9 in Chapter 14.

13.1 The Betway Handicap 2nd June 2020 at Newcastle

He was kept in training to be campaigned as a four-year-old and reappeared on 2nd June at the start of the truncated 2020 season at Newcastle on the "All-Weather." He was in the Betway Handicap a Class 2 race (0-105) for 4-year-olds +, over 1 mile and had by then an official rating of 97, and carried 9st 5 lbs. One of the features of the start of the "season" was that there were far too many horses entered to run, owing to the pent up demand, for the available places, so they were competitive. Another consequence was that the range of weights in these early "season" races was quite narrow. In this case only 9lbs between top and bottom weights.

He was drawn on the far rail, not the best draw as often over the straight mile the runners come down the middle or towards the stands rail. It was a clean break and with Silvestre de Sousa on board Dark Vision tracked across to take up a position at the rear of the field on the outside of the pack. Sir Busker, trained by William Knight was also at the rear tucked in behind. Arcanada, trained by Tom Dascombe took up the running but the field was close together at the half way stage. Dark Vision and Firmament, trained by David O'Meara set sail for home and well within the last furlong the former got the better of the latter only to be pipped to the post by the fast finishing Sir Busker.

A very promising run from the winner and a pleasing run from Dark Vision, who had looked to have had the race won, from what could be considered as a less than favourable draw, until he was collared in the final stages. The front two were almost 2 lengths clear of the third horse , Fifth Position, trained by Roger Varian.

Connections were pleased with Dark Vision's performance and he came out of the race well. On to better things?

Dark Vision swoops with a characteristic late surge to win The Royal Hunt Cup at Royal Ascot. *Megan Ridgewell*

13. 2 The Royal Hunt Cup 17th June 2020 at Royal Ascot

The Royal Hunt Cup was first run in 1843 and was for a long time run over a nominal 7½ furlongs. In 1956 it was extended to its present length of 1 mile and is run over the straight course. It is a Heritage Handicap for horses of 3 years old or older and attracts a large field to compete for the attractive prizes. One of which is a cup and it is one of the three races at Royal Ascot where the cup is kept by the winning owner in perpetuity, the others being the Gold Cup and the Queen's Vase. The Kingsley Park trophies are periodically auctioned off amongst the partners and I wonder what a Royal Ascot cup would have gone for? Mark had not trained the winner of the race before.

The event is highly competitive and only horses approaching a mark of 100 or above can get in. Thus in 2020 there was a "Silver Royal Hunt Cup" (a consolation race) which attracted horses rated in the lower to middle 90's. Sir Busker trained by William Knight won the race in 2020, the first race on the card. He did it with a late surge identical to his run at Newcastle. He was rated 96 and carried top weight of 9st 10lbs. Needless to say this result and the fact that the third horse in the Newcastle race had won last time out meant that Dark Vision's odds for the Royal Hunt Cup were affected and they came in from 14/1 in the morning of the race to around 15/2 after Sir Busker had won. In fact, he was quite fancied. He had been working well at home and the Racing Post's analyst had him as his nap in the "VERDICT" on the race card analysis page. Keith Melrose also of the Racing Post fancied him to win with the headline to his column *"Rejuvenated Dark Vision could take a tow from stablemate in stall next door"*. He went on to say that:

William Buick returns after winning the Royal Hunt Cup. Savroop Singh. *Megan Ridgewell*

Dark Vision is a personal fancy, having shaped best in a classy handicap at Newcastle. It is reasonable to infer that he is back to the form that won him the Vintage Stakes a couple of years back. Stall 11 does not readily count as "high" but one of the main pace angles is Vale of Kent, who is right next door in 12.

Inevitably in such a race there were almost as many opinions as to which horse was going to win as there were horses, with Pogo and Afaak (who had won the race the previous year) both trained by Charlie Hills, also fancied. Lord Tennyson, trained by John Gosden and Bell Rock, trained by Andrew Balding were touted. Montatham, trained by William Haggas was prominent in the betting and was rated 3lbs less than Dark Vision. Dark Vision in Godolphin's second colours (white cap) was ridden by William Buick. Johnston Racing's other two runners, Vale of Kent and Cardsharp were ridden by Joe Fanning and by Adam Kirby respectively.

They got away to an even break with three early groups. Pogo was on the nearside rail but Cardsharp led on the far side, with Willie John just behind. On the nearside Vale of Kent was prominent. Dark Vision was seemingly going well within himself at the back of the nearside group. Approaching the two furlongs marker Lord Tennyson made a move as did the grey Montatham with Pogo still very prominent on the rail. Cardsharp still led the quartet on the far side. Dark Vision now with a smooth passage came on the stand side to join Montatham and Pogo and sailed past them, with his big stride eating up the ground to win by just over a length going away. He had come from last to first to win. Montatham was second 1¼ lengths away, with Pogo in third a further half length back, and Vale of Kent a gallant fourth.

It would have been good to be able to describe the tremendous noise of the cheering crowd but this year it was not to be. I suspect there were plenty of Kingsley Park 10 followers shouting at the TV in their living rooms willing Dark Vision to win. Our once pride and joy was back. It was a relief, a delight and exciting in equal measure to see that the new owners really had bought a very good horse.

David Jennings's headline (writing in the following day's Racing Post) was "**Dark Vision reminds us of early days with late surge**". He certainly did and the social media chat between the stable staff and some of the partners was full of praise for the training performance and the horse's too. It was almost a carbon copy of the Goodwood race. It was a fast time, 1m 38.32 seconds, 0.28 seconds faster than standard. In fact the fastest time of the day.

David Jennings went on to report:

"Dark Vision, remember him? Yes he was the juvenile who won his first three starts for Mark Johnston and was subsequently snapped up by Godolphin after displaying a devastating turn of foot to win the Vintage Stakes at Glorious Goodwood back in 2018. Well he had not won since that race and his losing run had stretched to 13. That all changed in one of the hottest handicaps of the entire season he finally fulfilled his early potential with an unusually decisive victory in the 23-runner mile handicap. It was achieved in a similar manner to Goodwood too.

William Buick dropped him in stone last. All 22 rivals were still in front of him at half way, but what happened from there was a reminder that the talent he possessed during his early days is still intact. They went hard up front and he picked up the pieces to win going away by a length and a quarter from Montatham.

It was Buick at his brilliant best and while it might have looked further back than ideal, he said afterwards that he was always where he wanted to be.

Buick said that: he travelled beautifully through the race and I was always happy with the position we were in. We were tracking the right horses and everything fell into place. He ran very well at Newcastle on his return and that suggested that he was getting back to his best."

Mark Johnston explained after the race that he "was a pretty easy winner at Goodwood at two but has been nothing but a frustration since he changed ownership, so it is great for Sheikh Mohammed.

It was a drop in class into top handicap company and he did so well. They went hard all the way and it panned out well. He'd been working brilliantly at home. We'll see what the handicapper does to decide for us whether he stays in Handicaps or goes back to Group races."

Dark Vision being led down to the start at Pontefract by Bhanwar Singh

13.3 The Coral Challenge Handicap 5th July 2020 at Sandown.

Dark Vision was soon to meet the horse he had conquered in the Royal Hunt Cup, Montatham, trained by William Haggas and ridden by Jim Crowley, when they both were declared for the Coral Challenge Handicap on 5th July at Sandown Park. This race was on the same card as the Coral Eclipse, which saw the return of Enable up against the front running and improving Ghaiyyath. After his win in the the Royal Hunt Cup, Dark Vision was put up 6lbs by the handicapper and the second, Montatham 3lbs. The only other horse to have run at Ascot was Richard Hannon's Qaysar. The betting suggested that there was confidence in William Haggas's horse as the night before the race both Montatham and Dark Vision were close together in the betting at odds of around 4/1 or 7/2. On the day of the race Montatham was apparently supported much more than the rest and was backed down to 6/5 favourite. Dark Vision stayed more-or-less at the same overnight odds of 3/1. Most of the others apart from Acquitted, trained by Hugo Palmer at odds of 11/2 were 9/1 or much greater prices. The changes in the odds could not have been as a result of the way Dark Vision looked, or was turned out, as he was a picture. He was again admired by the ITV commentators as he had been previously at Glorious Goodwood.

There was some drama at the start as while Zwayyan was being re-shod Marronier trained by Stuart Williams reared up, disposed of Ben Curtis and ran away down the track. Jockey and horse were unscathed but the horse was withdrawn.

This did not seem to affect the other horses who were loaded quietly into the stalls without further incident. It was a clean break and Via Serendipity ran freely into the lead with Gallipoli after a slight jink at the start joined him. Qaysar was in third. These three stayed in the same order up to the bend into the straight but Montatham then took up a position at the bend on the rail in third place. Dark Vision at that stage, and until the 2½ furlongs marker, was in last place. William Buick seemed happy to be there as there was a strong headwind and he was in the slipstream of other horses.

He pulled him wide at about the two furlongs marker and the horse, with a clear run, got into his trademark long stride and powered towards Montatham who was now off the rail and heading for the line. Both horses and jockeys were flat out. It was a thrilling finish and "a photograph" was called. Richard Hoiles, the ITV Commentator, called Montatham as the winner. Not a good sign as he nearly always calls it correctly. Jason Weaver part of the ITV team thought it was close. It was but the ITV cameras, on the basis of their freeze frame of the line showed that Montatham had won and his victory was announced soon thereafter. *"Won by a whisker"* was Ed Chamberlain's comment and his colleague Jason Weaver thought the revenge was owing to *"a turn round in the weights."* It was indeed one of the the shorter winning distances - a short head.

Richard Lowther of the Racing Post thought it was a *"warm handicap"* and thought that Dark Vision had performed *"right up to the form"* of the Royal Hunt Cup and should *"continue to run well in these top handicaps."*

13.4 TheSky Bet Pomfret Stakes [Listed] 23rd July 2020 at Pontefract

The strange summer of 2020 was progressing and although horse racing was taking place *"behind closed doors"* there were plenty of meetings on the Flat and over the jumps. It was a very frustrating time for owners and everybody concerned with racing. Some of the landmark meetings were being held more-or-less at the time of year when they were supposed to be and Glorious Goodwood was due in the last week of July. It was two years since Dark Vision's famous victory there in 2018. Charlie Johnston told Oli Bell in an interview for "Sportinglife" that he had considered running Dark Vision in the Sussex Stakes at the Glorious Goodwood meeting but in view of some of the other entries he decided to go for *"the Pomfret"* instead.

The Listed Sky Bet Pomfret Stakes was run on 23rd July at Pontefract. It was over one mile and for 3-year-olds +. The going was described as Good to Firm and James Doyle was on board. There were only 5 runners and Dark Vision was drawn (2), which usually would be a slight advantage at this left handed uphill curve of a track. However, apart from a race at Beverley towards the end of 2019 when he had a commanding lead soon after the start, his racing style was not to shoot out of the stalls to attempt to make all but to come with a late surge to the line. He had gone up 3lbs for his very hard lines second place in his last race at Sandown and was top rated at 109. All of the colts of the five contenders carried 9st 5lbs whereas the sole filly Foxtrot Lady trained by Andrew Balding and ridden by Oisin Murphy received a 5lbs allowance. Dark Vision went off as the odds-on favourite at 4/5 with Wadilsafa, trained by Owen Burrows and ridden by Jim Crowley also fancied at 100/30. Beringer trained by Alan King and ridden by Martin Harley was not without support at 7/1. The outsider at 10/1 was Oh This Is Us, trained by Richard Hannon and ridden by Sean Levey.

The break was even and Jim Crowley brought Wadilsafa across to the running rail. James Doyle allowed him to do this and was a couple of lengths back also on the rail. Foxtrot Lady was prominent on the outside of Wadilsafa. Oh This Is Us was behind Foxtrot Lady, and Beringer at the half way stage was behind them all. They were closely bunched together. At the bend to the home straight

Jim Crowley was hard at work on Wadilsafa and well into the straight, just over a furlong out Dark Vision was trapped on the rail. Foxtrot Lady was still up there on the outside but Jim Crowley's mount was fading fast. James Doyle angled Dark Vision off the rail and came very close to the fast finishing Beringer. It was close at the line but Dark Vision had shown some characteristic finishing speed to win by a neck.

James Doyle was given a two-day ban for careless riding but the Stewards decided that Dark Vision should keep the race. The jockey said that *"the worry today was always going to be the lack of pace in a small field. You saw what he did in the Hunt Cup, he prefers those big fields and a good pace to run at. I tracked in behind Sheikh Hamdan's horse who didn't take me very far and he kind of stopped so I had to look for a bit of room. My fellow did it well enough once he got room and got striding."* Mark said that *"He's a really happy horse but you can see he is not the easiest because he goes when he wants to go, rather than when the jockey is asking him."*

Dave Toft of the Racing Post thought *"he had been in good heart this season in some big handicaps and had maintained his momentum with a hard fought success."* The comeback was well and truly on its way and since the resumption of racing, after his 277 day break, he had won twice and come second twice to take his earnings to £209,784. As Charlie said to Oli Bell *"let's hope he can kick on now from the Pontefract win."*

13.5 The Sky Bet and Symphony Group Strensall Stakes (Group 3) at York on 22nd August 2020

I have already described how the weight a horse carries in a race and the position in the starting stalls allotted by the draw can affect its finishing position. A third effect on performance is the going. This may not prevent the very best horses from winning but they might find it tougher to do so. For example Battash, trained by Charlie Hills and ridden by Jim Crowley won the 2020 renewal of the Nunthorpe, but not with his characteristic trailblazing style and any attempt at the track record, touted by the ITV pundits, was ruined by the soft or even "tacky" ground conditions. He won the race well but he had to dig in to fend off the challengers. A hallmark of a great horse.

Dark Vision and William Buick. *Jeremy Phillips*

David Hickin leads Dark Vision and William Buick. *Jeremy Phillips*

The weather for The Ebor Festival was poor with rain and at times together with very strong winds. Although a deserted scene had become the norm for the Covid-19 season it was still a very sad spectacle and shows how hard the excellent ITV team worked to present the action.

Montatham, trained by William Haggas and ridden by Jim Crowley had won the Clipper Logistics Handicap on the Thursday (20th August) on perhaps the driest day of the week and the ground was described as "Good." This form together with the second placed horse Sir Busker, trained by William Knight bode well for Dark Vision's chances in the Group 3 Strensall Stakes. However there had been rain since the Thursday and the ground on Saturday 22nd August was described as "Good To Soft." As I have explained before if Soft is mentioned in the description of the going at York the ground can be testing for the horses. In fact the awful weather conditions were wonderfully captured by photographer Jeremy Phillips as Dark Vision was led around the parade ring in front of the rain-soaked TV camera man. The race was won by Certain Lad, trained by Mick Channon and ridden by Hollie Doyle. Dark Vision never really got going and finished in 6th place beaten by almost 6 lengths.

13.6 Dark Vision Winner by a Nose in Group 2 Kronimus Oettingen Rennen Thriller at Baden-Baden 11th September 2020

In the south-west corner of Germany on the doorstep of the Black Forest and the French border, is the small village of Iffezheim. Nearby at the Baden-Baden racecourse horses have raced since 1858. From 1963 yearling sales have been held there and the Baden- Badener Auktiongesellschaft (BBAG) is now part of the European Yearlings Sales season.

The Oettingen Rennen is a Group 2 Flat race open to thoroughbreds aged 3 years or older and is held every year in late August or early September, over a distance of about 1 mile. The race was established in 1927 and was originally called the "Badener Miele." In 1970 it was renamed the "Oettingen Rennen", a Group 3 which was sponsored by Darley from 1999. In 2003 it was elevated to Group 2 level. The leading trainer with 4 wins is Albert Schlaefke and prior to the 2020 running Johnston Racing had won it twice; in 1999 with White Heart ridden by John Reid and in 2008 with Lovelace ridden by Jamie Spencer.

Tim Jarvis, Rhona Bagnall and Franny Norton

227

The 87th running of the race, sponsored by the local concrete factory Kronimus, took place on Friday 11th September with 8 runners going to the post. Six of the runners were trained in Germany and there were two foreign raiders; Half Light, trained by H-A Pantall in France and Dark Vision. Both were owned by Godolphin. Four of the German runners, had competed in the same Group 3, 1 mile race on 2nd August at Düsseldorf. Sanora, trained by A Wohler, Runnymede, trained by Frau S Steinberg, and Thorin, trained by Henk Grewe, were the first three home and Los Campos, trained by Dr A Bolte, came fifth. Rubaiyat, also trained by Henk Grewe had last run in June in Rome in a Group 3 where he came second. Half Light, ridden by Soufiane Saadi came to the race with good form having won a Listed race at Le Lion-d'Angers, a Group 3 in Hamburg and a second place in a Group 3 at Deauville. Not surprisingly she was the 19/10 favourite with Dark Vision the second favourite at 16/5, and Thorin the most prominent of the "local" horses at 39/10.

Franny Norton had travelled over to ride Dark Vision and to be reunited with him after he had won on him, first time out in 2018 at Yarmouth. The going in Germany was described as Good. The first prize was £16,949.15.

It was a fairly even break apart from Dark Vision who was characteristically slowly away. Los Campos led with Sanora and Rubaiyat close by. Runnymede and No Credit Limit were in midfield just in front of a pair of horses, Thorin and Half Light, who in turn were ahead of Dark Vision at the rear. As they came round the left hand bend and into the home straight the jockeys took most of the field to the centre of the track. At the 3 furlong marker Dark Vision was nudged along by Franny and he gained on the leaders Rubaiyat and Sanora who were at the front of the pack of contenders. Half Light towards the near, stand side rail was very much in touch and made progress to lead just inside the final furlong. Rubiaiyat and Runnymede were still there and were staying on for the fight. By this time Dark Vision had started to fly down the centre, with Franny horizontal in the saddle, and well within the last furlong hard driven he ran on strongly to get up on the line to win by the narrowest of margins - a nose from Half Light.

Rubyaiyat was a half a length behind in third and he had just beaten Runnymede in fourth by a neck. A thrilling victory and one that brought back memories of Dark Vision's tremendous acceleration in his first Group 2 race success in "the Vintage" in 2018.

Mark said: " *We had warned Franny Norton that Dark Vision could be slowly away but I was basically thinking that we couldn't win from there. Then I reminded myself that I had said exactly the same thing when he was a two-year-old in the Vintage Stakes. It was a little bit tighter today than the Vintage Stakes but was just as exciting a race, the gap opened and it was wonderful. It was a great ride from Franny, a typical never-give-up effort, and I am absolutely delighted.*

We have no immediate plans but obviously a Group1 victory would be the ultimate target and would repay Sheikh Mohammed for his faith in buying the horse. Dark Vision has had to wait a long time for another Group 2 victory and winning a Group 1 would be the ultimate aim, but I haven't really thought of a plan towards it."

Franny Norton said: "*I expected to win before we came over but I didn't down the back [straight] because Dark Vision ran into the race very lazily. William Buick said to me that I would feel at halfway whether he would win or not. I know exactly what he meant because I felt really good at halfway. Once we went up the straight this lad picked up well and finished them off like he always does.*"

That was Dark Vision's 6th victory and the third this year to add to the Royal Hunt Cup and the Listed Pomfret Stakes. His comeback was now well and truly established. Rohna Bagnall and Tim Jarvis had travelled with the horses (Communique and Rose of Kildare had also travelled) and Rhona had documented the journey, which included an overnight stay in Newmarket and an early exercise of the horses on the gallops. The collage shows the scenes at the racetrack and the photo finish image illustrated just how the close the victory was; Half Light on the nearside Dark Vision on the far side.

The following day Rose of Kildare, now with Franny wearing Qatar racing's colours, came third in the T von Zastrow Stutenpreis Group 2 race for 3-year-old + Fillies and Mares race over 1 mile 4 furlongs. Communique and Franny Norton then went one better on the Sunday finishing second to Barney Roy, trained by Charlie Appleby in the 148th Longines Grosser Preis von Baden Group 1, 3-year-old +, again over 1 mile 4 furlongs and on turf.

It is perhaps worth pointing out that Dark Vision was still an entire horse and then I thought the possibility of and potential for him to become a stallion took another small step closer to reality that weekend in Germany. This sadly was not to be the case.

13.7 The Queen Elizabeth II Stakes Group 1 (Sponsored by Qipco) (British Champions Mile) at Ascot on 17th October 2020.

After his success in Germany Mark promised to try to find a Group 1 race for Dark Vision. He certainly found one at Ascot on "Champions Day". This race was for horses of 3 years old and above and attracted some of the best milers in the business to compete for the £650,000 prize money. The going was described as "Soft" and at this time of year in England it should not have come as a surprise to find it so. It was too Soft for Enable and she was scratched from her race. William Buick took the ride.

Dark Vision was drawn (11) and the finishing positions indicated that the draw, even in this less than suitable ground did not appear to have much of an effect. He wasn't fancied at 80/1 but ran well and although he never lost sight of the leaders, equally he did not look as though he was going to land a blow in the finish. I am sure he found the soft ground not to his liking. Nevertheless he put in a good performance and came seventh out of 14 runners. The race was won by The Revenant, a Dubawi gelding, trained in France by F-H Graffard and ridden by Pierre- Charles Boudot who had come second in the 2019 race. He had beaten Dark Vision by only 6½ lengths.

CHAPTER 14
RESULTS SUMMARY

There can be no doubt that the results in the tables in this section represent a quite remarkable performance from the three KP 10 horses and indeed Johnston Racing's partnerships in general. To put this all in context the first table shows the number and percentage of horses that have won prize money and the respective range of amounts. It does not differentiate between horses that cost millions of guineas as yearlings or those that cost a few thousand pounds or euros. For example in 2019, only 171 horses out of 19,305 won more than £100,000 which was 0.9 % of the total running. Remarkably the previous year's figures were very similar namely 174 horses won more than £100,000 ie 0.90%. Sobering figures are that in 2019, 20% earned nothing and more than 50% less than £2500.

Table 1a Amounts of Prize Money Won by Horses in 2019

Prize Money +£	Number of Horses	Percentage
100,000	171	0.9
50,000	283	1.5
30,000	433	4.6
15,000	1350	11.6
7,500	2616	25.1
2,500	4125	46.5
1	6451	79.9
0	3876	20.0
	19305	

Table 1b Amounts of Prize Money won by Horses in 2018

Prize Money +£	Number of Horses	Percentage
100,000	174	0.9
50,000	306	2.5
30,000	481	4.9
15,000	1395	12.2
7,500	2727	26.4
2,500	4102	47.7
1	6363	80.7
0	3704	19.2
	19252	

The Golden Partnership horses won a total of 13 races and the details of these wins are set out in Table 2 below.

Table 2. KP 10: The 13 Winners, Date, Distance, Going, Weight and Jockey

Horse/Venue	Date	Distance/Going	Weight	Jockey
DARK VISION				
Yarmouth	05 July 2018	6 furlongs Good to Firm	9 st 2lbs	F Norton
York	14 July 2018	6 furlongs Good to Firm	9 st 8lbs	D Probert
Goodwood	31 July 2018	7 furlongs Good	9 st 1lb	S de Sousa
SEDUCTIVE MOMENT				
Windsor	28 May 2018	6 furlongs Good	8 st 2lbs	W Buick
Lingfield	31 December 2018	7 furlongs Standard	9 st 7lbs	R Kingscote
Windsor	22 July 2019	1 mile Good to Firm	9 st 12lbs	J Fanning
Newmarket July	27 July 2019	1 mile Good	9 st 12lbs	J Fanning
VICTORY COMMAND				
Doncaster	19 May 2018	5 furlongs Good to Firm	8 st 2lbs	J Mitchell
Beverley	19 June 2018	7 1/2 furlongs Good	9 st 9lbs	J Fanning
Beverley	26 June 2018	7 1/2 furlongs Good	9 st 10lbs	J Fanning
Ascot	28 July 2018	7 furlongs Good to Firm	9 st 3lbs	S de Sousa
Hamilton	02 July 2019	1 mile 1/2 furlong Good	9 st 2lbs	P J McDonald
Chelmsford	16 August 2019	1 mile 2 furlongs Standard	9 st 1lb	P J McDonald

Some of the financial details are included in Table 3. The prize money column is the amount that the owners received. Details of the prize money distribution has been explained in Chapter 6 and it is split between several of those associated with a horse: the owners receive 80%. The sums of money that changed hands at the Sales both as yearlings and as 3-year-olds has been covered in various pages of the narrative. The money received when the horses were sold has only been disclosed (elsewhere) when they were sold at public auction.

Table 3. KP 10: Some Financial Details: Prize Money, Training Fees and Entry Fees.

Horse	Prize Money £	Training Fees £	Entry Fees
Dark Vision	100,564	22,975	8,458
Seductive Moment	15,613	55,721	4,085
Victory Command	86,289	53,430	12,268

The three KP 10 horses ran a total of 38 times (of course Dark Vision continued to run after he was sold to Godolphin). Table 4 includes the venues where the KP horses ran and how many times they did so.

Table 4. KP 10: Locations and Number of Runs

Venue	Runs	Venue	Runs	Venue	Runs
Ascot	2	Hamilton	1	Newmarket Rowley	3
Beverley	4	Haydock	1	Pontefract	1
Carlisle	2	Lingfield	2	Sandown	1
Chelmsford	1	Meydan	3	Thirsk	1
Doncaster	1	Newbury	1	Windsor	2
Epsom	1	Newcastle	1	Yarmouth	1
Goodwood	2	Newmarket July	3	York	4

Three horses in separate partnerships caught the eye after the end of KP 10 and their best results have been included. Details of their breeding is included in Chapter 8 and their exploits have been referred to in the next chapter.

Table 5. KP 11: Best Results for Auchterarder

Date and Venue	Race, Distance, Going	Position	Jockey	Handicap Mark
14 May 2019 Beverley	Class 5 2-y-o Novice, 5f, Good to Soft	1/10	P J McDonald	
07 Nov 2019 Southwell	Class 5 2-y-o Novice, 5f, Standard	2/9	J Fanning	
18 Nov 2019 Wolverhampton	Class 5 2-y-o Novice, 5f, Standard	1/11	J Hart	
07 Dec 2019 Wolverhampton	Class 2 2-y-o Hcp, 6f, Standard	3/10	J Hart	87
25 Feb 2020 Lingfield	Class 3 Hcp, 6f, Standard	1/7	P J McDonald	87
15 October 2020 Chelmsford	Class 2 Hcp, 1m Standard	2/9	J Hart	89

Table 6. KP 13: Best Results for King's Caper

Date, Venue	Race, Distance, Going	Position	Jockey	Handicap Mark
28 Jun 2019 Chester	Class 4 2-y-o Maiden Auction, 7f, Good	2/7	F Norton	
06 July 2019 Beverley	Class 5 2-y-o Novice Auction, 71/2 f, Good to Firm	1/10	C Beasley	
17 Aug 2019 Ripon	Class 4 2-y-o Novice Auction, 1m, Soft	1/9	J Fanning	87
31 Aug 2019 Chelmsford	Class 2 , 2-y-o Hcp, 1m Standard	1/3	L Dettori	88
23 Oct 2019 Newmarket Rowley	Class 2, 2-y-o Hcp, 1m 2f Soft	2/6	F Norton	95
12 July 2020 Rome	Group 2, Italian Derby 3-y-o 1m 3f Good	2/13	L Dettori	

Table 7. KP 14: Best Results for Rose of Kildare

Date, Venue	Race, Distance, Going	Position	Jockey	Handicap Mark
30 Apr 2019 Brighton	Class 5 2-y-o Novice Auction, 51/2 f Good to Firm	2/8	J Fanning	
20 May 2019 Redcar	Class 2 2-y-o Novice Auction, 6f, Good to Firm	1/9	P J McDonald	
29 May 2019 Hamilton	Class 4 2-y-o Novice Auction, 5f, Good to Soft	1/7	P J McDonald	
8 Jun 2019 Beverley	Class 2 2-y-o Fillies Hcp, 5f, Good to Firm	2/8	F Norton	
03 Aug 2019 Newmarket July	Class 2 2-y-o Fillies Hcp, Good to Firm	1/13	W Buick	81
21 Aug 2019 York	Class 2 2-y-o Hcp, 6f, Good	3/20	J Fanning	87
21 Sept 2019 Ayr	Class 1 Group 3, 2-y-o, 6f, Good	1/9	J Fanning	94
11 Oct 2019 Newmarket Rowley	Class 1 Group 3, 2-y-o Fillies, 6f, Good	1/9	J Fanning	99
21 June 2020 Dusseldorf	Group 3 3-y-o Fillies, 1m, Good	3/11	I Mendizabal	
04 July 2020 Epsom	Class 1 Group 3, 3-y-o Fillies, 1m 1/2, Good	3/6	J Fanning	103
09 July 2020 York	Class 1 Group 3, 3-y-o Fillies, 1m 21/2 f, Good to Soft	1/6	F Norton	103
19 Aug 2020 York	Class 1 Group 1, Juddmonte International 1m 2f Good	5/5	F Norton	103
12 Sept 2020 Baden-Baden	Class1 Group 2, T von Zastrow Stutenpreis, 1m 4f	3/10	F Norton	103

The penultimate table below again is an attempt to put into context the remarkable achievements of the horses in KP 10. Twenty years of partnership horses have been avidly followed by their partners and the most successful ones are included in Table 8.

Table 8: Highest Official Ratings [90 +] for Horses in Always Trying and Kingsley Park partnerships. Purchase Price of the Yearlings.

Partnership	Horses	BHA Rating	Cost of Yearlings
AT II	Always Waining	91	9,000 gns.
AT III	Always Fruitful	97	10000 gns
AT V	Always Bold	91	14,000 gns
Ready to Run	Broxbourne	90	€8000
New Fairyhouse	Maid in Rio	103	€9000
KP 3 Originals	Cape Speed	96	
KP 7 Ready to Run	Sennockian Star	106	20000 gns.
KP 5	Teofonic	99	10000 gns
KP 9	Poet's Society	100	18000 gns
KP 10	Dark Vision	113	15000 gns
KP 10	Victory Command	103	6000 gns
KP 10	Seductive Moment	94	12000 gns
KP 11	Auchterarder	92	€18000
KP 13	King's Caper	102	11000 gns
KP 14	Rose of Kildare	103	€3000

After a disappointing 3-year-old career Dark Vision found his feet again in 2020 as a 4-year-old. The last table shows his consistent form "behind closed doors."

Table 9: Dark Vision's Results in 2020 when owned by Godolphin

Date /Venue	Race	Result	Jockey
02 June 2020 Newcastle	Class 2 Handicap 10K , 1 mile St/Slw	2/11	S de Sousa
17 June 2020 Royal Ascot	Class 2 Royal Hunt Cup 49K, 1 mile, Good	1/23	W Buick
05 Jul 2020 Sandown	Class 2 Handicap 19K Good to Firm	2/9	W Buick
23 July 2020 Pontefract	Listed "Pomfret" 14K Good to Firm	1/5	James Doyle
22 August 2020 York	Group 3 28K, 1mile 1 furlong Good to Soft	5/9	W Buick
11 September 2020 Baden- Baden	Group 2 17K, 1 mile Good	1/8	F Norton
17 October 2020 Ascot	Group 1 640K, 1 mile Soft	7/14	W Buick

CHAPTER 15
REFLECTIONS AND THE PERFECT SCIENCE OF HINDSIGHT
15.1 The Three Horses

Even during 2018, the first year of the KP 10 partnership it was obvious that it was becoming one of the most successful partnerships ever for Johnston Racing. There had been eight wins from the three two-year-olds. The average purchase price was less than 12,000 guineas, with the most successful of them, Dark Vision, costing 15,000 guineas. He won his first two races, at Yarmouth and York, before going on to complete his hat-trick in fine style when winning the Group 2 Vintage Stakes at Glorious Goodwood on 31st July to take his winnings to £128,000.

Dark Vision's Vintage win, with such an emphatic late surge, to come from last to first thrilled both the crowd and most definitely the attending KP 10 partners; he was the talk of the town that day. Soon after he was sold to Godolphin. Of course I will always remember his win at Goodwood. I will also look back with great pleasure, when at York he provided me with my first winner at my favourite track and in the company of mates with whom I had spent so many happy days there.

It was not just that he was victorious at York it was the manner in which he did it, cruising up to the pack, a casual look to the left by his jockey David Probert and then switching on the afterburners to storm away from the rest. Analysis of the Vintage by Simon Rowlands, using sectional times quantified the quality of the "burst" of speed and indicated that *"Dark Vision finished quickly- about 5% quicker compared to his average race speed."*

His next race was on 15th September 2018 at Doncaster in the Group 2 Howcroft Industrial Supplies Champagne Stakes for his new owners. He was soundly beaten by Too Darn Hot, trained by John Gosden and ridden by Frankie Dettori. Mark reported that Dark Vision was unsound after the race and was to be sent to the Equine Hospital at Newmarket, for a check up.

Nothing definite was diagnosed but he was treated as though he had a pelvis problem and was only gradually brought back into work. Obviously back in full training he still had to live with his official rating of 113, as he embarked on his Handicap career. We were able to see him quite often during the summer of 2019 as he ran in several Handicaps where Victory Command also took part. The latter carried a much lower weight, and managed to beat him on a few occasions.

One can't help but wonder if in fact history has been kind to the victory of Dark Vision in the Vintage Stakes as none of the horses involved in the finish, other than Dark Vision, has won a race since. Also the ground conditions during the spring and early summer of 2018 were probably deemed by some trainers to be unsuitable for some of their youngsters to be allowed out to perform. After the Vintage, when the ground conditions had eased, some very good 2-year-olds emerged. For example the John Gosden trained Too Darn Hot appeared and won the aforementioned Champagne Stakes at Doncaster and followed up in October to win the Group 1 Dewhurst Stakes at Newmarket. Nonetheless John Scanlon writing in the Klarion thought that in 2018 Dark Vision provided arguably the performance of the year from any Kingsley Park based horses when he landed the Group 2 Vintage Stakes under a tremendous ride from Silvestre de Sousa. Also the racing press generally supported the quality of his win.

He was kept in training as a four-year-old, with a handicap mark of 100 and showed signs of maybe being on the verge of a comeback when he ran well to finish second at Newcastle, behind Sir Busker on 2nd June 2020. This was one of the first races to be held "behind closed doors" after racing was allowed to restart after the "lockdown" imposed to combat the spread of Covid-19.

The promising signs at Newcastle foretold the remarkable comeback race on 17th June 2020 at an eerie Royal Ascot. There was no royal procession, no champagne, no fashion, no hangovers and no overt exhibition of wealth, apart from the fantastic riches of the horses on display. The government's aim, in the 1960's, to maintain a funereal atmosphere in the early betting shops was achieved on the racecourse at Royal Ascot. Dark Vision won the Royal Hunt Cup and afterwards Mark confirmed that the horse had been working well at home. This manifested itself in the race, which in the end he won rather cosily. The race panned out for him in a similar way to the Vintage Stakes, where in both cases he came from last to first in a scintillating show of great determination and finishing speed to win, expertly ridden at Ascot by William Buick.

He almost won his next race but Montatham, trained by William Haggas and with a weight advantage after his second place in the Royal Hunt Cup turned the tables and won by the narrowest of margins. The next race was at Pontefract where he confirmed his recovery was definitely on course when he won their "Pomfret" Listed race again in his customary last ditch style. Once more at the beginning of September he left it very late to win a Group 2 at Baden-Baden with his exhilarating turn of foot.

I am sure some readers may be wondering whether it would have been better to have kept Dark Vision rather than selling him to Godolphin. The rules of the Kingsley Park partnerships are clear that at the end of a horse's three-year-old career it is sold at public auction. So if we had kept him for the 2019 season that itself would have been full of disappointment and the sale in October of that year would have been perhaps an even bigger one. Rarely do decisions result in all sides winning. Godolphin got a good horse, the partners got a good price and Johnston Racing worked their magic and brought him back to success. Hindsight, the perfect science, confirms that Mark's decision to sell and Franny Norton's clear advice to do so was the correct choice.

Dark Vision did well for Godolphin as a 4-year-old, as I have described and was kept in training at Johnston Racing as a 5-year-old. Sadly in April 2021 tragedy struck when a small cut on his hock became infected (osteomyelitis) and as he failed to respond to treatment he was put down. The tragic end to such a beautiful animal serves to illustrate the vicissitudes of owning a racehorse. Fortunately in this case he has been immortalised by the oil painting on the front cover of this book and within it with the descriptions and photographs of his remarkable racing career. I will forever remember him.

Victory Command ran 26 times and 17 of those runs were as a 3-year-old. Right from the start of his career he showed promise, and like Dark Vision his career set off like a train. He won his second race and was not out of the first three places in his first seven starts. He completed a hat-trick with two wins at Beverley in June 2018 and the third win came on 28th July at Ascot with a most memorable win in a Listed event, with a virtuoso performance from Silvestre de Sousa on board. To his credit Victory Command was never out of the first four home in his 2-year-old career. This included when he ran in two Group races; he came fourth in both the Group 3 Solario and in the Group 2 Royal Lodge.

Early in the following year he had a winter "break" at the Dubai Carnival and arrived with an official handicap mark of 102. After a creditable third place on dirt for his first run he struggled a bit at Meydan on his subsequent runs on turf and returned at the end of February to Middleham with a handicap mark of 98. This proved to be a millstone around his neck.

In summary Victory Command won six times from twenty six starts and amassed a total of £106,574 in prize money. His highest official rating was 103. He was the only horse in this period by War Command, that raced in the UK to have such impressive statistics. As such, he was a truly wonderful servant, a genuine horse, and not only was he "Always Trying", but he always tried his best.

Seductive Moment was the son of the late Shamardal but did not reach his sire's dizzy heights. Even so he gave us some wonderful moments especially his two wins at Windsor, a memorable win at Newmarket's July course, and his gallant effort in his final race at York. He was temperamental, difficult to train and keep sound and he was often injured. However, the surge away from the field at Newmarket's July course was reminiscent of Dark Vision's wins at York and Goodwood. All three wins produced many smiling faces. Maybe that day he showed a flash of his late sire's greatness. He won £19,490 in prize money.

By the autumn of 2019 the Kingsley Park 10 horses had run in a total of 38 races. They had taken the partners and their friends to all the Grade 1 tracks, a total of 20 different venues in the UK and one in Dubai. They had won just over £250,000. Dark Vision was sold for a reported seven figure sum, Victory Command for 100,000 guineas and Seductive Moment for 30,000 guineas. A great partnership which truly deserved the accolade of The Golden Partnership. Mark has said that: *"buying a racehorse is the most expensive lottery ticket anybody can buy."* We did not win the lottery but it felt like we had.

15.2 The Reaction of Some of the Dramatis Personae

Not all of the partners were regular attendees at the races but like the horses many will have been busy and may have found it difficult to make arrangements sometimes at short notice. Those who were "regulars" have sent me their overall feelings of the success story I have told.

Lionel and Lorna Beecroft wrote:

Although it is difficult to pick out our best day's racing, two days really do stand out. One of them came when Dark Vision won the Group 2 Vintage Stakes at Goodwood in a style that was nothing short of sensational and it was only his third run. A truly memorable day! Secondly, we were there to see Poet's Society win the Clipper Logistics Stakes at York with an eye-popping tough and resolute performance, thereby giving Mark the record for the most wins ever by a trainer. That was an unforgettable experience.

Adele Brown wrote: Sadly KP 10 has come to an end. It has been a fabulous 2 years, all three horses did us proud. Very well done to the superb team at Johnston Racing

Liz Pescops wrote:

Goodwood came and the enigmatic Dark Vision, whom Mark had previously described as an ugly horse ran the race of his life. After the race Mark came over and said that we would not have to sell Victory Command after all. Dark Vision would go. Although I was sorry to see Dark Vision sold it didn't bother me. As I write this, I can look across my lounge at a very large picture of Dark Vision nearing the winning post and relive those thrilling moments. I also now have my dream kitchen from the proceeds and have been able to join KP 17 and KP 18. I was delighted when Ruth showed me the photograph of a very young Victory Command [whom Liz named]. Although I have had over 20 horses with Mark and enjoyed many exciting victories, Victory Command was my dream horse, who will always be my favourite. It's great to have the picture. Hopefully, when the curse of Covid-19 passes there will be many more happy race days ahead.

Sue Russell wrote:

Victory Command took us to all the big meetings in 2019 and never ran a bad race, he was sound and genuine- just a superstar. Dark Vision was a dream come true and wonderful to have the three wins and the sale to Godolphin. Seductive Moment was the reason why Bryan and I bought in to the partnership as I never thought we would have a chance to own a horse by Shamardal. He did well but unfortunately injuries and his temperamental behaviour played their part. When we turned up at Beverley last summer we expected another win but there was no way he was going into those stalls. Racing is such a fun game.

Peter Neumark who had won a charity auction with the prize being a visit to the stables, had not only bought a share for himself in KP 10 but also for his granddaughter Isdadora and explained:

Our visit to Park Farm was in April 2017 and come May 2018 the horses started winning…and winning….and winning. Victory Command was the first on the score sheet when he won at Doncaster on May 19, and Seductive Moment scored on his debut at Windsor on May 28. It was turning out to be a fantastic investment already, but the icing on the cake was provided when Dark Vision produced an extraordinary run to land the Group 2 Vintage Stakes at Goodwood.

Isadora with Mojo

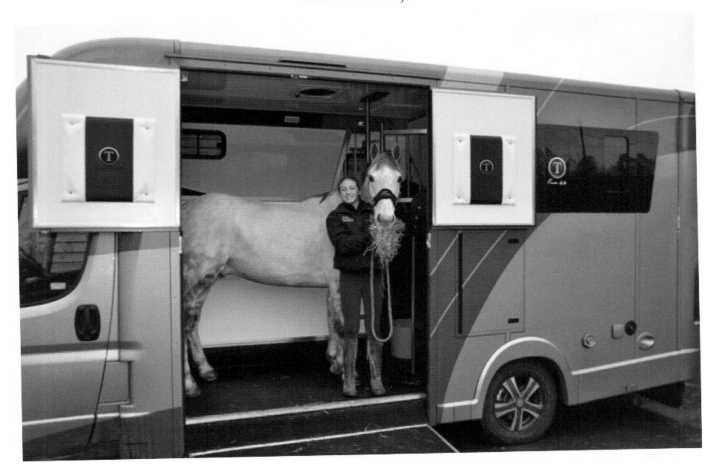

Isadora in her new Horsebox with Mojo

However, when Mark emailed us about the offer he had received for Dark Vision, we had no idea what sort of return we could expect to receive for our relatively small investment in the partnership.

When the figure came through, I sat down with my granddaughter and suggested there are two ways in which she could use her share of the proceeds. One option would have been for her to save it and put it aside for better horses as she grew older; alternatively, she could replace her existing trailer with a purpose built horsebox. Dora had clearly been doing her research, and immediately produced brochures from all the horse box manufacturers, so the die was cast! My daughter Rebecca then helped out by visiting four manufacturers before deciding to place an order with Tatton. Deirdre kindly popped into their pitch at the ``Horse of the Year Show'' at the National Exhibition Centre in Birmingham and gave Isadora's choice her seal of approval.

The 4.5 ton vehicle was delivered at the end of November. The look of sheer joy on my granddaughter's face when she saw it for the first time was something to behold and I understand the Connermara pony, Mojo, is very happy too! To say we were lucky with our investment is a huge understatement but we are absolutely thrilled with our experiences to date and immensely grateful to Mark, Deirdre, Charlie and the team at at Kingsley Park who have been instrumental in this incredible story. It's fantastic that Isadora should have such a tangible and valuable, reminder of how well the partnership has done.

Catherine and Billy Ross told me:

We were together at most of the winning races and the ones we were not at you probably were and vice versa. The best day's racing has to be Dark Vision's win at Goodwood. It was just an amazing day and a great few days at The Old Thorns Manor Hotel in good company!! We were at Windsor when Seductive Moment won his first race. Mark Chapman interviewed those there. I have to say that the trip to Dubai with Victory Command was brilliant too and a totally different experience from our earlier visit to the World Cup meeting. Visiting the stables, the race itself, the party afterwards in the Meydan Hotel terrace bar and the Friday brunch at the Westin hotel, with Dougie Livingston, Jock, Robynne and Emma were wonderful experiences. The second visit to watch Victory Command on turf was slightly disappointing. Following the success of KP 10 we joined further partnerships, KP 13, KP 15 and KP 18. It was an amazing two years with Dark Vision, Victory Command and Seductive Moment all doing us proud. It was a wonderful partnership with lots of happy memories. Friendships formed that will continue.

With regard to the sale of Dark Vision Sheikh Mohammed may have been influenced , not only by the horse's ability , but by the title of his internationally acclaimed book "White Vision".

Paul Walker wrote:

On 10th October 2018 I went to Kingsley Park to say my fond goodbyes to all three equine stars of this story. All three gave us so many tales to tell but Victory Command was simply a dude. For two magical seasons he took us to the best days on the best racecourses and tried his heart out every time. He was a credit to everyone involved with him at Kingsley Park and I will never have the pleasure of owning his like again.

Reg Witheridge wrote:

Val and I had joined KP 8 and when KP 10 was launched we joined that too to hopefully give us more opportunities to go racing as an owner. We were hoping for quantity rather than necessarily quality. How wrong we were! Although we travel a lot we were able to see Victory Command win 4 times, Seductive Moment win 4 times and Dark Vision win twice. Although Dark Vision's win at Goodwood was probably the highlight, his debut win at Yarmouth was memorable. It was a lovely summer's day and he absolutely outclassed the field. A very long trip for us to get there but so worthwhile. We were fortunate to see all of Seductive Moment's victories. As a 2-year-old he won on debut and also on New Year's Eve. We were mentioned in the Racing Post the following day. As a 3-year-old we had two memorable evenings with him. A win at Windsor on a Monday evening made the long journey worthwhile and this was followed by a brilliant win on a July evening at Newmarket. He started slowly but stormed through at the end to win with pounds in hand. The race was sponsored by the Heath Court Hotel, which happened to be where we stayed overnight. He went up quite a few pounds for this but was able to put in a solid performance when placed in a Class 2 handicap at York.

Victory Command seemed to have been around for ever and he provided a lot of excitement for us. We were very nervous when he won his "walk in the park" at Beverley, when a 1/14 odds-on shot. His Listed win at Ascot was a wonderful prelude to Dark Vision's win in the Vintage Stakes at Glorious Goodwood. We also really enjoyed his placed efforts in Group races at Newmarket and Sandown. We were unable to make the trip to Dubai but saw plenty of action during his 3-year-old campaign back in the UK. We particularly remember his win at Chelmsford. It was a cold, wet evening and he gave a gutsy performance to make all. We didn't notice the rain. We had some great days out when he ran well in big Handicaps at Royal Ascot, Goodwood and York. With Kingsley Park 10 we had so much quality action, and so much winning that we really got to know our fellow partners.

15.3 Could it Happen Again?

The remarkable success of the horses in KP 10 has led to suggestions that it was a one-off experience and, therefore, unlikely to be repeated. Comments such as *"a one in a million chance"* have been used to describe what many thought to be a very rare event. Past experiences of horse racing did suggest that, at least, it was a very unusual feat. It was the combination of all three horses in a partnership being so successful and the fact that they had cost so little as yearlings that caught everybody's imagination. Mine too of course, which led to this book. Unfortunately data on how many yearlings go on to be racehorses, how many that do then win a race, what type of race they win and the prize money won are hard to come by. One old statistic I found reputedly from the British Horse Racing Authority in 2007 was that year there were 8,556 horses in training and fewer than 50% of these won a race and less than 1% won a Stakes Race.

This last part of the quote does tie in with the data from the Racehorse Owners Association annual Prize-Money Pyramids, shown in Table 1 in Chapter 14. In 2018 and 2019 less than 1% of all horses won amounts of prize money greater than £100,000 and about 20% of horses won nothing. This latter figure shows they not only did not win but were not in the place money. Two of the KP 10 horses won more than £100k and the third won almost £20k. It is tempting, therefore, to suggest that two of the horses achieved a one in one hundred (1:100) sum in the sample of the horses for those years with the third about one in ten (1:10). So perhaps a rough guide of a one in a hundred thousand occurrence rather than one in a million could be used to describe the feat. Definitely a rare achievement.

However, the Prize-Money Pyramids do not take into account how much each horse cost at the Sales, or their potential value if they did not go through the sales ring. One can only guess as to what some of the offspring of Galileo or Dubawi would fetch. It has already been explained that paying large sums of money for yearlings does not guarantee the horses will win races, but it is generally agreed that this may increase their chance of doing so. Johnston Racing very rarely pay more than £20k for a partnership horse and often less than £10k. Ron Huggins told me that all of his successful horses had been bought cheaply by Mark, including Double Trigger who in 1992 cost just 7,200 Irish Pounds. They named a restaurant/bar and lawn (Goodwood) and a train (GNER) after him.

Statistics which are readily available and are reliable are those for the performances of the horses in the Always Trying partnerships and the Kingsley Park partnerships. The former 13 partnerships, which ran from 2000 to 2013 produced 49 winners. A feature of these partnerships was the relatively cheap purchase prices of the horses, which is also true of the prices paid by Mark and Charlie for the Kingsley Park versions of today (see Table 8 in Chapter 14). Those horses which achieved a BHA rating of 90 and over are the ones included in Table 8. Some of the horses in the table were in Ready to Run partnerships and were usually older horses bought back at the Horses in Training Sales. Although none of the Always Trying partnerships reached the dizzy heights of KP 10 with regard to the number of wins and prize money they produced some stable stars of their day.

Always Waining (ATII), Always Bold (AT V), Copperwood (AT VIII E), Maid in Rio (The New Fairyhouse) and Broxbourne (Ready to Run) took their partners to Grade 1 tracks and although only **Always Fruitful** (ATIII) achieved Black Type many won valuable races. The combination of prize money and sales proceeds often meant the partners went away with a healthy cheque and at least covered their costs, which only a few owners do. The first Kingsley Park partnership (Ready to Run) got the new venture off to a good start with 11 wins, five of those by Duke Street. Teofonic was the star of KP 5 and she contributed 6 wins to a partnership of 9 successes and greatly to the pockets of the partners. Poet's Society won 6 of the 9 wins of KP 9 and will forever be remembered as the horse that provided Mark with the record number of winners. This was, of course in the same period Dark Vision, Victory Command and Seductive Moment were breaking other records to provide Johnston Racing with its most successful partnership to date with Black Type for **Dark Vision** and **Victory Command**. The first ten Kingsley Park partnerships produced 62 winners.

However, hold on, as already mentioned and documented in Chapter 8, in 2018 Kingsley Park partnerships 11, 13 and 14 were launched. I remember Bryan Russell had told me, when we were up at the stables viewing these newcomers, that it had crossed his mind that the success of KP 10 would unlikely be repeated in the same way, the saying goes *"lightning never strikes in the same place twice."* I replied that this was probably true but it might, and if it did perhaps it would not be of the same intensity. I joined KP 11 and he and Sue joined KP 14.

The yearlings in the crop of 2018 were certainly not all superstars, some were to disappoint and in fact some of their careers emphasised yet again how precarious this wonderful sport can be and equally how dreadfully sad, at times it is. Blake's Vision (KP 13) and Golden Fountain (KP 11) were both fatally injured, the former at Doncaster and the latter at home on the gallops. Ironically an injury, although not a fatal one, to the Planteur colt, in KP 14 resulted in the filly **Rose of Kildare** being substituted to take his place.

Here the misfortune ended as she definitely did turn out to be a superstar winning three Group 3 Races and placed in two other Group 3s to secure **5 Black Type** entries for her "page". She was after Black Type again in the Group 1 Juddmonte International at York and ran very well and was not outclassed but was dwarfed by the colt and much older winner, the majestic Ghaiyyath, trained by Charlie Appleby. Early in the same week of the race it was announced that she had been purchased privately as a broodmare prospect by Qatar Racing for a reported *"substantial six figure sum."*

Auchterarder of KP 11 another filly also did well running 8 times, winning three races and being placed three times. She won very impressively first time out at Beverley and the Racing press were eager to plot her future plan of attack with a return to Beverley for their Hilary Needler, before tackling the Queen Mary at Royal Ascot. This was not to be as she was found to be lame in her right fore leg the morning after the race. A hairline crack of the knee on that leg kept her on the easy list for many months. When she did return 5 months later at Southwell she missed the break, was race rusty but managed to pick up speed and come a comfortable second. The winner broke the Juvenile 5 furlong track record. Eleven days later she won easily at Wolverhampton and was a fraction of a second off their track record. Injury struck again to the same right fore knee and she was off for 205 days. After this prolonged absence and two disappointing runs over 6 furlongs she found her feet again over a longer trip of 1 mile on 15th October in a Class 2 Handicap at Chelmsford under a crafty ride from Jason Hart. She was beaten into second place by a very good horse, Johan, trained by William Haggas, but left other good types in her wake. The race time was only 0.73 seconds slower than standard.

Auchterarder at Beverley first time out with the ever enthusiastic Paddy Trainor. *Brian Lunn*

On the last day of November 2020 trained by F Rossi in France she returned to 6½ furlongs at Deauville for her new owners in a €28000 Conditions race on the All-Weather. She ran strongly to the line and came second, only beaten by a length by Golden Boy trained by S Wattel. We are left with the feeling of what might have been if she had stayed fit?

King's Caper of KP 13 won 3 races and came second 3 times. One of the second places was at Campannelle in Rome in the Group 2 Italian Derby with Frankie Dettori on board.

He gave him a great ride and just could not get there to win and was beaten by Tuscan Rose by the narrowest of margins- a nose. So a partnership with these last three horses would perhaps have rivalled the exploits of KP 10 but they belonged, of course, to three different ones.

Some of the gloss was probably taken off most of the wins in 2020 owing to the restrictions in place, which prevented, or put off many of the owners from attending to watch the races live. I attended one race meeting in 2020, at Meydan at the end of January. I am sure the shine was not removed completely but did not return close to the original brightness, (apart from the private sale of Rose of Kildare) at the Newmarket Horses in Training Sales. The median price was 40% lower than in 2019. At the Sales Auchterarder fetched 37,000 guineas and was bought by Scea Marmion Vauville in France. King's Caper was bought by BBA Ireland for 45,000 guineas.

So how do Mark and Johnston Racing do it? I hope that I have provided the answer or at least some insight into the reasons for their success in this book. I have never believed that the correct use of the word "luck' is when it is meant to describe good fortune. Rather luck is an event which occurs completely by chance with no outside influences. The "luck of the draw" is an example in Racing of sheer luck, where a favourable stalls position is allotted to a horse by a ballot.

That circumstance is "luck', but it is not involved in the buying of good horses, their nurture, together with the training, and the placing of horses to win races. There are outside interests at play in these processes, namely the many skills exercised at Kingsley Park. The track record of Johnston Racing, perhaps in a small way, is epitomised by the successes of the horses in their partnerships. These are the result of the application of expertise, an attention to detail and hard work all of which are abundant and essential ingredients possessed by the training establishment called "Johnston Racing."

I think that a similar story to this one could happen again.

EPILOGUE

For as long as I can remember, racing has been known as 'the Sport of Kings.' In reality, this soubriquet has proved something of a mixed blessing for the sport over the years.

On the one hand, there's little doubt that the royal patronage which the sport has enjoyed in Britain over hundreds of years, typified by the splendour of the annual Royal Ascot meeting, British racing's premier summer festival, has imbued the sport with a prestige and glamour with which few other sports can compete.

British racing trades heavily on the traditions and history of the sport, often arising from royal and aristocratic connections, which have attracted much-needed inward investment in the British racing and bloodstock industries at a level which, arguably, is not in any way justified having regard to the derisory levels of prize-money available on the British turf.

The active involvement of the monarchy in breeding and racing their own horses has also given a massive boost to the sport over the years. I'm old enough to remember the fantastic reception given to the Queen's filly Dunfermline when she landed the Oaks and the St Leger double in her owner's Silver Jubilee year (1977).

On the other hand, the association of the sport with 'kings' has led to the perception that racing is 'a rich man's game'; that one needs to be very well off to get involved, at least at an ownership level. Certain other practices within the sport, including the manner in which crowds are segregated into separate enclosures within racecourses and treated very differently according to their rank, also contribute to the idea that the sport can be overtly exclusive.

In other racing jurisdictions, and notably in Australia, the notion of shared ownership has provided a means by which more and more people have been able to get involved more deeply in the sport. The idea is gaining traction in Britain, though racing institutions, and notably the racecourses, are still coming to terms with how best to serve the needs of racing clubs and partnerships with multiple owners, in terms of issues like entry badges, parade ring access and proper accommodation and hospitality within Owners and Trainers' facilities.

Crucially, these shared ownership vehicles allow racing enthusiasts to enjoy the benefits and thrills of being an owner without being exposed to the full financial implications of training and racing horses.

The Kingsley Park partnerships are operated by Johnston Racing and have been offered to individuals looking for routes into racehorse ownership since late 2014. They boast a number of advantages for potential owners, not least that the partnerships share the benefit of Johnston Racing's guarantee to all their owners that all veterinary costs are included in the stable's daily training fee for a horse.

Furthermore, each of the partnerships is underwritten by Johnston Racing. Each partner need contribute only the sum agreed at the outset of the partnership; thereafter, they will never be obliged to contribute any further sums, and if the partnership runs out of funds, the shortfall will be picked up by Johnston Racing.

With these safeguards in place, it's not difficult to see why Johnston Racing has been able to launch 26 of these partnerships in little over seven years. And with the horses selected by Mark and Charlie Johnston, it will come as no surprise to the reader to know that the popular partnerships have been spectacularly successful.

In early 2021, the Kingsley Park partnerships enjoyed their 100th win when Kingsley Park 16's Dancing King won a Wolverhampton Handicap. Robin has also written in some detail about Dark Vision's Group 2 win in the Vintage Stakes at Goodwood for KP 10, and KP 14 partners were thrilled when their Rose of Kildare won three Group 3 events before being sold on to Qatar Racing.

By simple virtue of having had the enthusiasm to research and then assemble this book, Robin Holleyhead has demonstrated the sheer enjoyment he has derived from his interest in racing generally and the Kingsley Park partnerships in particular.

In many ways, he has demonstrated the best way to enjoy these partnerships, resolving to go and see the horses run whenever possible; from enjoying the nervous anticipation of meeting with connections in the parade ring, through the thrill of watching the horses race, to celebrating with other partners in the winners' enclosure, he has made the most of the partnership experience in the process. As he has faithfully recorded, his share in Kingsley Park 10 and its horses took him to the premier meetings at home and abroad. From his account of those travels, the friendships forged along the way and the camaraderie he has enjoyed with fellow partners, Johnston racing staff and jockeys, have added hugely to a rich partnership experience.

And, at the heart of it all, are the horses themselves. Dark Vision, Victory Command and Seductive Moment all gave the partners of Kingsley Park 10 some moments to savour which they will never forget, memories of pure gold. Understandably, for Robin Holleyhead, he will always regard this as....'the Golden Partnership.'

John Scanlon

APPENDICES

MARKJOHNSTON
racing

Kingsley Park 10

- Kingsley Park 10 will consist of 20 shares and will purchase three yearlings at the coming sales to race in 2018/19.

- Partners may own more than one share but no subdivision of shares is allowable. The Partnership will run until the end of October 2019, at which time all remaining horses will be entered into the Horses in Training Sales and sold. The proceeds of sale will be added to the account, all debts will be paid, and if an end balance occurs, it will be distributed among all partners.

- A partnership bank account will be opened, into which all monies will be paid. Accounts will be audited by the MJR accounts department. Prospective partners can secure a 1/20th share by depositing a single sum of £7,000 into the partnership bank account. Alternatively, partners may pay a deposit of £3,300 and set up a standing order to the partnership account for six monthly payments of £700. A second payment of £1,500 (or a standing order for 12 monthly payments of £135/horse), **for each horse** we take on into a second year, will be due in November 2018. Mark Johnston Racing Limited will hold a 1/20th share at no cost but will waive our usual 5% commission on sale.

- All racing and training expenses will be drawn from the partnership account, as well as purchase price and insurance. Cheques can be made payable to Kingsley Park 10.

- All returns from prize money, any other income and sales proceeds will be deposited into the partnership account. Mark Johnston Racing Ltd. will charge its standard, all-inclusive, daily rate for training and will apply its standard terms and conditions. A copy of

Mark Johnston Racing, Kingsley Park, Middleham, North Yorkshire, DL8 4QZ Tel: 01969 622237 Fax: 01969 622484 VAT No. 499 3150 11
E-mail: info@markjohnstonracing.com Website: www.markjohnstonracing.com
Mark Johnston, B.V.M.S., M.R.C.V.S. Licensed Trainer of Flat and National Hunt Horses.
Company Registered in Scotland. Reg No. SC106428. Reg Office 29 Brandon Street, Hamilton ML3 6AB.
Directors M.S. Johnston. D.M. Johnston.

MARKJOHNSTON
racing

the current rates is attached. The partnership will be underwritten by Mark Johnston Racing Ltd. i.e. no further payments will be required beyond those detailed above and Mark Johnston Racing Ltd will continue to train the retained horses until the end of the partnership in October 2019.

- Charlie Johnston and Nicky McGrath will provide extra points of contact, short monthly progress reports on the horses, e-mail reports after each race, and regular photographic updates from the gallops. They will also ensure that all partners receive a regular financial statement and will endeavour to provide answers to any queries. MJR will also subscribe to the Weatherbys text messaging service (at no cost to the partnership) for all partners so that you are informed of all entries, declarations etc. In addition to this all partners will be informed of entries and declarations to run by e-mail. MJR's standard terms and conditions will apply unless otherwise stated in these rules.

- A meeting of partners will be held in the first quarter of the partnership and then in the first quarter of 2019. The meeting will take place at Kingsley Park Farm, Middleham, North Yorkshire DL8 4QZ. It is an opportunity for partners to meet Mark and he will offer an overall guideline for the season ahead.

- When the partnership is dissolved all moneys will be pooled in the partnership account and the balance will be distributed between partners.

- There shall be two 'nominated' partners for Weatherbys registration purposes.

- All partners will receive Mark Johnston Racing Limited's monthly newsletter by post. Partners are all welcome to visit the horses by prior arrangement. Each partner will be guaranteed a minimum of

Mark Johnston Racing, Kingsley Park, Middleham, North Yorkshire, DL8 4QZ Tel: 01969 622237 Fax: 01969 622484 VAT No. 499 3150 11
E-mail: info@markjohnstonracing.com Website: www.markjohnstonracing.com
Mark Johnston, B.V.M:S., M.R.C.V.S. Licensed Trainer of Flat and National Hunt Horses.
Company Registered in Scotland. Reg No. SC106428. Reg Office 29 Brandon Street, Hamilton ML3 6AB.
Directors M.S. Johnston. D.M. Johnston.

MARKJOHNSTON
racing

one racecourse badge per runner provided they have notified Mark Johnston Racing of their intention to attend by the end of the day prior to racing.

- The horses will race in Royal Blue, Green Epaulets, Royal Blue Sleeves, and a Royal Blue Cap.

- One name per animal will be put forward by each partner. A vote will take place and the most popular name will be selected for the animal, if available.

- Mark Johnston Racing Limited will make payment of £7,000 per share into the Partnership Account for any shares not taken up by 1st January 2018, and subsequent payments for second year as required, but shall reserve the right to pass those shares onto partners who wish to join at a later date.

- As owners with Mark Johnston Racing, all partners will automatically be entitled to membership of the Kingsley Park Owners Group. This group will race a number of leased horses in the Blue and Green colours of Kingsley Park. Members will have no financial interest in the horses (no costs – no prize money) but will be able to attend the races, as owners, if they wish. Badges will be allocated by ballot if necessary. Members may, if they wish, receive information on all entries and declarations for club horses via the Weatherbys text messaging service. All members will receive a Kingsley Park Owners Group annual metal badge.

Mark Johnston Racing, Kingsley Park, Middleham, North Yorkshire, DL8 4QZ Tel: 01969 622237 Fax: 01969 622484 VAT No. 499 3150 11
E-mail: info@markjohnstonracing.com Website: www.markjohnstonracing.com
Mark Johnston, B.V.M.S., M.R.C.V.S. Licensed Trainer of Flat and National Hunt Horses.
Company Registered in Scotland. Reg No. SC106428. Reg Office 29 Brandon Street, Hamilton ML3 6AB.
Directors M.S. Johnston. D.M. Johnston.

MARKJOHNSTON
racing

Further details and Rules.

Partners should ensure that they are in a position to provide an e-mail address and mobile telephone number.

The partnership shall be registered for VAT as with a business partnership. It will pay VAT on supplies and claim back VAT on qualifying expenses (including training fees etc.). VAT is not payable on owners' subscriptions into the partnership account.

Partners are all welcome to telephone the yard for news of their horses at any time during normal working hours.

Partners' input on preferred entries, running plans or jockey bookings will be welcomed but Mark Johnston will make final decisions on these matters.

If an offer is received for any horse during the term of the partnership, partners will be informed but Mark Johnston will make a final decision in the best interest of the partnership, on whether to sell or not.

For Jockey Club registration purposes two "nominated partners" will be required to be registered owners and to sign an "Authority to Act" in favour of Mark Johnston. These partners will not enjoy any privileges over other partners.

There will usually be a minimum of four badges available for a partnership runner. Mark Johnston Racing will endeavour to provide more badges from other stable runners on the day but any cost incurred for the purchase of extra badges to provide the minimum of one per partner will be met from partnership funds.

Mark Johnston Racing, Kingsley Park, Middleham, North Yorkshire, DL8 4QZ Tel: 01969 622237 Fax: 01969 622484 VAT No. 499 3150 11
E-mail: info@markjohnstonracing.com Website: www.markjohnstonracing.com
Mark Johnston, B.V.M.S., M.R.C.V.S. Licensed Trainer of Flat and National Hunt Horses.
Company Registered in Scotland. Reg No. SC106428. Reg Office 29 Brandon Street, Hamilton ML3 6AB.
Directors M.S. Johnston. D.M. Johnston.

The horses will be insured against death or humane slaughter. This value may be amended from time to time at the discretion of Mark Johnston.

The partnership will abide to the Mark Johnston Racing Ltd, Racehorse Training Agreement.

On joining, partners are committing to the two year term on the partnership for all three horses. Decisions to retain horses for a second year will, ultimately, be made by Mark Johnston after discussion with partners. Any partner who fails to pay their instalment/s for the second year will forfeit their share in the partnership and all its assets.

Mark Johnston Racing, Kingsley Park, Middleham, North Yorkshire, DL8 4QZ Tel: 01969 622237 Fax: 01969 622484 VAT No. 499 3150 11
E-mail: info@markjohnstonracing.com Website: www.markjohnstonracing.com
Mark Johnston, B.V.M.S., M.R.C.V.S. Licensed Trainer of Flat and National Hunt Horses.
Company Registered in Scotland. Reg No. SC106428. Reg Office 29 Brandon Street, Hamilton ML3 6AB.
Directors M.S. Johnston. D.M. Johnston.

WIll Stand at Park Paddocks, Highflyer Paddock BB, Box 709

+10

1064 (WITH VAT)

A BAY COLT (IRE)
Foaled
February 16th, 2016

Dream Ahead (USA)	Diktat (GB)	Warning
		Arvola (GB)
	Land of Dreams (GB)	Cadeaux Genereux
		Sahara Star (GB)
Black Dahlia (GB) (2005)	Dansili (GB)	Danehill (USA)
		Hasili (IRE)
	South Rock (GB)	Rock City
		South Shore

E.B.F. Nominated.   **B.C. Nominated.**

1st Dam
Black Dahlia (GB), **won** 5 races at 3 and 4 years and £38,522 and placed 18 times including second in betdaq.co.uk Ladybird Stakes, Kempton Park, **L.**;
dam of **two winners** from 2 runners and 2 foals of racing age viz-
>   **Al Hayyah (IRE)** (2013 f. by Lope de Vega (IRE)), won 1 race at 3 years, 2016 in France and £46,752 and placed 7 times including second in Prix Madame Jean Couturie, Vichy, **L.**, Prix La Sorellina, La Teste De Buch, **L.** and third in Prix Occitanie, Toulouse, **L.**
>   ANOTHER ECLIPSE (IRE) (2014 c. by Lope de Vega (IRE)), won 1 race at 3 years, 2017 and placed 5 times, all his starts.

2nd Dam
SOUTH ROCK (GB), **won** 4 races at 3 years at home and in France and £34,219 including Prix de Saint-Cyr, Evry, **L.**;
dam of **five winners** from 7 runners and 9 foals of racing age including-
>   **Black Dahlia (GB)** (f. by Dansili (GB)), see above.
>   COLD TURKEY (GB), won 16 races and £163,768, placed 23 times; also 1 race over hurdles.

3rd Dam
SOUTH SHORE, **won** 4 races at 3 years and placed 3 times;
dam of **six winners** from 9 runners and 10 foals of racing age including-
>   **SOUTH ROCK (GB)**, see above.
>   LEONICA (GB), won 1 race at 3 years and placed 3 times, all her starts; dam of winners.
>>   **Rodrigo de Torres (GB)**, 7 races, third in King Charles II Stakes, Newmarket, **L.**
>   Tidal Chorus (GB), ran twice at 3 years; dam of winners.
>>   **MAJESTIC DUBAWI (GB)**, 2 races at 2 years including Laundry Cottage Firth of Clyde Stakes, Ayr, **Gr.3**.

The next dam **Shore Line**, **won** 1 race at 3 years and placed fourth in Oaks Stakes, Epsom, **Gr.1**; Own sister to **QUAY LINE**, **ANCHOLIA**, **TRADE LINE** and **HIGH FINALE**;
dam of **five winners** from 12 runners and 12 foals of racing age including-
>   **SOVIET LINE (IRE)**, won 16 races at home, in Hong Kong, in U.A.E. and in U.S.A. including Juddmonte Lockinge Stakes, Newbury, **Gr.1** (twice), Kiveton Park Stakes, Doncaster, **Gr.3**, Charlton Hunt Supreme Stakes, Goodwood, **Gr.3**, Robert F Carey Memorial Handicap, Hawthorne, **Gr.3**, Firecracker Breeders' Cup Handicap, Churchill Downs, **Gr.3**, Fourstardave Stakes, Saratoga, **Gr.3**, Maker's Mark Mile Stakes, Keeneland, **Gr.3**, Hong Kong International Bowl, Sha Tin, **Gr.3**, second in Challenge Stakes, Newmarket, **Gr.2** (twice), Sandown Mile, Sandown Park, **Gr.2**, Keeneland Breeders' Cup Mile, Keeneland, **Gr.2**, third in Queen Elizabeth II Stakes, Ascot, **Gr.1**.
>   **MAMDOOH (GB)**, won 8 races at home and in Australia including CUB Onkaparinga Cup, Oakbank, **L.**; also won 1 race over jumps in Australia.
>   Lajna, ran twice at 2 years; dam of winners.
>>   **GOLD LAND (USA)**, won Bing Crosby Handicap, Del Mar, **Gr.3**, Los Angeles Handicap, Hollywood Park, **Gr.3**, Ancient Title Breeders' Cup Handicap, Santa Anita, **Gr.3**, second in Churchill Downs Handicap, Churchill Downs, **Gr.2**.
>>   SOLAR STAR (USA), 2 races at 2 years; dam of **SOLAR BOUND (USA)**, won Edgewood Stakes, Churchill Downs, **L.**; grandam of **FIRST CORNERSTONE (IRE)**, 2 races including Galileo EBF Futurity Stakes, Curragh, **Gr.2**, **STRATH BURN (GB)**, 2 races at 3 years including Al Basti Equiworld Hackwood Stakes, Newbury, **Gr.3**, second in Betfred Sprint Cup, Haydock Park, **Gr.1**.
>>   Western Friend (USA), ran once at 3 years; dam of **RESPLENDENT CEE (IRE)**, 6 races at 2 to 4 years including Ripon Champion 2yo Trophy, Ripon, **L.**
>>   The Strand (GB), unraced; dam of **PAUSANIAS (GB)**, 4 races at 2 to 4 years at home and in Hong Kong including European Free Handicap, Newmarket, **L.**
>   Embark (GB), ran once at 3 years; dam of winners.
>>   **CAN'THELPBELIEVING (IRE)**, 4 races at 3 to 5 years, 2016 in U.S.A. including Cliff Hanger Stakes, Monmouth Park, **Gr.3**, second in United Nations Stakes, Monmouth Park, **Gr.1** and third in Man O'War Stakes, Belmont Park, **Gr.1**.

HORSE IN TRAINING, consigned by Kingsley Park

Will Stand at Park Paddocks, Highflyer Paddock H, Box 98

662 (WITH VAT)
VICTORY COMMAND (IRE)
(2016)
A Bay Colt

War Command (USA)	War Front (USA)	Danzig (USA) / Starry Dreamer (USA)
	Wandering Star (USA)	Red Ransom (USA) / Beautiful Bedouin (USA)
Aguinaga (IRE) (1997)	Machiavellian (USA)	Mr Prospector (USA) / Coup de Folie (USA)
	Crystal Cup (USA)	Nijinsky (CAN) / Rose Bowl (USA)

VICTORY COMMAND (IRE): won 6 races at 2 and 3 years, 2019 and £106,213 including Pat Eddery Stakes, Ascot, **L.** and Almada Mile Handicap Stakes (Class 2), Hamilton Park, placed 12 times including second in EBF Stallions Youngsters Conditions Stakes (Class 2) (Plus 10 Race), Pontefract, third in Al Bastakiya Trial, Meydan, Amix Silver Bowl Handicap Stakes (Class 2), Haydock Park, Trucking By Brian Yeardley Two Year Old Trophy Conditions Stakes (Class 2) (Plus 10 Race), Beverley, fourth Royal Lodge Stakes, Newmarket, **Gr.2**, European Free Handicap Stakes, Newmarket, **L.** and Solario Stakes, Sandown Park, **Gr.3**.

Highest BHA Rating 103 (Flat) Latest BHA Rating 99 (Flat) *(prior to compilation)*

TURF	21 runs	5 wins 11 pl	£88,646	GF - G	5f 3y - 1m 68y
ALL WEATHER	1 run	1 win	£9,704	ST	1m 2f
FOREIGN FLAT	3 runs	1 pl	£7,863		

1st Dam
AGUINAGA (IRE), **won** 1 race at 3 years and placed 6 times;
dam of **five winners** from 9 runners and 9 foals of racing age viz-
  CONQUEST (IRE) (2004 g. by Invincible Spirit (IRE)), won 5 races at 2 and 4 years and £224,026 including Gimcrack Stakes, York, **Gr.2**, Bengough Mem. Stakes, Ascot, **Gr.3** and Hever Sprint Stakes, Lingfield Park, **L.**, placed 4 times including second in Windsor Castle Stakes, Ascot, **L.** and third in Altium Scarbrough Stakes, Doncaster, **L.**
  VICTORY COMMAND (IRE) (2016 c. by War Command (USA)), see above.
  STORM FORCE (IRE) (2005 c. by Cape Cross (IRE)), won 2 races at 2 years, all his starts.
  SECOND SERVE (IRE) (2013 c. by Cape Cross (IRE)), won 1 race at 3 years and £16,341 and placed 8 times, died at 3.
  NYMFIA (IRE) (2008 f. by Invincible Spirit (IRE)), won 1 race at 4 years in France and £14,453 and placed 3 times; dam of 2 winners.
    GREENSHOE (IRE), 3 races to 2019 in France and £60,130 and placed 10 times.
She also has a 2018 filly by Lawman (FR).

2nd Dam
CRYSTAL CUP (USA), ran in U.S.A. at 2 and 3 years;
dam of **eight winners** from 9 runners and 11 foals of racing age including-
  IKTAMAL (USA) (c. by Danzig Connection (USA)), won 7 races at 3 and 4 years and £155,153 including Haydock Park Sprint Cup, Haydock Park, **Gr.1** and Beeswing Stakes, Newcastle, **Gr.3**, placed second in Abernant Stakes, Newmarket, **L.**; sire.
  FIRST MAGNITUDE (IRE) (c. by Arazi (USA)), won 5 races at 3 and 4 years in France and £147,510 including Prix du Conseil de Paris, Longchamp, **Gr.2**, Prix Jean de Chaudenay, Saint-Cloud, **Gr.2** and Prix d'Hedouville, Longchamp, **Gr.3**.
  ROCKAMUNDO (USA) (c. by Key To The Mint (USA)), won 2 races in U.S.A. including Arkansas Derby, Oaklawn Park, **Gr.2**, second in Ak-Sar-Ben Juvenile Breeders' Cup Stakes, Ak-Sar-Ben, third in Arlington Washington Futurity, Arlington Int., **Gr.2**; sire.
  CRYSTAL CROSS (USA), won 4 races at 3 and 4 years; dam of winners.
    CRYSTAL VALKYRIE (IRE), 1 race at 2 years; dam of **ABOVE AVERAGE (IRE)**, 2 races at 3 and 4 years including Classic Trial, Sandown Park, **Gr.3**, placed second in Moonee Valley Gold Cup, Moonee Valley, **Gr.2**, **SENT FROM HEAVEN (IRE)**, 2 races at 2 years and £71,976 including Prestige Stakes, Goodwood, **Gr.3**, **Granddukeoftuscany (IRE)**, 2 races at 3 and 4 years, placed second in The Bart Cummings Handicap, Flemington, **Gr.3**; grandam of **Allegro Fiddle (TUR)**, winner to 2019 in Turkey, second in Ozdemir Atman Stakes, Veliefendi, **L.**
    BLUE CRYSTAL (IRE), 1 race at 3 years; dam of **Golden Liberty (IRE)**, 1 race at 2 years in Italy and placed 11 times including second in Criterium di Pisa, Pisa, **L.**
  SUSPENSE QUEEN (USA), won 3 races in Japan; dam of winners.
    YUKINO MERMAID (JPN), winner in Japan; dam of **BESTEN DANK (JPN)**, won Yonago Stakes, Hanshin, **L.**
  Cup Custard (USA), unraced; dam of winners.
    Afternoon Clinic (USA), winner, third in M Tyson Gilpin Stakes, Delaware Park, **R.**
    Wingate (USA), winner in U.S.A., second in Brookmeade Stakes, Colonial Downs.

YEARLING, consigned by Jamie Railton (Agent)

Will Stand at Park Paddocks, Wall Box V, Box 488

834 (WITH VAT)
A CHESNUT COLT (GER)
Foaled
April 10th, 2016

Shamardal (USA)	Giant's Causeway (USA)	Storm Cat (USA)
		Mariah's Storm (USA)
	Helsinki (GB)	Machiavellian (USA)
		Helen Street
Sexy Lady (GER) (2003)	Danehill Dancer (IRE)	Danehill (USA)
		Mira Adonde (USA)
	Sky Dancing (IRE)	Exit To Nowhere (USA)
		Saquiace (USA)

E.B.F. Nominated.   B.C. Nominated.

1st Dam
SEXY LADY (GER), won 4 races at 3 years in France and in Germany and £52,849 including Prix Chloe, Maisons-Laffitte, **Gr.3** and Festa-Rennen, Baden-Baden, **L.**, placed 3 times including second in Alice-Cup, Hamburg, **Gr.3**;
dam of **three winners** from 3 runners and 5 foals of racing age viz-
    SEXY GIRL (GB) (2011 f. by Lando (GER)), won 3 races at 5 and 6 years, 2017 in Germany and £11,527 and placed 6 times.
    SALAMATI (GER) (2012 f. by Dubawi (IRE)), won 2 races at 4 years, 2016 in Germany and placed 4 times.
    SHOWTIME (GER) (2014 f. by Pivotal (GB)), won 2 races at 3 years, 2017 in Germany.
    Sessanto (IRE) (2015 c. by Soldier Hollow (GB)), unraced to date.

2nd Dam
SKY DANCING (IRE), won 5 races at 2 and 4 years in Germany and in Italy and £45,970 including Premio Buontalenta, Rome, **L.**, placed 6 times;
dam of **nine winners** from 9 runners and 11 foals of racing age including-
    SCALO (GB) (c. by Lando (GER)), Champion 3yr old colt in Germany in 2010, won 6 races at 2 to 4 years in France and in Germany including Preis von Europa, Cologne, **Gr.1**, Prix Guillaume d'Ornano, Deauville, **Gr.2**, Gerling Preis, Cologne, **Gr.2**, Fruhjahrspreis des Bankhauses Metzler, Frankfurt, **Gr.3** and Bavarian Classic, Munich, **Gr.3**, second in Gran Premio di Milano Tris Int.7, Milan, **Gr.1**, Grosser Preis von Berlin, **Gr.1**; sire.
    SEXY LADY (GER) (f. by Danehill Dancer (IRE)), see above.
    Scolari (GB) (c. by Monsun (GER)), won 5 races at 4 and 5 years in France and in Germany and placed second in Grosser Preis der Dortmunder Wirtschaft, Dortmund, **Gr.3** and Preis der Sparkassen Finanzgruppe, Baden-Baden, **Gr.3**.

3rd Dam
Saquiace (USA), won 4 races at 3 and 4 years in France and placed 9 times including second in Grand Prix de Villeurbanne, Lyon, **L.**;
dam of **eight winners** from 11 runners and 12 foals of racing age including-
    SKY DANCING (IRE), see above.
    Starla (GER), won 3 races at 3 and 4 years in Germany and placed 7 times including third in Bremer Stuten Meile, Bremen, **L.**; dam of winners.
    SANGITA (GB), won 1 race at 4 years; dam of winners.
        WHAT'S UP PUSSYCAT (IRE), 2 races at 2 years including Blenheim Stakes, Curragh, **L.**, third in Loughbrown Stakes, Curragh, **L.**, IrishStall.Farms EBF Sweet Mimosa Stakes, Curragh, **L.** and Saoire Stakes, Curragh, **L.**

The next dam **LAQUIOLA (FR)**, won 2 races in France including Prix de la Seine, Longchamp, **L.**, placed once viz second in Prix Cleopatre, Saint-Cloud, **Gr.3**;
dam of **six winners** from 9 runners and 14 foals of racing age including-
    LAQUIFAN (USA), won 2 races at 2 and 3 years in France and placed twice; dam of winners.
    TZAR RODNEY (FR), won Prix La Force, Chantilly, **Gr.3**, All American Handicap, Golden Gate, **Gr.3** and second in Prix Maurice de Nieuil, M'-Laffitte, **Gr.2**; sire.
    Askmysecretary (USA), unraced; dam of winners.
        Carsona (USA), winner in U.S.A., second in Palo Alto Handicap, Bay Meadows, **L.** and third in Hollywood Oaks, Hollywood Park, **Gr.1**; dam of **SIPHON CITY (USA)**, won Cornhusker Breeders' Cup Handicap, Prairie Meadows, **Gr.2**.
    LISA DANIELLE (USA), winner in U.S.A.; dam of **WISE DAN (USA)**, Champion older horse in U.S.A. in 2012 and 2013, won Clark Handicap, Churchill Downs, **Gr.1**, Breeders' Cup Mile, Santa Anita, **Gr.1** (twice), Shadwell Turf Mile Stakes, Keeneland, **Gr.1** (twice), Turf Classic Stakes, Churchill Downs, **Gr.1** (twice), Ricoh Woodbine Mile Stakes, **Gr.1** (twice), **SUCCESSFUL DAN (USA)**, won Greenbrier Fayette Stakes, Keeneland, **Gr.2**, Alysheba Stakes, Churchill Downs, **Gr.2**, second in Whitney Invitational Handicap, Saratoga, **Gr.1**, **OUR ROYAL DANCER (USA)**, won West Long Branch Stakes, Monmouth Park.